Oklahoma Horizons Series

Oklahoma Horizons Series

An Oklahoma Adventure

The First National Bank, Muskogee, 1890. Courtesy First National Bank of Muskogee.

Oklahoma Horizons Series

An Oklahoma Adventure
Of Banks and Bankers

By James M. Smallwood

Kenny A. Franks, Series Editor

Published for the Oklahoma Heritage Association
by the University of Oklahoma Press : Norman

By James M. Smallwood

Studies in History (Editor) (Lubbock, Texas, 1973)
A History of Cooke County, Texas (Editor) (Gainesville, Texas, 1975)
A Century of Achievement: Blacks in Cooke County, Texas (Gainesville, Texas, 1975)
And Gladly Teach: Reminiscences of Teachers from Frontier Dugout to Modern Module (Editor) (Norman, 1976)
Urban Builder: The Life and Times of Stanley Draper (Norman, 1977)
Daily Telegrams of Will Rogers: The Coolidge Years, 1926–1929, Vol. I of *The Will Rogers Papers* (Editor) (Stillwater, 1978)
Five Faces of Oklahoma History (with Joe Stout) (Stillwater, 1978)
Daily Telegrams of Will Rogers: The Hoover Years, 1929–1931, Vol. II of *The Will Rogers Papers* (Editor) (Stillwater, 1978)
Daily Telegrams of Will Rogers: The Hoover Years, 1931–1933, Vol. III of *The Will Rogers Papers* (Editor) (Stillwater, 1979)
An Oklahoma Adventure: Of Banks and Bankers (Norman, 1979)

Library of Congress Cataloging in Publication Data

Smallwood, James.
An Oklahoma adventure.

(Oklahoma horizons series)
Bibliography: p. 229
Includes index.
1. Banks and banking—Oklahoma—History. I. Oklahoma Heritage Association. II. Title. III. Series.
HG2611.05S6 332.1'09766 79-4745

To my wife, Ruthie

Preface

Thomas J. Hartman, a financial leader with a long tenure in Oklahoma who served many years as the president of the Bank of Commerce in Sulphur and who, in 1911, served as president of the Oklahoma Bankers Association, had a favorite story he enjoyed relating. According to Hartman, at a time before the Oklahoma land run of 1889, a nameless entrepreneur of unknown origins found himself in a small white settlement in Indian Territory. On examining his opportunities for the main chance, the vagabond noticed that the village had a general store, a blacksmith's shop, several saloons, and various other business establishments, but the hamlet did not have a bank. After disappearing for several days, the young businessman returned driving a wagon hauling a cast-iron safe. He rented a storeroom, moved his safe inside, printed the word "BANK" on a piece of cardboard, and tacked it above the storehouse door. He then sat by his safe and waited to see what would happen. A nester soon came forward. Saying "so, this is the new bank," he deposited $150. Another appeared and deposited $200. Drunk with visions of gold and prosperity, the entrepreneur said, "I decided that maybe my bank was going to be a success . . . I had $100 in cash and thought that if the other fellow had confidence in my bank, I had better deposit my $100 to show my confidence."[1] Reportedly, the unnamed man prospered and lived long.

Although the names of the banker and of the settlement where he commenced operations are lost, the above story typifies the history of early banking in Oklahoma. Scores of individuals, some with a small amount of capital, some with no capital, performed banking functions without regard to federal or territorial regulations. Some failed. A few were corrupt. Many, with an abundance of business acumen and personal integrity, founded thriving establishments that won a place in rugged, frontier Oklahoma.

The task of surveying the growth of Oklahoma's banking industry from pioneer days to the modern era is awesome. Hundreds of individuals—many prominent, some notorious—and hundreds of banks parade across the researcher's note pad. And significant developments in the modern era alone are legion. Thus, the author of a one-volume study must necessarily be selective. Only the more important trends can be traced, and only a few individuals, chosen to be representative of their colleagues, can be mentioned.

Heretofore, no one has attempted to synthesize the history of banking in Oklahoma. Many textbooks have surveyed the history of the state, and countless monographs have examined one or another aspects of the story, but only a few brief articles have examined the banking industry. It is hoped that this survey, a volume in the Oklahoma Heritage Association's Horizons Series, will fill a void in the historiography of the state.

In the research and writing of this volume, I have incurred many debts. Joe Gilliland, executive director and vice-president of the Oklahoma Bankers Association (OBA), and Jack Conn, a premier financial leader in the state and the president of the Oklahoma Heritage Association, provided constant encouragement; as well, Gilliland opened the files of the OBA, a most valuable collection of sources. I thank other bankers who gave me interviews and/or who opened their files to me—they are noted in the bibliography. Also, I extend my gratitude to Paul Lambert, executive director of the Oklahoma Heritage Association, who coordinated this project and who helped arrange numerous interviews, and to Kenny Franks, editor of the association's Trackmaker and Horizons series. In addition, I acknowledge the advice and encouragement provided by LeRoy Fisher of Oklahoma State University. Cathy Camerer, Vicki Funkhouser, and Patty Nelson, who typed portions of the manuscript, also have my gratitude.

Finally, I thank my wife, Ruthie, and my children, Martha and Jim—for their patience.

JAMES M. SMALLWOOD

Stillwater, Oklahoma

Contents

Illustrations

An Oklahoma Adventure

CHAPTER 1.

The Beginnings

In old Indian Territory, banks were established by many people who were unfettered by regulations or laws. Any respected Anglo or Indian, be he trader, shopkeeper, farmer, or missionary, occasionally might hold money for or lend money to others. Of course, early adventurers and settlers, who came into Oklahoma during the eighteenth and the first half of the nineteenth centuries, engaged in rudimentary banking functions only on a part-time basis and in addition to their regular vocations. Under crude conditions their financial exchanges remained simple, basic. Only later—in the 1880s and 1890s—were "true" banks of a modern appearance founded.

Banking functions in Oklahoma were performed initially by traders who treated with Indians on a barter basis. Intrepid Spaniards and enterprising Frenchmen were the first. As early as 1718 the French explorer and entrepreneur Bernard de la Harpe received from a commercial company a grant of land on the Red River above the fort at Natchitoches, near present-day Texarkana. La Harpe traveled extensively in eastern Oklahoma, treating with Indians on every expedition, trading on a "wampum" basis, exchanging French firearms for horses, mules, and pelts. To maintain friendly relations with the tribes he treated with, he occasionally gave Indians firearms or other goods, although they had no items to barter. Once he gained their trust, they sometimes left pelts or other trade goods with him when he had no items to exchange. Such circumstances forced La Harpe to become a banker, for he had to maintain a ledger to keep the accounts in order.[1]

The Spaniards established a line of presidios and settlements north of the Río Grande, including Old Spanish Fort on the Red River near the Taovayas village north of Nacona, Texas. Like the French, the Spaniards traversed eastern Oklahoma, bartering with the Indians. Spanish traders maintained detailed accounts and managed trade goods—and profit and loss—much as bankers later managed money.[2]

Two years after the United States purchased the Louisiana Territory in 1803, Congress created what was known as the factor system to insure harmonious relations with the Indians. Designed to discourage British traders from entering the United States and trafficking with the Indians, the system was not abolished until 1822. Factors appointed by the government lived among the Indians and performed elementary banking functions, exchanging trade goods for pelts and keeping accounts.[3]

The most important trading posts in early Oklahoma were established by the Chouteau family. Rene Auguste Chouteau, with his partner Pierre Lacléde Liguest, known as Lacléde, founded a great fur industry in Saint Louis, Missouri. After Lacléde's death in 1778, Chouteau became the wealthiest and most influential trader in Missouri, and Jean Pierre Chouteau, his energetic younger brother, acted as agent for his extensive trade area. Although the brothers lost their trade monopoly of the Missouri country to Manuel Lisa in 1802, they continued to prosper while looking for new areas to conquer. Jean Pierre's son, Auguste Pierre, established a post in 1817 on the east bank of Grand River near present-day Salina in Mayes County. A West Point graduate who served in the War of 1812, Auguste Pierre Chouteau also established himself on the mouth of the Verdigris River, where he maintained a shipyard and trading post. Like many traders who would follow him, Chouteau kept a set of books and performed certain banking functions. He advanced credit to Indians and Anglos to allow them to outfit hunting expeditions. He sometimes held furs and other goods for trappers and traders for safekeeping. He also acted as a commercial agent, shipping from his post cargoes of beaver, wildcat, and raccoon hides, bearskins, deerskins, and buffalo robes in addition to many other items. His customers included Anglo traders and Cherokee, Delaware, Osage, Shawnee, Seneca, and other Indian hunters.[4]

Anglo traders entered Oklahoma early in the nineteenth century, and many engaged in banking. Hugh Glenn, a frontier entrepreneur who became a prominent banker and businessman in Cincinnati, Ohio, in the second decade of the century, only to lose his fortune during the panic of 1819, established a post in Oklahoma in 1820.

Faced with numerous court actions and with his career in ruins, he moved to a point sixty miles northwest of Fort Smith, Arkansas, and founded a trading post on the Verdigris River in the proximity of its confluence with the Arkansas, near present-day Chase, Oklahoma. In August, 1821, he received from the United States Army a license to trade with the Indians at selected points in northeastern Oklahoma. From his post on the Verdigris, Glenn performed rudimentary banking functions, usually on a barter basis, accepting deposits in the form of furs and other trade goods from Indians and Anglos. He kept books and allowed his customers to draw against their accounts for needed supplies. Occasionally he advanced credit, allowing customers to charge stores until they could deliver enough goods to Glenn to clear their accounts.[5]

With an influx of traders in the 1820s and 1830s, trading posts became more numerous in Oklahoma. The Department of War tried with limited success to regulate the traders, requiring them to give bond, secure a license, and treat with the Indians at designated places. Traders coming into Oklahoma often doubled as bankers; their financing was vital to the development of the region. To these merchants fell the responsibility of paying drafts for trade goods and livestock and of cashing drafts for Indian agents, army officers, and other customers, with most drafts payable at New Orleans, Fort Smith, or Washington, D.C. Merchants found that periodically they had to visit banks in one of the above locations, cash drafts, and bring gold and silver, usually packed in kegs, back to Indian Territory. Moreover, merchants found that they had to use caution in accepting bank notes because many were of a highly speculative character. After the banking panics of 1819 and 1827, notes varied greatly from their face value and were often negotiated at a sizable discount, if accepted at all.[6]

Bringing gold and silver into Oklahoma proved particularly hazardous for the merchant-bankers. Their presence in Fort Smith or New Orleans alerted highwaymen looking for easy marks. Scurvy outlaws who would kill for the price of a drink sometimes tracked the merchants and fell upon them when they crossed into Indian Territory. Several merchants lost their lives because they failed to take adequate security measures.[7] One of the most dangerous brigands was Henry Starr, who was born near old Fort Gibson in 1873.

Specializing in bank and train robbery and in waylaying weary travelers on the open road, Starr had a notorious career that began in the late 1880s. Operating as far north as Kansas and as far west as Arizona, he was not stopped until 1921 when he died after being shot in a holdup attempt at Harrison, Arkansas. When the dangers of the return trip became known, merchants hired extra guards and joined convoys to ensure safe journeys.[8]

Because there was little money in circulation in Indian country, the merchant-bankers conducted much business on credit. Indians purchased supplies with the understanding that they would pay with the proceeds of their hunts and farming activities or with government annuities. Whenever Indians did receive currency or coin, it usually passed quickly from the disbursing office to the merchants, who in turn paid their creditors and restocked their supplies.[9]

If those who performed banking functions in early Indian Territory did so haphazardly, their actions only mirrored the activities of financial leaders throughout the United States. Before the passage of the National Currency Act in February, 1863, the country's financial structure was chaotic. Prior to the legislation, more than 1,500 state-chartered banks, most only loosely regulated by their state governments, issued their own bank notes. There were more than 10,000 varieties of legitimate issues and an untold number of counterfeit bank drafts. Unscrupulous men often issued bills in excess of their banks' assets, never intending to cash the drafts, knowing that the worthless paper would continue in circulation at a heavy discount. "Wildcat" bankers sometimes established themselves temporarily in a rural, out-of-the-way place, issued unsound paper, and then moved to another location to begin new operations under different names.[10]

After the removal to Oklahoma of many tribes from east of the Mississippi, the Indians soon developed a need for financial houses; none existed, however, and the traders who also performed banking functions could not serve the entire region. Consequently, many of the merchants in Indian settlements assumed the duties of bankers. In the Choctaw Nation, for example, Doaksville, Skullyville, and Boggy Depot were among the towns that became leading trade centers. Each had mercantile firms that performed added duties as bankers. Originally, merchants simply set up a safe or a cash box in a nook of the store. For extra security some merchants enclosed the space in chicken wire through which a window was cut to permit the transaction of business.[11] The metropolis of the Choctaw Nation, Doaksville, had such private banks as the Doak and Tims Mercantile Company and Berthelet, Heald, and Company. At North Fork Town, Three Forks, and Micco in the Creek Nation, merchants performed financial functions similar to those in the Choctaw Nation. Likewise, at Tahlequah in the Cherokee Nation and at the trading centers of the other tribes, mercantile firms advanced credit, accepted deposits, and performed other banking duties.[12]

When whites began establishing settlements in Indian Territory, private banks were established. One early merchant-banker was J. J. McAlester, for whom McAlester, Oklahoma, was later named. A Confederate veteran, McAlester worked for a firm in Stonewall in the Chickasaw Nation from 1865 to 1870. Then, with a partner, who soon retired, he opened a store and a private bank at the "Crossroads" on the Texas Road. He also organized the Oklahoma Mining Company after he had discovered coal near present-day McAlester, thereby beginning a mineral boom destined to bring new demands for banking facilities in Oklahoma. Although J. J. McAlester soon sold his interests in his mining company, new fields were opened at Krebs, Coalgate, Lehigh, Alderson, and elsewhere. To a large extent, the mining towns were composed of European immigrants who were accustomed to conducting a limited amount of transactions with regular banks. Again, like their counterparts in earlier times, merchants responded to new demands by assuming extra duties as bankers.[13]

Early private banks sometimes started in tents before permanent facilities were completed and often conducted business amid rugged surroundings. As soon as wooden structures could be erected, the banks moved indoors, but usually occupied no more than a small area in a general store or other establishment. Furnishings consisted of an old crate or table, which served as a desk, and a locked box. But the progressive financial leader soon imported a real desk and a cast-iron safe and dignified his corner of the store by encasing his area in chicken wire. Most of the banker's customers were the same people who frequented the store. Those who had too much money to carry personally, but who wished to purchase three or six months of supplies, were sent toward the wire. There, if they had collateral, or could pass the bank officer's "eye" test for respectability, they received a loan.[14]

One firm that began offering banking services in the 1880s was the Degnan and McConnell Coal and Coke Company, which worked the mines in the Choctaw and Chickasaw nations. The firm primarily employed immigrants, particularly Italians who worked desperately to improve their economic status and who demanded the services of a financial institution. Establishing offices at Howe and Wilburton, the company's private bank offered only a safe-keeping service, making no loans or investments. It had no capital, no surplus, no directors. It was unsupervised, except by officers of the company, but until statehood the bank continued to function, offering European workers what they most needed: a safe place to store their savings.[15] After 1907 the company closed its books and urged old customers to patronize nearby banks.

Just as the mining frontier forced an expansion of banking activity, the railroad frontier also encouraged growth. The builders of the Union Pacific planned to lay rails from Kansas to the Gulf of Mexico, with lines running along the Texas Road. In 1869 the Missouri, Kansas, and Texas (MKT) Railroad acquired all rights to the southern branch of the Union Pacific and began building through Oklahoma. Although controversies with the Indian Nations slowed construction, the railroad reached Muskogee early in 1872. Pushing on, the company first established a new terminal in Eufaula, and then in Atoka, before reaching the Red River in 1873. Meanwhile, another company was building from the east. The Atlantic and Pacific (A & P) Railroad had reached western Missouri by 1871 and later that year formed a junction with the MKT at Vinita. Although financial considerations forced the A & P to suspend construction, it was reorganized in the 1880s as the Saint Louis and San Francisco (SL & SF) Railroad and pushed track to Sapulpa. Between 1882 and 1887 the company constructed another line through the Choctaw Nation from Fort Smith to Poteau, Wister, Antlers, Hugo, and eventually Paris, Texas. By the late 1880s other lines entered the region.[16]

As the railroads extended lines through Oklahoma, terminals along the routes temporarily became boom towns; some later developed into thriving communities that attracted both town dwellers and farmers. The MKT facilitated the growth of such towns as Vinita, Antlers, and Hugo. In each community demands were made for banking facilities, and merchants added the job to their other tasks.[17]

Despite the expansion of banking activities in old Oklahoma, no modern banks existed prior to 1889. Rather, respected citizens—Anglos or Indians—functioned as bankers as a sideline to their regular vocations. Private companies continued to organize quasi banks, and in some cases individuals performed similar functions. For example, the Reverend W. J. B. Lloyd often acted as a banker for the Choctaws. One day Lloyd, who maintained the Mission Church at Old Bennington, and his wife, Sarah, visited Governor Wilson W. Jones, principal chief of the Choctaws. As the Anglo couple left the Indian camp, Jones threw several sacks of gold over the saddle horn of Sarah's horse; he feared being robbed and asked the missionaries to keep his cache, which was worth $10,000. Sarah hid the gold under a mattress in her bedroom, holding it until the chief asked for the return of the money five years later.[18]

By the late 1870s traders P. S. Hoffman, J. B. Charles, and E. L. Conklin were acting as bankers at the Sac and Fox Agency. The traders extended credit, accepted deposits, and cashed government drafts. Operating the bank out of a corner of their general store, they patterned their operation to suit the needs of the Indians and Anglo farmers of the region. Open for business by sunrise, the bank remained available to customers until late evening. It was open six days a week and part of the day on Sundays. Always aware of their need for security, the firm hired armed guards to discourage desperadoes.[19]

Traders on the Cheyenne and Arapaho reservation also acted as bankers for their charges. At old Fort Cantonment in present-day Blaine County, government agents originally dispensed supplies to the Indians in exact portions according to the mandates of the federal Indian Bureau. By the 1880s the agents there had stopped that practice. Instead they issued checks or vouchers to the heads of families, who could then buy from the post store at their convenience and have their bills deducted from amounts due them.[20]

Beginning late in the 1870s at Muskogee, the firm of J. A. Patterson and Company acted as bankers for the Cherokee, Creek, and Choctaw, as did merchants J. E. Turner and H. P. Spaulding, one of the founders of a great banking family that for many years had banking interests in Muskogee and Sapulpa. Although there were no banks, the trio of mercantile firms accepted deposits and advanced loans if sufficient collateral was posted. They also issued scrip, which was used as a convenient medium of exchange and accepted by all local merchants. Most often such scrip was of a homemade, handwritten variety, but Spaulding—a man of vision and ego—issued printed, green paper money of varying denominations, all carrying his picture.[21] Most of those connected with the first "banks" continued to hold interests in financial institutions as the territories grew.

The experience of Patterson's company provided one illustration of how banking evolved in early Indian Territory. Originally, the Patterson Mercantile Company dealt in the buying and selling of cattle herds and other products. In 1879, as a convenience to out-of-town customers and cattlemen, the firm began accepting currency and coin for safekeeping, with the money being sealed in heavy canvas bags. Large cattle sales and other business transactions did not result in withdrawals from the bags held by the company; rather, other labels with the new owners' names attached were put on the bags. When $30,000 had accumulated, a worried Patterson bought a new safe to house the money and then decided to enlarge his banking functions. Accepting deposits, he issued passbooks and checks to customers. Soon his deposits reached $90,000. As mentioned before, like other merchants, he also made loans and issued scrip. But Patterson was no banker. His major interests were commercial, and he worried about the liability of the $90,000 in deposited funds. Moreover, in 1889 he organized a large department store in Muskogee, the first of its size in Indian Territory. With the store taking more and more of his time, and that of his staff, Patterson urged his depositors to transfer their banking business to the First National of Muskogee after it was formed by the leading businessmen of Muskogee—a group that included J. L. Dabbs and B. A. Randle—and chartered in 1890. Yet, it was not until January, 1905 that the firm had liquidated all the accounts of its unincorporated bank.[22]

Like the merchants at Muskogee, businessmen and ranchers at Spaulding, near Okmulgee, acted as bankers, accepting deposits, making loans, and issuing scrip. However, one rancher, Jake Simmons, disliked the practice of issuing paper money. Although he paid his men with scrip, they complained because the medium of exchange was of use only in Spaulding. If anyone planned a trip and wanted to exchange the paper for real money, the scrip was discounted and the customer took a loss.[23]

Occasionally, Anglo traders and merchants had difficulty in their banking negotiations with their Indian customers. A banker from Tahlequah, whose name is unknown, once related a story concerning a transaction with a Cherokee. Inquiring of the businessman for a loan, the Indian was asked in turn about collateral. "What is collateral?" the Indian asked. After explaining the term, the merchant questioned his customer to determine if he had any assets. The Cherokee, uncooperative when discussing his personal possessions, finally mentioned that he had ten ponies; the banker made the loan. Several months later the Indian repaid his loan and accrued interest in full, and the merchant noticed that his customer had begun to prosper. The entrepreneur then reminded the Cherokee of their past business dealings. Talking of friends in need and of reciprocation, the banker asked the Indian whether he had any money to deposit. The Indian turned and walked away, muttering that he would never loan money to a banker who did not own a string of ponies.[24]

Another banker in Indian Territory, whose name is lost in the misty past, loaned money not to an Indian but to an Anglo who listed a few head of cattle as his collateral. When the note came due and the farmer did not pay, the financier went to the countryside to investigate. The banker found no animals on the place except a few stray dogs and a mount. Exasperated because he intended to take his customer's collateral as payment for the debt, the disgruntled financier asked the debtor but one question: "Where are the cattle?" The farmer replied enthusiastically: "I et 'em. I et every damned one."[25]

Although early private bankers sometimes took risks with the money of their depositors, in most instances financial leaders took pride in their institutions, were judicious, and—in the absence of outside regulations—policed themselves to maintain the public trust. Most private institutions stood periodic inspections by their directors, who might be untrained in accounting but who instinctively knew when books were in order. In typical reports from Indian Territory in the 1890s the directors stated that "we examined the books and found the bank solvent. The crops were better than usual and we only have nineteen notes left on hand and they are good. The deposits have climbed back to $11,000, but will run down again when the spring demand for loans comes around." Continuing, the directors stated that "the salary of the cashier who runs the bank has been increased to $25 per month and he has been granted part time to keep books for the livery stable which the president owns. All accounts are balanced and the books are in good shape."[26]

Some patrons of early-day bankers complained about interest rates that they believed usurious. Most merchants and traders maintained reasonable rates, but some charged all that the traffic would bear, with rates climbing from 15 percent to 35 percent per annum of the note. Infrequently, rates climbed to a high of 60 percent a year. In response to those who criticized the high rates, merchants referred to the law of supply and demand and quickly pointed out that they took high risks in making many of their loans.[27]

A variety of people performed banking functions in early Oklahoma, and the major criteria for success appeared to be honor and trust. Despite the fact that most early bankers were honorable, however, their depositors' money was rarely safe. The aforementioned Reverend Lloyd and wife, Sarah, once entertained the notorious Frank James while they held $10,000 for the Choctaws. They did not know James's true identity until he had departed, and he did not know of their cache of gold. Doubtless he would have robbed the Lloyds had he known of the wealth they held.[28] Similarly, E. L. Conklin, one of the traders at the Sac and Fox Agency, lamented that his firm could not keep large amounts of cash on hand to conduct business. "The Dalton boys and others who happened along," Conklin said, "would make free with the cash but would fail to leave a check for the same."[29]

Because of the unstable conditions in Oklahoma and the lack of any real banking facility, the tribes and Anglo settlers of Indian Territory usually relied on stable institutions outside the territory when dealing in large sums of money. In fact, merchants in the territory who performed banking functions also turned to established banks elsewhere if sums were particularly large. In the Choctaw Nation, for example, by the 1870s most residents, as well as the tribal government, usually banked in nearby Texas at Denison, Sherman, or Paris, or in Arkansas at Fort Smith.[30]

One interesting experiment in banking occurred while David L. Payne was organizing the Boomers in the 1880s. In June, 1884, Payne and a thousand of his followers established a camp called Rock Falls on the Chickaskia River near the junction of Bois d'Arc, south of Hunnewell, Kansas. Within two months a village had grown to include four box houses, hundreds of tents, an underground workshop, a printing office, and a well for drinking water. The little settlement did not have a bank, however. Because people needed to secure their valuables, Payne got a cast-iron safe and began a form of purse-and-package banking. Broader and longer than its depth, the safe, when sitting on wooden horses, was concealed with a tablecloth and served as a desk. Certificates of membership in the colony, attached to each purse, identified each owner. No ledgers were kept, and deposit and withdrawal were always in whole, never in part.[31]

Once when General Edward Hatch led a detachment of soldiers to disperse the colony, the bank was broken. As the soldiers approached, leaders gave purses to owners present, left the other packaged valuables in the safe, caulked it, and tossed it into the well, which was filled with brush. When the troops arrived on August 7, they burned the village and arrested Payne and six other leaders but overlooked the purse-and-package bank. After the soldiers departed, colonists who still had possessions in the bank returned and, with block and tackle, hoisted the safe from the well and liquidated the bank.[32]

In the 1880s another experiment in banking began in Indian Territory, an experiment that centered in the Choctaw Nation. Licensed traders with the Choctaw introduced the "nickel-savings-stamp" system. Working with the Denison (Texas) National Bank, such prominent businessmen in North Texas and Indian Territory as D. W. Hopkins in McAlester, D. N. Garland in Lehigh, and J. D. Lankford, later state bank commissioner, in Atoka acted as stamp agents. Customers purchased stamps from the merchants at a cost of one nickel apiece and pasted them in a savings book, with sheets divided into twenty squares. The bank at Denison accepted deposits by the book or by the sheet. Thus when a purchaser was ready to open an account, he signed a signature card and gave his stamps to a "stamp banker" who mailed them to Denison. By return mail customers received a passbook and a check pad. The system of stamp banking worked well in the Choctaw Nation for several years. Although the marketing of stamps declined after 1890 because of the competition brought by new banks in Indian Territory, during the 1880s the system allowed many people to save money who would not otherwise have been able to do so.[33]

Meanwhile, settlers in isolated western Oklahoma had problems that not even the nickel-savings-stamp system could solve; there, settlement was very sparse, and only cattlemen had the resources to act as bankers. Until 1887 No Man's Land (the Oklahoma Panhandle) was almost totally without law and order. That year, however, Panhandle settlers formed the Territory of the Cimarron, headquartered at Kenton. Although a committee made laws for the area, it was not recognized by the federal government. Only in 1889 did Washington establish sway over the region and place it under jurisdiction of a court situated in Muskogee, 500 miles from Kenton. As a result, for many years after 1889 settlers in the Panhandle continued to live an autonomous, isolated existence. For their banking needs they turned to the 101 Ranch, which opened a private bank in the 1870s. The bank accepted deposits, made loans, and gave its customers a check-writing service. The bank used Caldwell, Kansas, as a reserve center, and a financial institution in that town supplied the ranch with forms and ledger books and dispatched examiners for periodic inspections.[34] The 101 bank was liquidated after the turn of the century when "real" banks were established in the Panhandle.

Although the Panhandle was more isolated than the rest of Oklahoma, no real banking industry existed in Indian Territory. Early traders had performed banking functions, but only in addition to other endeavors. Later merchants also performed banking functions, but they, too, offered only those services that benefited their commercial transactions. And of the few private banks existent before 1889, most were limited if not unsound. When dealing with large sums of money, the majority of people—both Indians and Anglos—patronized banks in Texas, Kansas, or Arkansas. Only after the land run of 1889, and subsequent other openings, did the great expansion of the banking industry begin.

Chapter 2.

The First Expansion

When the first Oklahoma land run occurred on April 22, 1889, the history of banking in the region entered a new phase. On that day thousands of land seekers gathered for the rush into the "Unassigned Lands," a one thousand-square-mile, heart-shaped area, bounded by a line running near present-day Stillwater, west to Kingfisher, south through El Reno, to a point near Purcell, to Guthrie. More than six thousand people made the first run, and Oklahoma towns like Guthrie and Oklahoma City literally were "born grown." Immediately tent cities grew from the rolling prairies of central Oklahoma. Merchants, saloonkeepers, gamblers, land speculators, farmers—all sought the main chance, a once-in-a-lifetime opportunity to get rich. Farmers, although they thought less of getting rich, wanted a claim on which to rear a family, on which to grow roots. Immediately in countless areas a restless, ever growing populace demanded financial services that only full-time bankers could provide. Many banks were born grown, along with the towns that spawned them.

Most early banks in Oklahoma Territory were private institutions. As towns were founded, people were obligated to establish their own government and social institutions. For more than a year there was no territorial government, and they were forced to "make do" while waiting for federal officials to complete the cumbersome process of organizing the Territory of Oklahoma. Consequently, anyone—with or without capital—could open a private bank unrestrained by any charter, code, or law. Occasionally an entrepreneur opened a bank with no capital by just pitching an IOU to himself in the bank's safe. When profits later allowed the creation of a capital fund, the IOU was destroyed.[1] On other occasions, bankers listed capital, but the account was in the form of fixed assets—tables, benches, chairs, a safe—with no cash reserves. One enterprising group of five entrepreneurs, whose names and locations have been long forgotten, decided to found a bank but had no capital whatsoever. They overcame that small problem easily. Each of the five threw IOUs for $1,000 into a tool box. With $5,000 capital, the bank was founded. Later, after the financial institution made a profit, the IOUs were withdrawn and destroyed. Yet another unidentified financier opened a private bank with no capital. Worse, he had liabilities in the form of charges with a Saint Louis firm that had sold him a safe on credit and with a railroad company for freight charges. However, the money he received from his first few depositors paid his debts, and the banker was established.[2] He could not have passed an audit by any regulatory agency, but audits were not required. Had depositors known of the unstable nature of the banker's developing financial "empire," a run certainly would have destroyed him. Yet, he survived and prospered into the twentieth century.

If almost anyone could establish a bank, so could he operate unrestrained by law. When balancing his books, he might follow his own accounting process; when making decisions affecting his bank's future, he might keep his own counsel, his decisions unchallenged by any board of directors or regulatory agency. When making loans, for example, financiers had complete freedom, subject to market conditions. They might charge a rate as low as 10 percent for short term, ninety-day notes, but 5 percent per month was closer to the norm. Likewise, most early bankers did not pay interest on deposits. Rather, they charged depositors a fee, usually a small one, for the privilege of storing money in the bank. Simply put, in the absence of regulations financial leaders did what seemed right at the time, what common sense told them to do; some charged high interest rates, for example, not because they wanted unreasonable profits, but because they knew that some bad risks would never pay, or that some natural calamity might prevent even an honest man from paying.[3] Consequently, those who could and did pay had to make up for losses.

One of the first "regular" banks opened during the rush was the Bank of Guthrie (later the Guthrie National Bank), which on April 22, 1889, was conducting business in the open air. Later the institution was moved into a tent. J. M. Ragsdale, C. R. McLain, and associates from Newton, Kansas, controlled another institution, the Commercial Bank. Later accused by some critics of being a Sooner,

Ragsdale apparently was simply a farsighted, well-organized businessman who reached Guthrie before his competition. At first doing business with no capital, he received $1,000 in silver from his bank, the Newton National, on April 23. A going concern, the Commercial Bank averaged $1,800 a day in deposits for its first three months.[4] By 1890, Ragsdale, McLain, and associates were active in several other towns in Oklahoma Territory. In addition to their Guthrie bank, which had moved into permanent quarters, they controlled the Commercial Bank of Norman, the Commercial Bank of Stillwater, and the Bank of Kingfisher.[5]

Ragsdale and McLain, two of the most active bankers during and immediately after the run, organized an impressive chain of establishments. In fact, when national banking laws were extended to Oklahoma Territory in 1890, Ragsdale claimed that his Guthrie bank was granted a charter and advertised $300,000 in paid-in capital. Depositors doing business with any one of the firm's five banks must have been chagrined, however, when they read their Oklahoma newspapers on November 21. Glaring headlines reported to a surprised populace that Ragsdale, McLain, and all the officers of their banks had "flown from the territory." Accompanied by his private guard, Ragsdale left Guthrie in the early morning hours. He tried to charter a private train to get him out of the territory but finding that impossible, booked an early morning, regularly scheduled run. Leaving the keys to his banks and empty vaults in the hands of Guthrie's sheriff and swearing that he had securities worth twice as much as his depositors' accounts, Ragsdale absconded. Visiting all of his banks and collecting all coins and currency in flour barrels, which he left at the home of one of his domestic servants, he left many of Oklahoma's depositors penniless.[6]

In El Reno, Norman, Kingfisher, and Stillwater, businessmen were surprised by the failure. As he left the Guthrie depot, heading for parts unknown, Ragsdale took all central Oklahoma "for a ride." He may have taken pride in the fact that he left his banks the same way he found them, without a penny. Although law enforcement agents and disgruntled private citizens acting as vigilantes combed the Midwest looking for Ragsdale, he was never found. Such escapades demonstrated how dishonest men could exploit many Oklahoma pioneers who tended to be too trusting and whose admiration for financiers made them too gullible. In fact, Ragsdale had apparently planned well in advance to rob his depositors. Even his boasts about the capital structure of his Guthrie bank were flights of fancy, for although he advertised it as a national institution, it never was.[7]

Scoundrels like Ragsdale took advantage of the unsettled conditions of early Oklahoma and the lack of regulations in banking. However, most bankers were honest, upright businessmen who wanted fair returns for their investments and labor but who watched depositors' accounts much as shepherds guard their sheep. Most realized that while scoundrels might make "quick" money, profits and long-term growth depended on developing the trust of the community and helping it prosper. In Guthrie, for example, although the Commercial Bank was the first of Ragsdale's to fold, four other banks survived: the Bank of Guthrie, the McNeal-Little Banking Company, the Capital City Bank, and the Bank of Indian Territory. These establishments, and others in Stillwater, El Reno, Norman, and Kingfisher helped the settlers recover from the damages wrought by such men as Ragsdale.[8]

Hard-working, civic-minded men headed most banks in early Oklahoma. One such man was the aforementioned McNeal, of Medicine Lodge, Kansas, who, along with his partner A. W. Little of Kansas City, Missouri, organized the McNeal-Little Banking Company in Guthrie in May, 1889. Opening his bank in a tent, he had no safe and carried his deposits in a money belt and in his pockets, while an armed guard protected him. Although he later switched to a Boston ledger, originally he kept accounts in a memo book that he also carried on his person. Protected day and night by two guards armed with Winchesters, McNeal never lost a penny. Nor did he make unsound investments that would have cost his depositors dearly.[9]

McNeal remained active in Guthrie's banking fraternity until 1910 and served a term as president of the Oklahoma Bankers Association. In 1910 his banking interests were purchased by Ned Holman and P. A. Norris—other pioneer bankers in Oklahoma—who merged several holdings into the First National Bank using an original charter that later allowed the firm to advertise itself as the oldest bank in Oklahoma.

Oklahoma City, like Guthrie, became the home of several of the territory's most stable institutions. By 1890 the city had four thriving banks, one of which was the Oklahoma Bank (later known as the First National Bank). Organized by T. M. Richardson—originally from Albany, Texas, and the founder of a great Oklahoma banking family—and J. P. Boyle, the institution was operating out of a tent and accepting deposits on April 22, 1889. Bringing the fixtures for his bank in by wagon, Richardson unloaded and went immediately to work promoting his establishment. After using several temporary quarters, the founders erected a substantial three-story building in 1891. As could be said of McNeal and Little, the hard work and honesty of Richardson, Boyle, and other early financial leaders helped bankers regain the trust that men such as Ragsdale damaged.[10]

Honest bankers also continued to found stable institutions in Indian Territory. In August, 1889, J. R. Anderson organized a private bank in Ardmore. Originally known as J. R. Anderson and Son Bank, the institution began with a paid-in capital of $3,200. Deposits on its first day, August 17, aggregated $203.75. After one year in operation the bank received a federal charter and became the First National Bank of Ardmore.[11] Except for national banks, there were no provisions for incorporating banks in Indian Territory prior to 1901. That year Congress passed a statute extending the corporation laws of Arkansas to Indian Territory. As aforementioned, requirements for a national charter were stringent. Consequently, most financial institutions were founded as private banks, subject to no regulations whatever.[12]

Occasionally, a trusting nature and unfamiliarity with banking procedure did more to harm unsuspecting merchants and settlers than dishonest men. One shopkeeper in Guthrie learned a hard lesson in 1889 when he went to the Merchants Bank to cash a $600 draft received from a customer. Informed that the bank would not cash the draft, the shopkeeper became irate. Bank officials could only explain that the signer of the draft, one John Doe, did not have an account at the bank.[13]

In May, 1890, the federal government imposed regulations on banks in Oklahoma Territory. The Organic Act passed by Congress created Oklahoma Territory and divided it into six counties, encompassing all of former Indian Territory except the tribal reservations of the Five Civilized Tribes, seven smaller reserves in the Quapaw Agency, and the unoccupied part of the Cherokee Outlet. Providing a government for the territory, the bill instructed the governor and legislature to follow the laws of the older states when framing legal codes. On banking, the statute directed the territory to follow the Arkansas laws.[14] The Organic Act also extended the National Banking Acts of 1863 and 1864 to the territory. Under their provisions a bank could receive a federal charter if it had $30,000 paid-in capital and if it invested at least one-third in United States banks. Banks could then receive federal deposits, conduct federal business, and issue currency in an amount up to 90 percent of the value of the capital held.[15]

The new territorial government of Oklahoma loosely followed the Arkansas banking codes, as did the white settlements in Indian Territory. The Arkansas codes were lenient, allowing almost anyone to secure a bank charter on payment of a small filing fee of fifteen dollars. Under the law no minimum capital or supervision was required. After Ragsdale escaped, however, the territorial legislature strengthened the banking laws. In December, 1890, it became unlawful for insolvent institutions to accept deposits. Moreover, all officers of such banks were held individually liable if they broke the law, and usury was forbidden. In addition, a maximum interest rate of 12 percent was established, but it was repealed in 1895 (later a usury law of 10 percent was placed in the Oklahoma State Constitution and was not removed until 1969). Also, corporate laws pertained to financial institutions when applicable. Yet no comprehensive, regulatory banking code was written until 1897.[16]

Occasionally, institutions chartered in Kansas, Texas, or other nearby states established branches in the territories where they were unrestrained by their state charters. Often such branches failed even to establish a physical presence in the territories. In November, 1889, for example, the Chickasaw Bank of Indian Territory was organized by H. P. Farrar in Cowley County, Kansas, and received a Kansas charter for ninety-nine years. Capitalized at $50,000, the bank for a time continued to operate in Kansas, and its only connection with the territory was a rented post-office box in Purcell, Chickasaw Nation. Depositors used the post to send in their money and to receive their passbooks. It was not until early 1890 that the bank moved to Purcell, where it faced stiff competition from the Bank of Purcell, a private institution owned by George, John, and B. F. Beeler.

Curiously, the fate of the Chickasaw Bank demonstrates the state of flux that permeated the development of banking in early Oklahoma. Organized under the laws of Arkansas, the bank was taxed under acts of the Chickasaw Nation. Later, in 1891, the institution merged with the private Bank of Purcell, and Farrar sought a national charter, which he received in June of 1892. Despite the constantly changing conditions and reorganizations, however, the Chickasaw National Bank served its surrounding agricultural region until 1927, when it was absorbed by the McClain County State Bank which had been founded in 1920.[17]

While the Kansas bank was bringing its services to Purcell, John Henry Dill opened a private bank in Muskogee in 1890. A businessman who learned the Creek language in order to deal better with the Indians, Dill was originally a sewing machine salesman. He saved his money and loaned it at interest. Finding the lending business profitable, he waited until he had amassed $750 capital, rented a small storeroom, added office fixtures, and opened a bank. F. B. Severs, a wealthy merchant and cattleman who lived in the area, allowed Dill to manage his account and thereby put the bank on a solid foundation. Although Dill soon sold his interests in the bank, the institution prospered and eventually became the Commercial National Bank.[18]

Dill's success convinced Robert L. Owen, who later represented Oklahoma in the United States Senate and who helped draft the Federal Reserve Act, to organize the First National Bank of Muskogee, which received its national charter on August 1, 1890. Well situated geographically and a hub of military and economic activity, Muskogee could support more than one bank. By 1890 the town was a thriving business settlement in the heart of the Creek Nation. Only a few Anglos were present, save those working for the government. Nevertheless, having one of the few gins in the area, the town was a headquarters for a flourishing cotton culture. Led by Owen, the local businessmen decided in 1889 to establish a commercial bank, and they applied for a national charter. The attorney general of the United States ruled, however, that a charter could not be granted until the status of Indian Territory was clarified. Dissatisfied, Owen—using the aid of influential friends—went to Washington, D.C., in 1890 and persuaded Congress to extend national banking laws to Indian Territory. Owen then became the first president of the First National of Muskogee.[19]

One year after Dill opened his bank in Muskogee, James and John Staples—members of a prominent mercantile family in Indian Territory—opened the Bank of Tahlequah in the Cherokee Nation.[20] Accepting deposits and making loans, when a dearth of hard money threatened to send the local economy into a tailspin, the Staples brothers were forced to provide a local means of exchange. Their firm issued brass coins (backed by deposits) that were accepted by all the businessmen in Tahlequah and in the surrounding area. Such improvisation, which was a hallmark of early bankers, facilitated the growth of the local economy.[21]

Soon after the Staples brothers had founded their institution, S. S. Cobb and other businessmen in Vinita decided that their community needed a bank. Settlers had been depositing money with leading merchants, or hiding it at home in flour sacks, salt barrels, and other such places. The merchants held a directors meeting in July, 1891, and founded the Bank of Vinita with Cobb as the first president. He was replaced in 1892 by Oliver Bagby, a physician who later acquired interests in banks in Tulsa, Claremore, Chelsea, and Miami. After Bagby took over, the institution applied for and received a national charter, becoming the First National Bank in Vinita.[22]

While Cobb was organizing his bank in Vinita, settlers in Pauls Valley began clamoring for a bank. Apparently the publicity about the success of a bank in one area inspired settlers in other areas to lobby for the creation of their own local institutions, which could serve their needs better than distant banks. As a result, C. J. Grant, Thomas P. Howell, and Sam Garvin founded a private bank that accepted deposits and lent money at interest rates of 10 to 15 percent per annum. Howell and Grant, along with Noah Lael and Perry Froman, also established a bank in nearby Davis. Likewise, the Miners Exchange Bank of Lehigh, in the Choctaw Nation, opened in March, 1891. In addition, the Choctaw Mercantile Company engaged in general banking.[23]

The opening of a number of new banks in Indian Territory after 1890 severely crippled the old savings-stamp system of banking. While banks had been few in the territory, settlers, particularly those in Choctaw and Chickasaw country had flocked to their merchants to buy stamps. Then when their savings warranted, they opened accounts with the First National of Denison, Texas. However, when institutions such as the Miners Exchange opened, frontiersmen stopped purchasing stamps, closed their accounts in Texas, and opened accounts at banks closer to home. Moreover, for those who mistrusted the small, fledgling institutions in the territory, banks in Arkansas, such as the German Bank owned by Gus Gill and H. T. Jackman, began bombarding the Indian Nations with advertising, offering to pay 4 percent on demand deposits of any amount. Eventually Gill and Jackman organized the permanent Bank of South McAlester and dealt the nickel-savings-stamp system its final blow.[24]

After Lincoln County was opened for settlement in September, 1891, Hoffman, Charles, Conklin, and Company, which was engaged in banking functions as an adjunct to its general store on the Sac and Fox Agency in the 1880s, enlarged its operations. The company hired H. C. Brunt, later president of the Union National Bank, a firm that eventually grew out of the original company, as cashier for a new private bank in Chandler. Housed in a box-frame building, ten by twenty feet, it was operated for five years as an auxiliary for the company's expanding network of department-general stores at Sac and Fox, Chandler, Stroud, Cushing, and other points. The institution's major function was to centralize the handling of credit for the company. In 1893 and 1895 the bank's stability was increased by the opening of the Cherokee Strip and Kickapoo lands. The latter opening added six townships to Lincoln County and helped to assure the bank's future. By that time there was enough business in the area to support a second financial institution, the Lincoln County Bank, which was founded in 1894 by O. B. Kee, Fred Hogt, and W. E. Meredith.[25]

Brunt sometimes had difficulty managing the affairs of Hoffman, Charles, Conklin, and Company, problems that doubtless were mirrored by many institutions in frontier Oklahoma. The bank at Chandler furnished cash for the annuity checks sent to the Sac and Fox Indians. Generally, the checks could be handled by crediting a customer's account and letting him draw goods as needed, but currency was also required, and it had to be shipped by stagecoach from Guthrie to Chandler, often at the risk of holdups. On one occasion Ed Conklin went to Joe McNeal at the Guthrie National to pick up funds. Conklin remarked that he was always nervous about taking money to Chandler and that he wished he could get his $10,000 delivered to him. For a $100 fee, the Guthrie banker agreed to transport the money. Accompanied by armed guards, McNeal fulfilled his commitment, but he remarked afterwards: "Never again. I had a feeling I would be held up at every black-jack tree we passed."[26] The problem of transporting its cash, a major difficulty, remained the responsibility of the Chandler bank.[27]

In 1893 the new financial institutions of Oklahoma underwent a severe test when a national bank panic and subsequent depression began. When word of the panic reached Oklahoma, there were runs on several banks as restlessness and fear gripped the territories. Most banks survived, but two firms in Oklahoma City were less fortunate. The Oklahoma National Bank, an outgrowth of the Citizens Bank founded during the run, and the Bank of Oklahoma City, organized a few months later, were forced to close their doors on April 23 when runs depleted their cash reserves. After witnessing several weeks of irregular openings, people in the city lost all confidence in the two banks, and the runs intensified. Finally at midday on July 19, James Wheeler, cashier of the Bank of Oklahoma City, posted a notice that his institution was insolvent and closed. Like a prairie fire, the news spread. Depositors of all the banks in the community began withdrawing their money. The Oklahoma National Bank could not complete the day; it, too, closed its doors.[28]

A run such as that which occurred in Oklahoma City was both exciting and horrible to view. Calm observers were amazed at the intensity of emotions, at the "mob psychology" engendered by a developing panic. First, rumors spread, perhaps hitting the farmers' market or the saloons first—wherever men gathered to converse. Then the rumors became the "news" that was heard throughout the town. Families discussed the stories at home and pondered their futures, and many men decided to withdraw their money before it was too late, before they lost all.[29]

Ordinarily, bankers could withstand the first early withdrawals, but as new rumors brought more and more depositors to the institutions, reserves began to evaporate. Moreover, as people gathered, lines became long, because it was impossible for the staff to serve all customers simultaneously. The sight of the long lines in turn convinced bystanders that indeed something was wrong. They then clamored to get into the bank to withdraw their funds. Soon, crowds spilled into the street and threatened mob action if their demands were not satisfied. Shouting, chanting, and pushing matches sometimes characterized the crowds, while bank officials could only look on in consternation—before closing their doors and perhaps readying bankruptcy papers.[30]

Although all the banks in Oklahoma City threatened to go under, T. M. Richardson, president of the First National Bank, devised a plan that saved his bank and most of the others in the city. The First National had withstood the run of July 19 and had remained open into the night, paying all customers in full. But reserves ran dangerously low. Then, in the middle of the night, with people still gathering in the street in front of the bank, Richardson addressed the crowd. He announced that he intended to close but would reopen early the next morning. Although his bank had depleted its cash reserve, he enthusiastically announced that "there is enough money to pay off every depositor." Then pointing to a pole down the street, he vowed that "if any man loses a dollar in this bank, I want to be hanged to that telephone post over there."[31]

Just then, prearranged by bank officials, employees of the bank—who had left by a rear door and circled the block—rounded a corner carrying full money sacks. With the sacks thrown over their shoulders and the contents jingling with each step, the employees marched single file into the front door of the bank. For moments amazed members of the crowd stood silently in awe, but then began whispering about the development. Although the crowd did not know it, the money sacks had been filled not with coins and currency but with iron washers. Richardson's ploy worked, nevertheless. He gained time. That night M. L. Turner and Joe McNeal, bankers from Guthrie, drove to the city with the necessary money to save the First National. The trip proved unnecessary. Richardson's quick-thinking gamesmanship had ended the run. The crowd had been so impressed by the jingling of the iron washers that it dispersed. The next day, lines formed outside the bank, but the now sheepish horde wanted the privilege of depositing, not withdrawing, money.[32]

The failure of the Oklahoma City banks—in addition to the failure on July 18, 1893, of one of the region's largest banks in Kansas

City, where many of the bankers in Oklahoma held accounts—caused a panic in many towns in the twin territories. In Guthrie, for example, as the national panic progressed, bankers, businessmen, and newspaper editors joined to assure depositors that their money was safe. The banks were besieged, however, by restless, worried depositors. On July 20 a run on the Guthrie National began, but by noon withdrawals ceased—partly because a group of local businessmen had purposely attracted public attention while making timely deposits, as though to prove the bank was stable. Following the example of the leaders of the Guthrie National, other bankers in the territorial capital announced that they could easily meet all demands, but the panic had by then subsided, and the other bankers experienced little trouble.[33]

Many areas of Oklahoma experienced an extreme money shortage during the panic. Currency and coin in circulation simply disappeared. Consequently, many financial institutions issued their own scrip. The Oklahoma City Clearing House, for example, printed its own paper money, which was slightly larger than United States currency. Likewise, merchants issued trade notes. Mine operators and bankers in McAlester jointly issued metal scrip to serve the town and the coal fields.[34]

Recovery from the Panic of 1893 was rapid. Within one year there was new expansion in the banking industry, particularly in Indian Territory. In 1894, Gus A. Gill established a private bank in McAlester. Operating with $25,000 capital, he received deposits, made loans, and engaged in other primary banking functions. Two years later, C. C. Hemming organized a second bank and secured a national charter as the First National Bank of South McAlester.[35]

Following the developments inspired by Gill and Hemming, several new banks were established in Indian Territory the following year. John Cheyene opened the Bank of Miami, which was destined to have a long history, and John Foresythe founded the Tulsa Banking Company, another bank that would survive and prosper. Foresythe, a rancher from Texas who leased land near Tulsa, joined B. F. Colley and C. W. Brown to organize the Tulsa firm at a time when the settlement was a cow town of 650 people. Foresythe noted that there was no bank nearer than Vinita or Muskogee, and the thriving farm and ranch community needed a local bank. With initial capital of

$10,000, the three men received deposits and loaned money on notes that ranged up to ten years maximum, at interest rates of between 8 and 10 percent per annum. Reorganized in 1899, the bank received a federal charter, becoming the First National Bank of Tulsa. Foresythe and Colley remained on the board, but W. E. Halsell became the new president.[36]

The continuing mining boom in southern and southeastern Oklahoma culminated in the opening of several new institutions. Owing much of their prosperity to the coal fields, the private Bank of Hartshorne and the chartered Hartshorne State Bank along with the Citizens Bank of Wilburton began in 1901 to advertise for the miners' trade. By 1904 other new banks in Krebs, Haileyville, Wilburton, Alderson, and Red Oak were likewise depending on the coal fields for the bulk of their business. Hearty, thrifty immigrants, working to save enough money to return to the old country, comprised the clientele of many of these banks. However, far more hoped to amass capital, a "grubstake," that would allow them to become yeomen farmers or merchants.[37]

Banks in Oklahoma Territory were founded even more rapidly than those in Indian Territory. All of the towns organized in the original run had several banks by 1892. On September 22, 1891, the surplus lands of the Iowas and the Sac and Fox, along with ceded lands of the Pottawatomie and Shawnee, were opened to settlement by lottery. In addition, a second land run opened the area east of the original Oklahoma counties. Approximately twenty thousand individuals participated in the run. People hoping to build a new life or to claim a fortune on the untamed frontier established townsites at Tecumseh and Chandler. A third rush came in April 1892 when lands on the Cheyenne and Arapaho Reservation were opened with approximately twenty-five thousand settlers making the rush. As towns were created so were banks, and many entrepreneurs founded private institutions that received and lent money. In the area were five national banks that averaged $50,000 in paid-in capital and $150,000 in deposits; four territorial banks were chartered, with two capitalized at $50,000 and two at $30,000; and fourteen private banks were established with an average capitalization at $15,000.[38]

In 1893 and 1895 new runs brought an influx of more settlers and the creation of new townsites. The Cherokee Outlet was opened

The Run for the Cherokee Strip, 1893. Courtesy Oklahoma Bankers Association.

in September, 1893, and the Kickapoo lands in May, 1895. In every community enterprising businessmen founded banks. In Enid, settled during the outlet run, H. H. Champlin founded a private bank in 1893. With $10,000 paid-in capital, the bank proved to be a valuable asset to a community where businessmen needed loans to begin operations and farmers needed "grubstakes" to survive until harvest. In 1899, Champlin sold his bank, only to repurchase an interest in it later. It became the First National Bank of Enid after another prominent banking family, the Stephensons, acquired interests in it.[39] While Champlin was organizing his bank in Enid, John J. Gerloch opened a private bank in Woodward. On the first day of the run, Gerloch pitched a tent, moved supplies inside, and opened a general store. A safe in a corner became the Bank of Woodward, where Gerloch received deposits and made loans.[40]

In Waynoka, another town founded during the run for the outlet, Frank Nickerson assumed the duties of a banker in 1893, ten years before a regular bank was founded. The owner of a general store, Nickerson had accounts with a bank in Kiowa, Kansas. In his store he cashed checks and accepted deposits for which he gave due bills. Settlers could redeem the due bills for cash or for supplies. Because most settlers took supplies rather than money, the Nickersons usually had ample amounts of working capital with which to make loans.[41]

Perhaps typical in the days of rugged, frontier Oklahoma was the experience of settlers who founded Pawnee during the Cherokee Outlet run. Settled on September 16, Pawnee was "born grown" as a tent city. As box houses and buildings replaced the tents, a Kansan, C. L. Berry, who founded a banking family still active in the Stillwater-Pawnee area, became Pawnee's first banker. Erecting a fourteen-by-sixteen-foot frame structure in which he placed a safe that he had hauled from Kansas, Berry made his business prosper as he handled the deposits of the town's merchants. Once in late 1893, however, Berry received a scare when several members of the Bill Doolin gang invaded his bank. They had no deposits with Berry but intended to make a sizable withdrawal. Claiming that he was only an employee and did not know the combination of the safe, the financier declined to open the lock. Although the bandits threatened his life, Berry refused to be intimidated. Failing to secure Berry's cooperation, the gang had to be content with loose change lying around the office.[42]

To Berry's horror, the outlaws decided to take him hostage to ensure a safe getaway. At gunpoint and surrounded by the bandits, he was forced upon a mount. Much to his consternation, he could think of no avenue of escape as they rode from town. The banker's pleadings with the members of the gang are not recorded, but his entreaties apparently were effective. A murderous horde not known for charity, the Doolins turned Berry loose after crossing Blackbear Creek. The banker returned to town somewhat upset, but secure in the knowledge that he had protected his depositors' money.[43]

Not all the early bankers in the Cherokee Outlet and Kickapoo opening were as scrupulous as Berry. In fact, the area became known in the mid-1890s for its "wildcat" banking institutions, several of which were opened with little or no capital and several of which folded within one year after their opening. The wildcat banks operated in remote areas, and many of the officers of such institutions sought only to make a quick personal profit. Taking depositors' money with no intention of ever returning it, issuing scrip for local exchange with no thought of ever redeeming that scrip, the scoundrels usually fled whenever their coffers were full or there was a hint of trouble—but only to move to another part of the territories to begin another wildcat scheme.[44]

Although wildcat banks brought hardships to some Oklahoma communities, most financial leaders, like Berry in Pawnee, facilitated rapid progress in their communities. In Alva, for instance, bankers had experiences similar to Berry's, but were perhaps better organized to face the run. Alva was first settled on September 16, and within three weeks Elmer Williams, representing the McPherson (Kansas) National Bank, arrived in town. Bringing a safe and office furniture and fixtures, he rented a structure and opened the Bank of Alva, a private unchartered institution. Eli P. Williams, president of the bank in McPherson, was listed as chief executive officer, but Elmer Williams, who became the cashier, actually ran the bank. Soon after the opening of the Williams brothers' bank, C. Q. Chandler organized the Alva State Bank, which remained a private institution until June, 1894, when it was incorporated under territorial law. Incorporating his bank for a good reason, Chandler, an astute businessman, realized that he needed an advantage if he were to compete successfully with the Williams brothers, who had a parent bank and more capital stability. By incorporating, Chandler hoped to present his institution as being associated with territorial government. Advertising itself as "the only incorporated bank in 'M' County," it attracted hundreds of depositors and by November had driven the Bank of Alva out of business. Later, the Exchange Bank of Alva bought the state bank. Yet in all the early bank liquidations and sales in Alva, no depositors suffered a loss; at least one sound bank always existed to serve the populace.[45]

Perry, Oklahoma, also settled during the opening of the Cherokee Outlet, existed without banking facilities for more than three years. Although the town had 110 saloons within three months of its founding, it waited until February 20, 1896, for the first bank. The Exchange Bank, destined to have a long history as the Exchange National Bank, under its president Fred G. Moore opened its doors to $1,008 of deposits that first day.[46] Because the bank occupied an old remodeled building that had once housed Jake Leon's Kentucky Liquor Store, it came as no surprise to bank officials that some of its

Stillwater National Bank, 1894. Courtesy Oklahoma Bankers Association.

early customers were Leon's patrons who were unaware that he had moved his establishment. In fact, one of the bank's first customers was an elderly black woman who came to the teller's window, laid \$0.15 on the counter, and asked cashier Harry McCandless for her morning shot of whisky.[47]

Institutions in western Oklahoma were continuing to develop in the early 1890s when one famous early-day banking family settled in Cheyenne. Erasmus G. Thurmond brought his wife and family to the town and initially established a general store. Soon the Thurmonds began to loan out money in small amounts, but as their accounts grew more numerous, Erasmus and his son, Arthur L., opened a bank, the first of thirty-eight the family ultimately founded. In the banking business for decade after decade, the family still controlled three—in Elk City, Sayre, and Cheyenne—in the 1970s.[48]

The First National Bank, Cleveland, 1895. Courtesy Oklahoma Bankers Association.

The First National Bank, Tulsa, 1895. Courtesy Oklahoma Bankers Association.

The Exchange Bank and Bank of Perry, Perry, 1896. Courtesy Oklahoma Bankers Association.

Estimates vary widely on the total number of banks in the territories by 1895–96. No central agency—territorial or federal—produced a reliable tally. Certainly by the mid-1890s the twin territories had a banking industry that had expanded greatly since 1889. Altogether, there were probably 175 territorial, national, and private banks in operation. Private, unchartered institutions, which were undercapitalized, were continuously merging, moving, or going bankrupt, and those factors caused the number of banks to fluctuate wildly. There was no doubt, however, that the industry was more stable than it had been when the early Boomers of 1889 threw IOUs for capital into tool boxes and proclaimed the opening of a bank. In the move toward statehood, the banking industry would achieve yet more progress, more stability.

CHAPTER 3.

Toward Statehood

Oklahoma's banking industry underwent tremendous growth in the years from 1889 to 1896, but as the twin territories moved toward statehood, even greater expansion occurred. In addition, innovations in day-to-day operations were implemented to create a more efficient system. In the latter 1890s, in urban centers with large populations that supported several banks, local clearinghouse associations were formed. While a clearinghouse need be nothing more than a room where messengers of a community's banks meet to transfer the checks that each bank wants to present to the others for payment, most in Oklahoma had roomy facilities maintained by members of the associations that sponsored them. Moreover, as banks grew, clearinghouses undertook more than the physical exchange of checks. Elaborate bookkeeping allowed the accounts of member banks to be posted and balanced as needed. Thus the innovation provided more speed, ease, and convenience in processing checks. By the first decade of the twentieth century there were, for example, twelve clearinghouse banks in Oklahoma City, while smaller towns such as Lawton and Enid had six and five, respectively.[1]

As the work of clearinghouses became more complex, the state's bankers were developing a host of correspondent relationships to make financial transactions more efficient. In establishing correspondent networks, smaller banks in Oklahoma created accounts with larger, urban institutions, both in and out of the state, that accepted the small bankers' deposits of surplus monies. In return, the larger institutions made periodic loans to the smaller banks and accepted their checks and other negotiable paper. To find correspondents, Oklahoma's bankers initially turned to such large metropolitan centers as Kansas City, Dallas, or Saint Louis. Later, bankers in Oklahoma City and Tulsa began servicing their smaller, rural sisters, especially as the banking industry continued to expand.[2] By mid-1897

Beaver County Bank, about 1897. Courtesy Oklahoma Bankers Association.

there were five national and forty-nine territorial or private banks in Oklahoma Territory. The total resources of the national banks showed assets of $866,042, and those of the territorial and private banks were $2,294,263. All banks appeared to be in sound condition, with all showing increases in deposits and cash on hand.[3] Statistics on Indian Territory were more difficult to find because of the existence of numerous private institutions, but there were approximately eighty assets of $3 million.

Bankers in the territories came from varied backgrounds, but most had common traits such as honesty, willingness to work, and a driving ambition to succeed. Key assets of most country bankers included a convenient location near the bank's customers and a willingness to cooperate with farmers and ranchers in arranging loans to carry them from one season to the next. In addition, common sense was needed and, when necessary, a two-fisted approach to problems. In April, 1897, for example, J. C. Post, of the Bank of Kingfisher, became concerned about an outstanding loan made by D. K. Cunningham, a local attorney. One day while Post sat whittling in front of a dry-goods store, Cunningham came along and began conversing with the financier. Post mentioned the attorney's past-due note at the bank, whereupon heated words were exchanged, and the two men came to blows. When Cunningham appeared to have the better of the banker, Post pulled his knife and cut the attorney's face. Although he was bleeding profusely, Cunningham continued to give battle. Bystanders finally separated the combatants and took Cunningham to the doctor's office. The next time Post saw the bandaged and bruised attorney, the latter paid his debt in full.[4]

Although Post received his money, many territorial bankers were occasionally stung by bad loans. With an ever-increasing number of people coming into the twin territories, financiers had great difficulty in determining whether a customer had adequate security for a loan. In Enid in the mid-1890s, one unidentified banker loaned $200 at 5 percent interest per month to a man he thought was a local farmer who gave a chattel mortgage on four mules, two mares, and two farm wagons. When the note expired ninety days later, the banker notified the farmer that his note was due. A few days later a stranger whom the financier had never seen before walked into the bank and asked to see the aforementioned note. Puzzled, the banker showed him the document. The stranger said, "That's my name . . . but I have no mules, no mares, and only one old farm wagon." Most important, he added, "That's not my signature at all." In a scene reenacted scores of times in the twin territories, the farmer's name had been forged and the banker swindled, while a rogue left town $200 richer.[5]

In addition to swindles and bad loans, territorial financial leaders had to protect themselves from robbers. In the early days before banks were equipped with vaults of steel, time locks, and automatic alarms, bankers improvised to establish some sort of security system. Most hired security guards and had their safes and strong boxes watched twenty-four hours a day. In addition, most financial leaders enlisted the help of local businessmen in organizing makeshift security systems. T. M. Richardson, of the First National Bank of Oklahoma City, placed electric call bells in nearby drug and clothing stores.

Push-button alarms were installed around the bank—some under counters, some on the floor—and rifles were given to local merchants with the understanding that all would form a posse if bandits tried to rob the bank.[6]

As ever-increasing numbers of banks were founded in Oklahoma Territory, many bankers joined voluntary, informal associations and lobbied for greater regulation of financial institutions. The Organic Act of 1890 and the work of the First Territorial Legislature included mention of banking, but early laws provided no comprehensive code. In several of the first legislatures Post, the pioneer banker from Kingfisher, introduced such a code, but it had little support. Hard times caused by the Panic of 1893 brought new demands by both bankers and laymen for regulation, but again nothing was done. In subsequent legislatures all new attempts failed until 1897, when a banking code finally was passed. The statute created a territorial banking board composed of the governor, secretary, treasurer, auditor, and attorney-general. The position of bank examiner was established, and the code called for each territorial bank to stand a periodic inspection. All financial institutions wishing to receive territorial charters had to file papers of incorporation and pay a small filing fee. Requirements for a charter included having paid in capital of $5,000, but such capital could be in the form of furniture, fixtures, and real estate. The law also required that each bank maintain a reserve fund amounting to 15 percent of the bank's deposits and that 10 percent of that reserve be maintained in cash. Further, the statute forbade banks from buying and selling merchandise. In the event of a loss, all shareholders were liable for assessments that would be used to pay depositors. The statute also set a maximum legal interest rate at 12 percent. The latter provision, however, was seldom enforced.[7]

The legislation of 1897 was amended in 1899; originally banks needed $5,000 capital to begin operations, but the new law set varying amounts, depending on the size of the community in which the bank was situated. In towns with a population of 2,500 or less, financial institutions still needed only $5,000, but in towns of 2,500 to 5,000 population, $10,000 was necessary. The law required $15,000 in paid-in capital if the populace numbered from 5,000 to 10,000, and $25,000 if it numbered 10,000 or more. The legislation also created the post of bank commissioner to supervise the system.[8]

While the new regulations put territorial banks on a more sound basis, critics still lamented that the proliferation of small communities in Oklahoma allowed most banks to begin operations undercapitalized, with \$5,000 to \$10,000, and with much of the amount represented by furniture and fixtures. Such regulations offered depositors little protection.[9] Moreover, some bankers played fast and loose with the regulations. As was typical in the territorial years, many country banks, which needed \$5,000 capital under the law of 1897, were begun when several partners joined and threw their IOUs amounting to \$5,000 into a cash box—that was paid-in capital. Many financiers continued to charge usurious interest rates on loans, escaping the legislature's ceiling of 12 percent by levying extra "fees" or additional service charges on loans. Oftentimes early bankers charged all the traffic would bear, with rates sometimes climbing to 5 percent per month, but with an annual rate from 24 to 36 percent being average.[10]

The task of adequately supervising territorial banks under the laws of 1897 and 1899 proved a major undertaking. The secretary of the territory processed incoming correspondence, accepted fees, and granted charters while the bank examiner toured the territory, making inspections and filing field reports.[11] Occasionally, conflicts among bankers consumed much of the time and energy of the territorial officials. H. Clay Willis, president of a bank in Fairview and the longtime leader of one of the first banking families of Oklahoma, applied for and received a charter in 1903 that listed his establishment as the Fairview State Bank. Later he was chagrined when a competitor opened the First State Bank of Fairview. Although he knew he would not lose his old customers, Willis complained to Territorial Secretary William Grimes that the new residents in the town—potential depositors—might believe that the competition's bank was the older and therefore the more stable. In the future, territorial officials took more care in designating the names of newly chartered banks.[12]

Early examiners of the territorial banks were underpaid and overworked. Consequently, there was a rapid employee turnover in the office. From 1900 to 1902, for example, four different men served as commissioner. The appropriation for the post was meager: \$500 annually for office expenses, supplies, and travel allowances. Although turnover was rapid, and regardless of the fact that they were not always well-schooled for their position, on-the-job training transformed most commissioners and examiners into well-qualified workers. Most important, commissioners always instructed examiners to analyze carefully the notes made by the banks.[13] Assistants could count money, balance ledgers, and check bonds, but at a time when many loans were secured by a horse, a mule, or a few acres of corn, the notes made by the banks proved to be the most important items and were inspected personally by the examiners. And if loans were made on insufficient collateral, examiners usually chided the guilty bank officials.[14]

H. C. Brunt, of Chandler State Bank, had an interesting experience when he was first audited by a territorial official in 1898. On learning that an examiner was coming to visit him, Brunt had to ask more knowledgeable townfolk what the official did. When told that the examiner would analyze all notes and ledgers, Brunt decided he was in a passel of trouble. "I had just about enough bookkeeping knowledge to know," he said, "if we made anything that day to add it to what we had and if we lost to subtract it." But Brunt survived his first inspection: "When he [the examiner] left, saying we were alright [sic], I concluded he was a good fellow [who] didn't know much more than I did."[15]

The early territorial commissioners and examiners were a hearty breed. Traveling almost constantly, they had to cope with many unusual situations and people, including bankers like Brunt, who said himself he knew little about accounting when he entered the banking business. In addition to their other problems, examiners often went to audit banks that they could not find. Under territorial laws, banks were permitted to move without giving notice and frequently did so. On other occasions a commissioner or one of his examiners might find an auditing job made more difficult by a sudden run on the bank being inspected. Depositors often suspected there was something amiss if an examiner came to town, and they rushed to withdraw their money. Thus, inadvertently, state officials sometimes caused runs.[16]

Like those officials responsible for supervising territorial banks, examiners of national institutions, who reported to the United States Comptroller of Currency, were also overworked. One early examiner, Myron M. Sturtevant, maintained a workload almost too heavy for one man. Traveling constantly, he examined banks operating in the open air, banks in storerooms, and banks in tents guarded by vigilantes. Once he went to Asher, Indian Territory, to inspect a national bank there. After riding all day in the rain, he arrived in Asher and looked down the main street. There he saw a heavy, square-door safe lying on its back in the middle of the street, submerged up to its doors in a mudhole. Bank officials had attempted to move the safe into the bank, but it had fallen from a wagon into the mud. Then the officials had decided that a safe buried in mud out in the street was better than no safe at all. Consequently, they deposited their cash reserves in it and used the safe while awaiting a crew to move it inside. Sturtevant rode into the situation and had no choice but to wade through the mud to get to the safe and to count the currency while standing in the rain. Several days later the safe was moved into the bank. After Sturtevant filed his report, he was criticized by the comptroller for allowing the financiers to leave their safe outside and to work in the street. The overworked, ill-paid examiner responded heatedly that he was "hired to examine safes and their contents, not move them."[17]

Although the pioneer examiners and commissioners were members of a hearty breed, circumstances forced a rapid turnover in the territorial commissioner's office. As mentioned earlier, between 1900 and 1902 four different commissioners resigned because of hardships caused by inadequate funds, but the territorial legislature continued to appropriate only $500 a year to pay all office overhead and traveling expenses. Yet, the state office had to supervise the organization of 124 banks during the period and to examine all others. Commissioners were sometimes harassed further when banks moved without giving notice, as they often did. If they did not prosper in one place, financiers simply moved to a better location, perhaps counties away. Early reports always noted that examiners failed to inspect several, usually from seven to ten, banks because they could not find the institutions.[10]

In June, 1897, a most significant event occurred when the Oklahoma Bankers Association (OBA) was organized. Meeting in Guthrie, a group of twelve leaders assembled and chose U. C. Guss of the Guthrie National Bank as president. State leaders present included Dan Hogan, a young man who in 1892 established the Bank of Yukon (now the First National of Yukon), who would serve as

U. C. Guss, president of the OBA, 1897. Courtesy Oklahoma Bankers Association.

W. S. Search, president of the OBA, 1897–98. Courtesy Oklahoma Bankers Association.

the OBA president in 1902–1903, and who was destined to provide leadership in a career that would span seventy years. At a second meeting in December, 1897, which was held in El Reno, W. S. Search, of Shawnee, a well-known state leader, was chosen president. Within five years membership in the association grew to 175, a small percentage compared to the number of banks in Oklahoma Territory.[19]

The purposes of the bankers association, which has existed to the present day, were varied. It was a voluntary association, enabling the members to meet and discuss common problems and common aspirations. Formal papers were presented on topics of interest, studies that delved into such matters as problems caused by undercapitalized banks. The association also performed work that was in the interest of all members and served as a middleman between certain com-

J. W. McNeal, president of the OBA, 1898–99. Courtesy Oklahoma Bankers Association.

Otto A. Shuttee, president of the OBA, 1899–1900. Courtesy Oklahoma Bankers Association.

panies marketing safes, safety devices, and bank supplies in order to get the lowest price possible.[20]

In the name of a group the association could accomplish many goals that individual bankers could not achieve for themselves. For example, the secretary of the association could negotiate for cheaper premiums on fire, burglary, and robbery insurance. In one such negotiation in 1901, H. W. Pointer, secretary of the association, approached the American representative of the Ocean Accident and Guarantee Corporation of London, England. Pointer, as secretary, agreed to act as the company's agent in Oklahoma, and, of course, the company's business in the state soared. Not only were substantial amounts in premiums saved, but the association profited from commissions that the company paid. In turn, the commissions were placed in a reward fund for the capture and conviction of bank burglars and robbers. To receive the designation of Ocean Accident's agent in

P. W. Smith, president of the OBA, 1900–1901. Courtesy Oklahoma Bankers Association.

Oklahoma, the association had to take action that proved advantageous to bankers in the future, for the association demanded that policy holders upgrade their security by installing, if they had not already done so, new, modern safes equipped with time locks.[21]

Likewise, Pointer became the agent in Oklahoma for several other companies that offered products or services to bankers. As agent, he acquired discount prices for members of the association. He represented the American Bank Protection Company, a company that marketed a new electric burglar-alarm system that would be set off by anyone trying to open a vault at any time before or after a time lock was scheduled to open.[22]

Early bankers were interested in more than undercapitalization, balance sheets, and ledger reports. Most were involved in all phases of community development, including social life. John Foresythe, B. F. Colley, and C. W. Brown, all officers in the Tulsa Banking Company, were most cooperative, for example, when in the late 1890s a group of Tulsans tried to form a baseball team to play on a circuit with teams from Vinita, Bartlesville, Muskogee, and other towns in Indian Territory.[23] Yet Tulsa did not have a first-class pitcher, and its team was certain to be defeated by those with more experienced lineups. The Tulsa Banking Company remedied the situation by hiring an excellent baseball player, James H. McBirney. McBirney later organized the Bank of Commerce, which eventually became the National Bank of Commerce. Working at a bank in Coffeyville, Kansas, for forty dollars a month, McBirney excelled in baseball. Foresythe lured him away from Coffeyville by offering him fifty dollars a month to work for the Tulsa Bank—and to pitch for the baseball team. Later James's brother Sam, also an outstanding player, was hired.[24]

The duo employed by Foresythe transformed the Tulsa team into champions, but trouble developed late in the 1898 season. Tulsa was playing Vinita in an important series, and although McBirney pitched winning baseball, illness forced him to leave the game at the end of six innings. Tulsa promptly lost the game. Led by the president, W. E. Halsell, a group of bitter Tulsans who also happened to be stockholders and officials in the Tulsa Banking Company, demanded McBirney's job, but Foresythe sprang to his pitcher's defense, arguing that his illness justified his leaving the playing field. McBirney retained his job with the bank and remained on the team; Foresythe and his associates held 51 percent of the bank's stock.[25]

Representative of other early leaders in Oklahoma's banking circles, Foresythe and his banking firm were interested in more than recreation, more than baseball. Always supportive of civic projects, officers of the firm helped Tulsa acquire its first permanent public school facility in 1898 by purchasing an old mission school for a thousand dollars and transferring the deed to the school board. Later, in 1905, when oil was discovered near Tulsa, the firm was in the forefront of investors who supported drilling and who knew that the petroleum industry would be a dynamic force in the future development of Oklahoma and the nation.[26]

Other bankers in the twin territories showed concern for their communities. For example, officials stood helpless when a cyclone leveled the town on March 30, 1897, and left twenty people dead and a hundred injured. Many believed the settlement was doomed. However, the populace and officials of the Chandler State Bank and the Lincoln County Bank did not want the town to die. For more than a year, the leaders of the two banks marshaled all their resources to rebuild the community, a decision which proved to be a wise one when in 1898 the Frisco Railroad built through Chandler and started a local boom.[27]

It was not unusual to find early-day bankers who showed concern for all phases of community developments, especially those who worked for country banks in small towns where people were on a first-name basis. In fact, some settlers often imposed on their bankers, almost to the point of unfair advantage. In 1899, J. W. Schaff, a contractor in Holdenville, was building a house and delivered a load of lumber to the site. Although Schaff received a due bill for fifty dollars, he had no money. However, he did have an account at the Bank of Holdenville, but unfortunately no bank draft on his person. A quick-thinking capitalist, Schaff cavalierly sawed a piece of lumber approximately the size of his hand. He then drew a check form on it, wrote a draft for fifty dollars, and gave it to his creditor, who later took it to the bank. Officers there, surprised to receive a wooden check, knew of Schaff's excellent reputation and honored the draft, returning it to him along with his other canceled checks.[28]

During the latter part of the 1890s there were many mergers that strengthened the banks of the twin territories. One of the more important was the combination that created the First National of Stillwater. In May, 1899, directors of the Payne County Bank, the first bank in the county, and the directors of the Farmers and Merchants Bank of Stillwater met with Alexander Campbell, representing the Farmers and Merchants Bank, and Clifford P. Rock of the Payne County Bank and other executives. In a series of conferences the stockholders decided to combine the two banks. Campbell was elected president and Rock was named a director. He would later assume the presidency after Campbell's retirement. The creation of the First National from the merger of two strong, established institutions ensured that the bank would succeed.

There was a new expansion in the banking network in 1901 when Kiowa and Comanche Indian country was opened for settlement. There was no run into the area; settlers met in El Reno and drew lots for land. County seats were quickly organized: Anadarko in Caddo, Lawton in Comanche, and Hobart in Kiowa. In all three towns tent banks were organized as settlers first arrived. Bankers conducted business out of cast-iron safes or tool chests surrounded by armed

First National Bank, Stillwater, 1899. Courtesy Oklahoma Bankers Association.

Interior, First National Bank, Stillwater, 1899. Courtesy Oklahoma Bankers Association.

guards who remained on duty day and night. Not all the early banks in the three counties survived, but some, like the Anadarko Bank and Trust Company, organized by Dennis Flynn on June 7, 1901, were destined for long existence. Receiving its charter in July, the Anadarko Bank and Trust began operations with $25,000 paid-in capital and six months later had resources of $135,072.[29]

The same year, the Indian Territory Bankers' Association (ITBA) was created. Edmund McKenna, founder of the Bank of Poteau, was president. Meeting with the Oklahoma Bankers Association in its first year, it held its own annual convention in 1903. Beginning with a membership of 16, the organization had 147 members by 1904. Like its sister in Oklahoma Territory, the association was created in order that the region's bankers might become better acquainted, form closer working relationships, and benefit from exchanges of ideas and experiences. The founders of the association also wanted the group to take firm stands on public policies, stands that would give the general welfare priority. And like the Oklahoma Bankers' Association, the ITBA worked to secure lower insurance rates for its membership and to get the best prices on bank fixtures and supplies.[30]

First State Bank, Canute, 1900. Courtesy Oklahoma Bankers Association.

By 1903 tremendous expansion had taken place in the banking industry. There were 339 territorial, national, and private banks in Oklahoma Territory and 192 in Indian Territory. Although the capital stock of institutions varied from $5,000 to $200,000, the typical institution was still a small country bank with limited capital, serving a rural, agriculturally oriented populace. Yet, there were several metropolitan institutions that had outstanding capital and resources. In Oklahoma Territory the Oklahoma Trust and Banking Company, Oklahoma Station, under John Threadgill, had the largest amount of paid-in capital: $200,000. In Indian Territory several banks had a paid-in capital stock of $100,000 or more, including the Muskogee Title and Trust Company with $250,000.[31]

The banking network in the twin territories experienced rapid growth in the years immediately before statehood. One encouraging

Bank of Commerce, Kaw City, 1902. Courtesy Oklahoma Bankers Association.

development was the merger of the twin banking organizations into the Oklahoma-Indian Territory Bankers' Association in 1904. Now the banks of the twin territories could unify to enlarge the banking network of the region and plan programs that would affect the future of what would become the state of Oklahoma. And the network was growing. By mid-year there were 112 national and 290 state banks in Oklahoma Territory, commanding resources of $41 million. In addition, there were 142 national banks in Indian Territory and an

A. B. Dunlap Banking Company, Okemah, 1903. Courtesy Oklahoma Bankers Association.

estimated 100 state and private institutions with combined resources of approximately $39 million.[32]

Despite the expansion of the banking network and the apparent stability of the financial institutions, depositors worried constantly about their accounts, and honest bankers sometimes had their reputations sullied by the actions of a few unscrupulous men. On May 3, 1906, in Atoka, W. W. Allen, president of the Citizens National Bank, was reportedly "long gone and far away." The respected businessman, who had diverse interests throughout Indian Territory, absconded with $35,000 of his bank's money. He had left the territory on April 22 and had not been seen since. Detectives, carrying warrants charging him with forgery and embezzlement, were on his trail but could not find him. His wife, who was preparing to leave

Atoka, was detained temporarily, but after she swore that she knew nothing of her husband's whereabouts, she was released. As was customary in Oklahoma, town leaders soon filled the void created by the bank failure. Businessmen of Atoka reacted quickly to the failure of the Citizens National. The Atoka State Bank was organized with A. S. Burrows as president, and it assumed the deposits of the old bank. Burrows, also president of the First State Bank in Denison, Texas, advanced $35,000 to begin operations.[33]

Both before statehood and after, financiers were most concerned about agriculture, since loans to farmers represented the banking community's biggest single investment and biggest source of return. Many pioneer bankers remembered making farm loans with no collateral except a man's word, or perhaps a yoke, a chain, and a pair of oxen. Because of the uncertain nature of such loans, many turn-of-the-century bankers began to follow what became known as the Bokchito Plan. The president of the First State Bank of Bokchito, Harve Wilson, an advocate of the plan, told bank examiners in 1904 that "grubstaking can never be a part of good banking. If a farmer cannot feed his family and livestock while making a crop, he is a poor risk and a year behind."[34]

Like most developing banks in Oklahoma, the institutions in the Bokchito area depended on agriculture. By 1904 ten banks in the region had come and gone. All had gone into liquidation except the First State, and contemporaries believed Wilson's Bokchito Plan explained the latter's success. Wilson strictly regulated the loans he made. He visited a man's farm before he approved a loan application and personally inspected production of milk, butter, chickens, eggs, ham, bacon, and lard. He instructed the applicant to plant an early and a late garden, and he personally set aside a well-described plot of land for livestock feed, which could not be confused with crops under mortgage. Wilson then recommended the planting of such early crops as small grains and hay that would thrive in spring rains and mature before the July heat. He asked farmers to plant their cotton and corn late, after other crops were harvested.[35]

Wilson also financed the purchase of milk cows, swine, and turkeys, but he kept strict accounts and reinspected farms to make certain his customers were developing their herds and flocks in accordance with the principles of scientific agri-management. The devel-

Interior, First National Bank, Muskogee, 1905. Courtesy Oklahoma Bankers Association.

oper of the Bokchito Plan provided one final service to his customers. He, along with his directors, offered a guaranteed market for all mortgaged crops. If a farmer could not dispose of all his crops and other products, Wilson purchased the remainder at the market price. Harve Wilson was such a success that the territorial governor, Thompson B. Ferguson, offered to name him as Oklahoma's bank commissioner, but Wilson, choosing to remain "in the field" with his own bank, declined the position.[36]

First National Bank, Haskell, 1905. Courtesy Oklahoma Bankers Association.

The Panic of 1907, although it had origins in the financial centers of the East, had ramifications in Oklahoma when the flow of money into the territories was interrupted. A run on banks in Oklahoma Territory necessitated rapid action. Acting Governor Charles Filson, in the absence of Governor Frank Frantz, decreed a banking holiday to begin October 28, 1907. Then bank commissioner Herbert Smock asked representatives of all territorial and national institutions to come to Guthrie for a conference. He also invited all banks in Indian Territory. In the emergency meeting financial leaders evolved a two-sided program. Bankers decided to reopen as soon as possible, but not later than one week after the meeting. Then they agreed to pay in cash no more than five dollars on demand account withdrawals

Farmers National Bank (left) and The National Bank (right), Kaw City, about 1905. Courtesy Oklahoma Bankers Association.

in any one day and no more than fifteen dollars in one week—until new money shipments arrived from the East. Because of the money shortage, clearinghouses in Oklahoma City, Tulsa, McAlester, Muskogee, and other points in the territories issued scrip to aid transactions of business and exchange of goods. The holiday never formally ended, but the money crunch began to ease within two weeks, and conditions returned to normal.[37]

The majority of banks in Oklahoma survived the Panic of 1907, and most financial leaders considered the events of the past decade and reflected upon themes of constant growth and development. Only the most farsighted, however, could dream of the tremendous expansion that would follow statehood.

CHAPTER 4.

Halting Steps Forward

In November, 1907, a new watershed was reached in the history of banking in Oklahoma. The twin territories joined to become the forty-sixth state in the Union. At the time of statehood a total of 665 banks served a population of 1,414,042; total resources of the commercial banks exceeded $95 million.[1] Most financiers welcomed statehood because of the benefits it would bring. They knew that banks always tended to flourish during eras of stable economic development and to suffer during times of upheaval. Statehood, leaders knew, would have a settling influence on the local economy and naturally would produce a favorable climate for the banking industry. Moreover, the first legislatures in Oklahoma passed regulatory laws that put banks on a sounder basis.

Article XIV of the Constitution of Oklahoma contained an enabling clause that called for the legislature to create a banking department under a commissioner who was to be appointed for a four-year term by the governor with the consent of the Senate. Further, the constitution stated that the commissioner was to be given "sufficient" power to regulate all state bank, loan, trust, and guaranty companies. Section two of the article set maximum legal interest rates at 6 percent per annum, unless a contract stipulated a higher rate. By contract, parties could agree to 10 percent maximum, a ceiling that stood until 1969. A final section forbade usury, declaring that parties who charged more than the legal rates would forfeit all interest on a loan.[2]

The first state legislature enacted banking laws that included the constitutional provisions just mentioned and also passed in 1908 a guaranty law, which was partially a reaction to the Bankers' Panic of 1907. William Jennings Bryan, titular leader of the national Democratic Party, advocated such a law. In 1908 he visited Oklahoma and addressed the solons to urge the adoption of a state bill that would guarantee deposits. An orator of national prominence, and perennial candidate for president, Bryan stressed the need to protect the "little" man—the yeoman farmer and town laborer—as well as the landowner and businessman. The guarantee, Bryan asserted, also would benefit bankers. If potential depositors knew beyond all doubt that their funds would be safe, they would be more inclined to allow banks to manage their savings; thus, deposits would soar. Swayed by Bryan's arguments, the legislature passed the Oklahoma Guaranty Law.[3]

A forerunner of the Federal Deposit Insurance Corporation, the law was supported by Governor C. N. Haskell. Earlier, Haskell had tried to write the guaranty into the state constitution but had failed by one vote to secure its adoption. Later, he appeared before the Democratic Convention in Denver and lobbied for a guaranty plank in the national platform. Although he failed to gather the support of national Democrats, he was successful in Oklahoma. Under the law, any bank receiving a state charter had to contribute 1 percent of its average daily balance to a fund to protect depositors against failures. Although some critics believed the law to be socialistic, it was received warmly by most financiers and the general public.[4] In fact, many national banks dropped their federal charters and applied for state charters, because deposits rose rapidly in state institutions after the statute became effective. Depositors, time proved, had great confidence in the law and rushed to put money in state institutions. On February 14, the day the guaranty took effect, state banks had resources of $26,544,281 and national banks, $70,036,033. On September 1, 1909, state banks showed resources of $65,821,048, a figure indicative of a steady gain and of the influence of the guaranty fund.[5]

However, the guaranty law caused some problems. When the act became effective, a question arose as to whether a state bank could continue in operation if it did not join the program. The attorney general ruled that all state banks had to comply with the guaranty law and join the program. Then another question surfaced: If banks were unsound, should they be permitted to participate in the benefits of the program? On that issue the attorney general simply ruled that unsound banks must be closed. Yet, the state banking board and its commissioner never wished to close an institution unless it was impossible to save. Ordinarily, banks operating in violation of state statutes were sternly warned, and upon their promise to correct the objectionable features of their businesses, they were allowed to continue in operation and join the guaranty program.[6]

Occasionally, however, officials had to act forcefully, because financiers sometimes refused to obey the regulations of the banking department. For example, the International Bank of Coalgate was closed because it would not comply with the orders of the department. Organized under an Indian Territory charter in 1905, the International Bank was first audited in February, 1908, and examiners objected to several unsound practices. Although the bank listed capital of $38,000 and deposits of $32,424, the examiners found notes for $9,923 in unsecured loans made to officers of the bank and also unsecured, speculative stock loans for another $7,812. In addition, furniture and fixtures were carried at $900 in excess of their actual value. After being warned, bank officials promised to adjust the objectionable items. Yet, by May nothing had been done. Another audit revealed that loans to bank officials had, in fact, increased to $10,181. Immediately, State Commissioner H. H. Smock ordered the bank closed and sent his assistant, H. C. Schultz, to liquidate its accounts. Although $24,844 was taken from the guaranty fund to pay depositors, the sale of the bank's assets allowed a full reimbursement. Later the bank was reorganized as the Citizens State Bank of Coalgate, and its new officers followed all of the state board's guidelines.[7]

Although the guaranty program appeared to be an immediate success, a rash of bank failures jeopardized the new program. The system continued to operate, however, and demonstrated to the citizenry that the state government was fully committed to it. On September 21, 1909, the Columbia Bank and Trust Company of Oklahoma City closed its doors. Although $2,800,000 was required to satisfy depositors, Governor Haskell took the money out of the guaranty fund and ordered the institution reopened the next day. In the aftermath of the Columbia failure the Farmers National Bank of Tulsa, under President E. F. Blaise, closed its doors, and a national bank examiner, F. W. Bryant, was named receiver. Then, following the failure of the bank in Tulsa, the First State Bank of Kiefer, owned by Blaise and others who had interests in Farmers National, also was forced to

Okemah National Bank, about 1910. Courtesy Oklahoma Bankers Association.

close. Funds available under the state's Guaranty Law protected the depositors of the state bank, while those who had done business with Farmers National had no recourse. Seeing that the legislature and the governor fully supported the guaranty program, more financiers holding national charters rushed into the state system after the series of failures.[8]

By January of 1910, state banks numbered 695 and national banks, 221. Although the program appeared successful, bank failures in 1910 and 1911 continued to deplete the fund. In that latter year the legislature amended the Guaranty Law to require that state banks contribute 5 percent of their average daily balance to the fund, with 1 percent due immediately and the balance payable in installments.

A. J. Martin, president of Okemah National Bank, 1910–60. Courtesy Oklahoma Bankers Association.

The high levy persuaded many more bankers to drop their state charters and apply for national charters. A new law in 1913 reduced the levy, but the guaranty program never recovered its earlier popularity.[9] By October, 1913, the number of state banks had dropped to 596 while that of national banks had risen to 326.[10]

While the state government and responsible bankers grappled with the problems of protecting their depositors' money, the banking network continued to expand. By 1916 Oklahoma had 335 national and 553 state banks with resources of $162,941,010, and $68,494,010, respectively.[11] By that time, in the larger cities and towns, innovations in clearinghouse activities helped bring more stability to the

Tom J. Hartman, president of the OBA, 1911–12. Courtesy Oklahoma Bankers Association.

banking industry. Following a national precedent set in 1906 by the houses of Chicago, clearinghouses in Oklahoma, led by one in Oklahoma City, appointed an examiner who made a periodic audit of all member banks. F. G. Dennis, the first examiner hired by the Oklahoma City Clearing House Association, inspected member banks four times annually and reported its findings to all members. Under the system member banks need not speculate on the solvency and soundness of another bank, because a weak bank following unsound practices would be barred from the association. Regular audits uncovered other problems. Earlier, some bankers had unwisely allowed the granting of excessive lines of credit to individuals and corporations. Sometimes a customer who had exceeded his line of credit at one bank merely went to another bank to borrow the money to repay the first. In this way dramatic losses often occurred when a debtor with notes due at several banks finally defaulted. With a clearinghouse examiner at work, however, those customers with excessive lines at member banks were exposed and forced to liquidate their debts.[12] In addition to its other work, the Oklahoma City Clearing

House Association opened a transit department to process the checks of all Oklahoma banks. It became only the second association in the United States to offer such a service.[13]

Although urban bankers thus made rapid progress and cooperated closely with each other, the typical bank in Oklahoma was still a country bank with deposits of less than $100,000. Situated in a small town, which had a population of fewer than a thousand people, it served as a trading center for surrounding farms. Small as the town might be, it probably had one, two, or even three other banks. Each of the country banks had only a few hundred depositors and fewer borrowers. To keep accounts and perform other banking duties, only a small staff of four or five was needed, and that staff required only a space of one or two rooms. Except for a typewriter, the industrial revolution was not conspicuously represented. Most bookkeeping and calculating was done by hand. The financial publications of the day advertised new Burroughs posting machines and other mechanical marvels, but most banks acquired the new accounting aids slowly. Rather, the country banks continued to use the familiar Boston Ledger for their records.

Perhaps typical were the financial institutions of Pontotoc County. By 1910 there were five banks in Ada and thirteen others scattered across the county. The major crop of the agricultural region was cotton; bankers loaned out most of their money in January and February and hoped that yeoman farmers and sharecroppers "made a crop." Frequently, Johnson grass or some kind of blight took the crop; thereupon financiers gave borrowers more money and enjoined them to increase their acreage. In good years bankers and agriculturalists all prospered, but in lean years they suffered alike.[14]

In the country communities the banker was usually more than a financier; he was one of the original promoters or early boosters of the town. His efforts helped the town take root and, with the expansion of surrounding farms and ranches, grow. Such bankers, like other leaders, were carried along by great expectations in the great age of enterprise.[15] Typical operations revolved around deposits and loans. Most loans, usually small in dollar amounts, were made to farmers who needed credit to bring the surrounding countryside into cultivation. The loans covered the seasonal expenses for seed, feed, and labor. Bankers made other loans to farmers when they were ready

Interior, First National Bank, Enid, about 1915. From front to back: seated, F. A. ("Fred") Champlin; standing, A. F. ("Arch") Butts; first window to left, Homer Green and Orville Butts; second window, Earl Butts; third window, Russel Henry. Courtesy Oklahoma Bankers Association.

to experiment with such new, complicated equipment as reapers, threshing machines, and big, alien, smoke-belching, chugging, adventurous steam-driven tractors. The bank's loan customers also included merchants who borrowed to increase their stock of goods, to pay bills, or to finance the credit they extended to farmers and other debtors. Dealers in produce needed seasonal loans at harvest time in order to pay the farmer for crops to be marketed. Likewise, contractors and dealers in real estate needed loans to purchase lots and to construct housing and business buildings. Almost all citizens, it seemed, needed loans on one occasion or another. Interest the bank received on loans served as the income with which to pay salaries, interest on deposits, and dividends.[16]

Farmers, however, remained the most important single group with whom the typical bankers did business. From early statehood to approximately 1921, agriculture, particularly the growing of cotton and wheat, continued to dominate the Oklahoma economy, and bankers—like the farmers they served—relied on those crops. In good years when crops flourished, bankers also prospered, but when crops failed, banks also suffered. No less than farmers, financial leaders, particularly those in small country banks, were hard pressed in 1921. In that year cotton dropped from thirty-nine cents to five cents a pound.

Financiers were aware of their dependence on the farm community, and realizing that their prosperity depended upon it, they took great interest in the farm economy. When farmers applied for loans, it was not unusual for financiers to inspect crops or to advise the farmers on what to plant. From its inception in 1897, the Oklahoma Bankers Association in its advertisements and publications—principally the *Oklahoma Banker*—always gave "tips" to farmers. In 1913 the Western Oklahoma Bankers' Association, which had been founded in 1905 as a branch of the OBA and included bankers in Dewey, Ellis, Woods, Woodward, Harper, Beaver, Texas, and Cimarron counties, devoted its entire program to the utilization of better farming methods.[17] Led by the OBA, bankers and farmers from towns throughout eastern Oklahoma met in Muskogee in February 1914 to hold seminars on farming methods and the proper crops to be planted in the coming year.[18]

By early 1914 statistics revealed that farmers in Oklahoma lost a million dollars the previous year from planting Indian corn. Financiers then led a drive to persuade them to plant kafir corn; by the end of the year farmers had harvested twenty million bushels of the more hearty hybrid. In 1913 the farmers also lost money on cotton; financial leaders persuaded many of them to reduce cotton acreage and to plant milo maize. Some bankers, in fact, regulated planting by forcing farmers to follow their advice as a condition for securing loans.[19]

Bankers were also interested in animal husbandry. In 1916, for

Interior, First Wagoner Bank, Wagoner, about 1915. Courtesy Oklahoma Bankers Association.

example, members of the OBA became involved in developing swine herds that would result in profits for the farmers and their financial backers alike. To encourage the breeding of the herds, bankers started swine clubs for boys throughout the state and furnished the young members with purebred gilts. By 1920 bankers had loaned $88,745 on 100 contracts for 1,038 pigs. Such institutions as the Vinita National, the First National in Durant, and the First State in Oklahoma City were among the one hundred banks participating in the state-wide program. Successful, the work of the pig clubs led to the development of huge swine herds and added a new dimension to animal husbandry in the state.[20]

As the twentieth century entered its second decade, there were more than seven hundred country banks in Oklahoma. Perhaps typical was the Bank of Ringwood, situated in a town of 225 people in Major County, twenty miles west of Enid. C. R. ("Bill") Williams, cashier, had charge of the day-to-day management of the bank, while his daughter helped him at the "wicket." Williams was on a first-name basis with everyone in town, and he was acquainted with most of the farmers in the surrounding countryside as well. And everyone knew and respected Williams. They eagerly sought his advice on nearly all subjects. Therefore, he had to remain informed. He had to know whether the price of wheat was likely to go up or down, how the weather would affect crops, whether the town could support another merchant or another artisan's shop. All were important when he was called upon to make loans based upon these and other considerations. Farmers asked him to look over their swine herds and estimate values. Ranchers had him inspect their cattle herds. Williams always responded. He knew it was his duty to help his community if possible. Moreover, he recognized his obligation to learn all he could about the community and its economy so that he could make wise decisions on loan applications, decisions based on exact knowledge.[21]

Although many institutions could be labeled "typical," some defied description. One bank, organized soon after statehood, experienced peculiar difficulties. Opened on April Fool's Day in 1908, the Cimarron County State Bank was situated in Kenton, where a small settlement of adobe and rock shelters surrounded an old trading post. The bank's experience provided an excellent example of the problems involved in state-line banking, because Kenton was situated fifty-six miles southwest of Kansas, twenty miles north of Texas, six miles south of Colorado, and two miles east of New Mexico. The only bank in the last town in northwestern Oklahoma, Cimarron County State Bank had a paid-in capital of $25,000. In its first six months after opening, it had attracted $22,000 in deposits, most of which came from New Mexico, Colorado, and Oklahoma, with a few deposits coming from Texas.[22]

Because the bank wished to serve all its customers, its staff had to become familiar with the laws of four states. Small services such as notarizing documents caused the bank's officers headaches, as did the constant worry about making loans on out-of-state collateral. Once a settler in the Texas Panhandle made a sizable loan, using a section of his land for collateral. A bank officer processed the account and made the loan. Later, horrified examiners discovered that the loan papers were in order with one exception: unfamiliar with out-of-state deeds and landmark terminology, the loan officer had described land not in the Texas Panhandle but land hundreds of miles to the southeast—in the South Texas Valley. Despite such problems, the bank survived for fifteen years. It finally folded in 1923, when declining population in the area led to a drop in deposits.[23]

Of course, there were controversies that arose in some communities between bankers and their constituents. Many financiers as late as 1915 still charged what borrowers considered usurious interest rates; state usury laws were not enforced except on an individual basis. And such cases were fraught with danger for those who brought suit. In 1912 in Lincoln County, for example, farmers formed a voluntary association that brought suits against bankers who charged more than the legal maximum rates. Although the farmers won several court struggles, bankers in the county simply stopped making loans unless potential borrowers had perfect credit ratings and "absolute" security for their loans. Consequently, many farmers who had opposed the high rates found they could not qualify for a loan at lower interest.[24]

Yet, the problem of usury in Oklahoma appeared real when comparisons were made with other states. By 1915 there were 7,615 national banks in the United States, and only 1,022 charged an averaged interest of 10 percent per annum or higher on loans, but 300 of that number were situated in Oklahoma. National banks in Arkansas, Louisiana, Mississippi, and Alabama charged lower rates. Likewise, state banks in Oklahoma charged high rates that ranged from 10 percent to 36 percent per annum. One banker, on short-term loans, charged 5 percent per month.[25]

The farm community brought pressure in 1915 to regulate the interest rates that financiers could charge, but a bill to set maximum interest at 10 percent per annum was defeated in the state House of Representatives by a vote of fifty-two to thirty-eight. Continuous pressure, however, resulted in the enactment of an Anti-Usury Law in 1916, which the House approved sixty-four to twenty-five, and the

Senate, twenty-five to twelve. The new law limited the maximum legal interest to 10 percent per annum. Penalties provided that the banker would forfeit twice the amount of interest he charged if he charged more than the legal rate.[26]

Many of the financial leaders of Oklahoma lobbied against the Anti-Usury Law. They argued that they paid out-of-state banks 10 percent on money that they borrowed and that they had to charge more interest to make a decent profit. Others said that only under-secured loans were made at higher rates and that lower rates made this class of loan too great a risk. Bankers contended that higher rates were charged only to new, unknown customers who, after they proved themselves and their ability to pay, might receive lower rates. In addition, some leaders pointed out—rightly in fact—that unstable risks (farmers struggling through a bad year) would be denied loans by institutions operating under the new regulations, and only the most secure borrowers would receive money. Incentive, free enterprise, the bankers said, would be thwarted by the Anti-Usury Law. Yet, acting on the advice of the best counsel in the state, most financiers accepted the new law and stayed within its bounds.[27]

Other controversies arose that drew the ire of the rural communities against a few bankers whose actions, unfortunately, damaged the reputations of their colleagues, the great majority of whom were responsible and ethical. Some financial leaders occasionally used depositors' funds to make unsecured loans to themselves, to relatives, or to friends. For example, officials in charge of the Bank of Bennington, near Durant, sometimes make "insider" loans, wherein officers of the bank, or their influential friends, received unsecured, low-interest loans. In 1914 one officer, Lewis T. Martin, had a loan of $5,282, secured by only $110 in notes.[28]

Ethical bankers, of course, refused to allow such practices. Robert Lee Williams, a state supreme court justice who served as governor of Oklahoma from 1915 to 1919, was one of the wealthiest men in southeastern Oklahoma. He had interests in real estate, insurance, and banking, including stock in the Bank of Bennington. When he learned that Martin and several other officers and relatives of officers had insider loans, he became adamant. He had allowed the state land office to deposit $10,000 in the bank, and he feared a scandal if the institution went bankrupt. Moreover, he objected to insider loans on principle. Martin and others had to pay their unsecured loans immediately, when Williams forced his bank to stop the practice.[29]

Although insider loans and some unscrupulous officials caused the banking fraternity worry, financiers had other problems. The banks of early Oklahoma were often victimized by swindlers, embezzlers, and outlaws. Almost every issue of the *Oklahoma Banker* reported the activities of "hot check" artists or swindlers who gained money by other devious means. Embezzlers, too, were most active. But by far the most dramatic and serious blows to Oklahoma's banks were perpetrated by outlaws. For example, the Bank of Stuart was burgled on April 5, 1910. Under the cover of night, robbers gained entrance by breaking the lock on the backdoor, blew the safe with dynamite, and collected $1,600 in cash and $750 in checks. The town marshal and his deputies exchanged shots with the highwaymen, who put a handcar on railroad tracks outside of town and made good an escape toward McAlester. Eleven days after the robbery at Stuart, the First Bank of Haskell was robbed of $6,200 and suffered $300 property damage. Five bandits had made a backdoor entrance and had blown the safe. But before they could sack all their booty, several citizens who had heard the explosion alerted authorities, who chased the robbers out of town. In both instances, the outlaws were not apprehended.[30]

Soon after the attacks on the banks in Stuart and Haskell, a pair of particularly resourceful bandits robbed the People's National Bank in Wapanucka on May 19. Because the unidentified outlaws wanted a fail-safe escape, they planned their movements carefully. They entered Wapanucka on a railroad handcar that brought them within two blocks of the bank. Then at 12:30 A.M. they broke into the People's National and blew the safe with dynamite. The town only had one night watchman, who was nowhere near the bank. Consequently, the bandits experienced scant resistance in their escape as they left town the way they came, by railroad handcar.[31] Robberies, always a problem, convinced most bankers in Oklahoma of the value of insurance, and most banks carried policies that protected against robbery as well as natural calamities. The OBA negotiated an agreement with the Ocean Insurance Company of New York and offered policies to members at discounted rates.[32]

Some robberies were inside jobs. In 1908, C. W. Jones, the assis-

People's National Bank, Wapanucka, after an attempted robbery, 1910. Courtesy Oklahoma Bankers Association.

tant cashier at the Bank of Texola, claimed he was robbed of $5,000 when, in fact, he had taken the money. Found in the bank's vault with his hands tied and handcuffs on his wrists, Jones knew no one would question his story. After a decent interval the assistant cashier, $5,000 richer, disappeared. He retired in beautiful, lush timber country in Oregon. Although the ex-cashier enjoyed six years in the Northwest, he eventually became troubled. In 1914 the entrepreneur's conscience started to bother him. He had, at some time in his six years in Oregon, converted to Christ. He could not live with his past sin; he returned to Oklahoma and confessed all. A state judge rewarded him with a two-year sentence to the prison in McAlester.[33]

More often, robberies were planned by outlaws who had no inside connections. Usually a small gang of would-be bandits would recruit at least one "yegg" (an expert safeblower) and plan a group assault. The banks at Prue, Oklahoma, near Tulsa, were victimized with such regularity in the early years of the twentieth century that settlers began referring to a bank robbery as "our annual event." Then, because robberies there became even more frequent, the citizenry started referring simply to "another of our events." Once, however, an outlaw who attempted to rob the Prue State Bank in 1912 met a dire fate. The yegg robbed the bank, absconded with $2,200 and appeared to be making a clean getaway. But once outside the bank, he made a mistake. He jumped on the first horse he saw, an action that proved to be his undoing. The horse belonged to farmer H. C. Burke, who apparently tolerated bank robbers but hated horse thieves—especially if his horse were involved. As the outlaw rode down the street, Burke grabbed his rifle, took deliberate aim, and calmly shot him out of the saddle. The bandit died instantly. While bank officials reclaimed their deposits, Burke reclaimed his horse.[34]

Easterners who read accounts of bank holdups in Oklahoma must have believed that there was no law west of the Mississippi River. The week of the Prue holdup, for instance, there were at least six other robberies. Banks at Kremlin, Douglas, and Keystone were attacked by a gang operating out of Enid, with the yeggs unsuccessful in their attempt to rob the first two, but $2,200 richer for the latter raid. Immediately after the successful Keystone burglary, the Council Hill State Bank in Muskogee County was robbed in a holdup, the outlaws absconding with $2,000. In addition, outlaws burgled the Vera State Bank and the Chouteau Trust and Bank Company, but were successful at the latter only, taking $600 in silver.[35]

Occasionally, would-be bandits botched their holdup attempts so badly that their escapades took on a comical air. Soon after the burglaries at Vera and Chouteau, a lone, masked man entered the Bank of Bixby at 10:30 A.M. Armed with a revolver, he demanded all the currency and coin in the bank. While the robbery was in progress, Jim Crowell, a bank customer, entered the building. With the outlaw temporarily distracted, cashier Charles Lipscomb, intent on going for help, ran into the back room toward the rear door. The bandit chased the cashier, but fell over a table in the back room. Aided by the clumsiness of the outlaw, Lipscomb managed to give an alarm, which eventually brought aid.[36]

Meanwhile, as the bandit lay sprawled on the floor of the back room, Crowell left the bank by the front door. Struggling to his feet, the bandit shouted at Crowell and tried to chase him, but again tripped on the table and fell. Then Crowell dashed into a hardware store adjacent to the bank and returned with a shotgun. Believing that discretion was a virtue, the bandit ran for his horse—with Crowell firing at him from the back door of the bank. The outlaw mounted and spurred his horse but the steed reared, dumping the inept robber—sacks of money in one hand and gun in the other—to the ground. Surrounded by armed men, the man, later identified as O. C. Brock, surrendered. Then, on the way to a jail cell in Tulsa, Brock engaged in polite conversation with several of his captors and in passing implicated the two other men who had helped him plan the robbery attempt. They, too, were quickly arrested and taken to the jail in Tulsa.[37]

In the fall of 1914 Oklahoma was the scene of the worst series of bank robberies to occur in the Southwest. Between September of that year and January 13, 1915, fourteen banks were robbed, with the holdup men attacking the following banks and taking the amounts listed:[38]

September 8—Keystone State Bank, $3,000
30—Kiefer Central Bank, $6,400
October 6—Farmers' National Bank of Tupelo, $800
14—Pontotoc Bank of Pontotoc, $1,100
20—Byars State Bank of Byars, $700
November 13—Farmers' State Bank of Glencoe, $2,400
20—Citizens' State Bank of Wardville, $800
December 16—Prue State Bank of Prue, $1,400
29—Carney State Bank of Carney, $2,853
January 4—Oklahoma State Bank of Preston ($1,200 damage to vault, no money taken)
5—First National Bank of Owasso, $1,500
12—First National Bank of Terlton, $1,800
12—Garber State Bank of Garber, $2,500
13—Vera State Bank of Vera, $1,300

Throughout the Southwest, men stood aghast when they heard of the rapid succession of robberies. Insurance companies threatened to cancel bank policies; the legislature of Oklahoma passed a bank-robber bill that empowered the governor to place a reward of $1,000 on the heads of known bandits and that appropriated $15,000 to hire a force of men to track down outlaws.[39]

When the robberies first began, authorities were unable to unearth a clue regarding the identity of the bandits, but after the holdup of the Carney State Bank on December 29, witnesses identified the leader of the gang as Henry Starr, an outlaw who had a long and unsavory career in crime in the Midwest and Southwest.[40] A massive manhunt began, while Starr relaxed in a five-room house in the heart of Tulsa and planned his most daring robbery.

On March 27, Starr left Tulsa and led a gang of seven men into Stroud. Leaving one man to watch their horses, the bandits split into two groups and simultaneously entered the First National Bank and the Stroud State Bank. Starr led his party into the latter bank where they emptied the cash drawers of approximately $1,600. Starr then demanded that the bank's bookkeeper, J. B. Charles, Jr., open the safe, but Charles claimed he did not know the combination of the lock. After threatening to kill the bookkeeper, Starr turned to the bank's vice-president, Samuel Lee Patrick, but Patrick swore that the time lock would not allow the safe to be opened until the next day. Starr and his cohorts then marched Patrick, Charles, and another bank employee out the door to join the other bandits who had had better luck at the First National. There, Starr's men had invaded the safe and sacked $4,215 in silver and currency. Soon the two groups and their hostages had formed one big parade and headed for the outlaws' horses.[41]

Ultimately, Starr's band was thwarted in its attempted getaway. Word of the robberies had spread, and townspeople had rushed to recover their deposits. Apparently, there were few good marksmen in Stroud, and the townsfolk did little but delay the outlaws while they exchanged shots with them. But a slight delay was enough for Paul Curry, a seventeen-year-old boy. While the older citizens of Stroud occupied Starr and his bandits, Curry entered a butcher shop and grabbed a 30-30 Winchester, a "hog" rifle, and took cover behind some salt barrels at the rear of the shop. As Starr came into range, the boy fired a slug that shattered the outlaw's leg. Then he calmly threw another cartridge into the "hog" and threatened to kill Starr with the next volley. The bandit surrendered. Then Curry chased

Tulsa, about 1915, a city that needed the services of several banks. Courtesy Oklahoma Bankers Association.

the other outlaws who were escaping on horseback. The boy fired the "hog" once more, knocking another brigand from his horse, but the robber's compatriots helped him remount and escape—temporarily. Eventually, the wounded man, who was identified as Lewis Estes, and three other members of Starr's gang were captured. All except one, Charley Johnson, who was acquitted because of the lack of positive identification, were convicted and sentenced to terms in the state prison. Two other members of the gang thwarted justice by escaping into Arkansas.[42]

Because of the numerous robberies and embezzlements, many people were hesitant to trust banks. They hoarded their surplus money in coffee tins, salt barrels, and mattresses. Moreover, many potential depositors remained ignorant as to the functions of the bank, believing that it cost money to keep a savings account. As a result, it sometimes took a bank decades to build confidence. One day in 1912, a financier in Oklahoma City noticed a railroad workman who had for many weeks been cashing his paycheck but who had never opened an account with the bank. "Look here," the banker said, "why don't you let some of the money stay in the bank?" The worker looked quizzically at the financial leader, taking particular notice of the derby hat that the banker wore day in and day out. The worker then replied: "Boss, I'se jes' afeared. You look like you was always ready to start somewhere."[43] One day in 1920, an elderly man entered the First National of Tulsa. At a teller's window he laid down a hundred dollars in damp currency and mildewed silver. As he opened his first bank account, the old man told the teller that he had always buried his money but that he had "been reading about . . . fellows [who got] bumped off [because they] kept money hid." Continuing, the man declared that "I allowed me and the money would both be safer if it was in the bank. What does it cost to keep it here?"[44]

Although many Oklahomans never became sophisticated in their knowledge of bankers and banks, the state prospered from the early 1900s to 1914, and the outbreak of World War I further stimulated Oklahoma's economy. All sectors of the state's economy grew. Financial leaders realized, however, that the war would place new demands on the banking industry.

CHAPTER 5.

The Changing Times: The War and the Roaring Twenties

When World War I started in Europe, the economy of the United States experienced a sharp recession as international trade patterns temporarily collapsed. In Oklahoma the producers of goods sold abroad, particularly those marketing alcoholic beverages, cotton, and processed meats, suffered a decline in business that extended into 1915. Rapidly, however, the general economy turned upward as war orders poured into the United States. The new demands by European nations for food, clothing, and munitions generated a business boom. Soon, Oklahomans were furnishing the beleaguered Allies with these goods and other products, such as saddles, horses, mules, flour, and lumber.[1]

The bankers of Oklahoma experienced their first direct involvement in the European crisis in the autumn of 1915. An Anglo-French team of financiers arrived in the United States to negotiate a loan of $500 million. Oklahomans were divided as to the merits of subscribing to the loan, especially "ethnic" Oklahomans who could trace their ancestors to Germany, Italy, or Austria-Hungary. Yet, most people realized that allied war purchases would have a positive effect on the economic viability of the state. Most segments of the economy were involved, and the question of loans directly affected bankers, farmers, miners, packers, munition makers, and manufacturers. Although some critics believed that subscribing to a foreign bond issue constituted an unneutral act, the *Oklahoma Banker* mentioned that the German government also had floated bonds overseas. However, the editor pointed out that both the Anglo-French and the German issues appeared to be poor prospects for Oklahoma bankers, who could make other investments and loans that would yield a higher return.[2]

While the bankers of Oklahoma were slow to invest in international bonds, by late 1916 most of them had purchased Anglo-French bonds. As war orders from Europe stimulated the United States economy, financial leaders in Oklahoma, like their counterparts throughout the country, watched their deposits and profits soar. By 1916 most bankers reported record transactions. In December of that year, 337 national banks reported resources of $218,457,000, while 547 banks showed $96,588,176.[3] "The chief difficulty which American bankers have to face today is not securing money," said Oklahoma's Senator Robert L. Owen, "but disposing of what they have."[4] For example, the First National Bank of Muskogee reported end-of-the-year deposits of $5 million, the highest in the bank's history. And like other banks in Muskogee and throughout the state, it had invested heavily in Anglo-French securities. By December the First National had purchased $500,000 in British bonds and continued to buy issues at the rate of $100,000 a week for as long as the paper was on the market.[5]

As the war in Europe continued on its disastrous course, neutrality became a hotly debated issue in Oklahoma. Such incidents as the sinking of the *Lusitania* led an increasing number of citizens to support the Allies, and finally, the resumption of unrestricted submarine warfare led President Woodrow Wilson to ask for American involvement. Pursuant to his message, Congress declared war on Germany on April 6, 1917.

Immediately, national and state leaders began the task of mobilizing the nation's industrial, agricultural, and financial resources, the latter task of particular interest to Oklahoma's bankers. Less than three weeks after the United States entered the war, President Wilson signed the Liberty Loan Act. It authorized the Treasury to market a maximum of $5 billion in bonds at 3.5 percent interest, exempt from all taxes except estate and inheritance. Anticipating the revenue from the bonds, Congress authorized the immediate marketing of $2 billion worth of short-term Liberty bonds; the issue was successful. Led by the Federal Reserve Bank in Kansas City, Oklahoma's financial leaders joined the bond drives, which stressed the stability of the issue and the need to support the government.[6] "We capitalized the profound impulse called patriotism," said Secretary of the Treasury William Gibbs McAdoo in explaining the success of the drive.[7]

A second Liberty bond drive began in 1917, with the final push in the campaign coming in October. Bankers again were in the forefront, calling on the citizenry to show their support for their country. Because of scattered opposition to the draft in Oklahoma, some eastern critics had lambasted the entire population of the state as "slackers" who would not do their part. Quick to defend their state, bankers asked the people to prove that Oklahomans were patriotic.[8] And the people responded. Financiers from throughout Brady County assembled in Chickasha and formed committees and subcommittees to canvass the county. Aided by an address by former Vice-President Charles W. Fairbanks, the bankers sold $425,000 in bonds, a $50,000 oversubscription. In Comanche County Guy C. Robertson, cashier of the First National Bank of Lawton, headed the local drive. In an intensive two-day effort near the end of October, he sold $380,000 in bonds, $5,000 more than his quota. With bankers and chamber of commerce executives leading the campaign, Oklahoma County subscribed more than $3,250,000, another oversubscription. At Shawnee, Chandler, and McAlester, the results of the Liberty drives were similar. At Muskogee, Bartlesville, Vinita—indeed throughout the entire state—bankers led a major campaign in which Oklahomans subscribed a total of $35 million in bonds.[9]

Five other Liberty-bond issues followed in rapid succession. Led by the banking community, Oklahomans oversubscribed to each one. In the fifth drive, the victory loan, the people of the state purchased $28,506,000, an amount that again was more than the state's quota and that pushed the entire Tenth Federal Reserve District over its goal. For all issues the example of Tulsa perhaps best typifies the state. With bankers and other financial leaders heading each drive, the Tulsans' total purchases of war bonds are reflected as follows:[10]

Bond Drive	*Amount of bonds purchased by Tulsans*
1	$5,685,000
2	6,450,000
3	4,623,400
4	8,240,560
5	5,000,000

Oklahomans did their part to aid the war effort.

In addition to leading the drives to sell Liberty bonds, bankers also supported the government's efforts to sell war-savings stamps (called "baby" bonds) in small denominations.[11] Those who led the campaign constantly repeated to customers that "a dollar unnecessarily spent is a traitor. A dollar in the bank is a slacker. A dollar in loan savings stamps is a soldier."[12] While the drive was ongoing, leaders in Oklahoma City spawned a novel idea, a first for the nation. At a chamber of commerce meeting, bankers and other businessmen developed the concept of a war-savings bank, a special institution for which bankers volunteered their time and in which the marketing of baby bonds would be the only item of business. Quickly, the businessmen financed the building of such an establishment. No ordinary financial institution, situated at Main and Broadway, the bank had no liabilities and no expenses; however, after 12,000 people marched into it on opening day to buy baby bonds, it had assets. An effective innovation for financing the war effort, it started a statewide, then regional, then national movement as other cities established similar institutions.[13]

Bankers in Oklahoma aided the war effort in yet another way. Agricultural production proved vital, and financiers did all possible to encourage farmers to increase output. Financial leaders extended more credit to allow the farmers to put more acreage under the plow and sponsored programs related to scientific management, which increased yield per acre. The program was successful. Production of cereals increased by 21 percent, cotton by 45 percent, and potatoes by 20 percent. Overall, the value of crops in the state increased by 114 percent, from $185,311,204 to $397,722,470.[14] Oklahoma thus became one of the nation's breadbaskets in the war effort, and the state's bankers deserved much of the credit for stimulating the wartime economy.

The end of the war in 1918 drastically altered the national economy. Again the skills of the bankers of Oklahoma were needed to ensure a smooth transition to a peacetime economy. At the annual convention of the American Academy of Political and Social Science in 1918, six weeks after the signing of the Armistice, Adolph C. Miller delivered a prophetic address entitled "After-War Readjustments." A founding member of the Federal Reserve Board, Miller observed that during the war the government had floated $18.5 billion in loans, of which banks subscribed an estimated $6 billion. The expansion of bank credit came into existence, Miller pointed out, because not all purchases had been made with cash. Many had been made with bank loans. Such expansion of credit, Miller feared, would result in runaway inflation. His proposed remedy placed him in the school of classic economics. Simply put, he warned that deflation must follow inflation as a corrective for the economy.[15]

In January 1920 the Federal Reserve Board, as though to accept Miller's argument, increased its rediscount rate to 6 percent on ninety-day commercial paper and on six-month agricultural paper. A few weeks later the price of cotton, corn, and wheat collapsed. The drop in farm prices began an agricultural depression in Oklahoma, just as it did in the other agricultural regions of the country. Institutions in Oklahoma that had overextended credit faced a crisis. For the economic dump, most critics blamed the policy of "drastic deflation" that the Federal Reserve Board had inaugurated. The vocal Senator Owen of Oklahoma lamented that the board had promoted the depression with its "arbitrary higher interest rate."[16]

But the board could not be held solely responsible. Between 1903 and 1920 the number of banks in Oklahoma had increased from 531 to 978. However, not all were healthy, or welcomed by conservative financiers. The proliferation of banks came as population in the state expanded. More commercial houses were needed to serve more people. The boom was also facilitated after 1897 by two decades of agricultural prosperity. The Bankers' Panic of 1907 and a brief recession prior to the outbreak of World War I did little to shake the confidence of financial leaders who were intent on expansion. The continued prosperity of the war years encouraged more men to enter the banking field, their optimism based on the need they saw for financial service to the agricultural sector of the economy. But prices for farm products fell after World War I as the overseas demand for America's food returned to normal. Bankers in Oklahoma felt the effects of the postwar agricultural depression. When farmers could not repay their loans, bankers in the countryside experienced difficulty in meeting their obligations, and an increasing number of banks failed. From 1921 to 1923 a total of 70 banks in the state closed their doors.[17] One bank, however, was founded during the era, a bank that was destined to have a major impact. The Liberty National Bank of Oklahoma City was organized in 1918 by a small group of businessmen who contributed a capital stock of $300,000 and a surplus of

$30,000. L. T. Sammons, the first president, watched $726,265 accumulate as the first day's deposits were made, and he set the bank on a course of sound expansion. By 1921 the bank had doubled its assets.[18]

Still tied predominantly to an agricultural economy, particularly cotton and wheat, bank fortunes ebbed and flowed, depending on markets for those crops. In 1921, when cotton dropped from thirty-nine cents to five cents a pound, many small country banks folded, and those in urban centers were hard pressed. At Ada, for example, the Norrises had to foreclose on many farm notes, although they did so only as a last resort. Suffering through a particularly severe slump, all the bankers in Ada had to rent large barns in order to house the plows, mules, and horses they repossessed. For a period, local bankers spent more time at their barns trying to get rid of their inventory than they did managing their institutions.[19]

Revolutionary changes had been taking place that affected banking in Oklahoma as well as in the rest of the nation. The census of 1920 reflected that for the first time a majority of the population lived in urban centers. After 1920 the number of people engaged in farming began gradually to decline. That reduction sounded the death knell for many country banks that had catered to that segment of the population. Not only did the rural population decrease further, but farmers in Oklahoma experienced tremendous problems in the 1920s as prices for farm commodities continued a downward trend. Many farmers were driven from the land, and tenancy increased. In 1910 tenants operated 54.8 percent of the farms in the state; by 1925 the percentage was 58.6, with some counties having 75 to 80 percent tenants. From 1920 to 1925 the value of farm lands and buildings in the state declined by 23 percent, or a total of $314 million (census). The gross value of all crops produced also declined. In 1919 gross income for all farmers in the state averaged $2,865, but in 1925 that average had dropped to $1,656.[20]

The following table reflects the decline in the number of banks in Oklahoma in the twenty-year period from 1908 to 1928; yet, the figures divulge the ever-growing amounts of capital and resources of those banks that survived:[21]

Oklahoma Banks, 1908–1928

	Number	*Capital*	*Resources*
1908			
State Banks	520	7,456,250	36,186,208
National Banks	298	11,890,000	68,202,205
Totals	818	19,346,250	104,388,413
1910			
State Banks	694	11,543,800	78,394,089
National Banks	227	10,692,500	81,816,928
Totals	921	22,236,300	158,211,017
1912			
State Banks	617	9,286,250	59,187,855
National Banks	306	13,810,000	106,739,048
Totals	923	23,096,250	165,926,903
1914			
State Banks	563	8,387,250	57,057,404
National Banks	350	15,099,650	117,758,604
Totals	913	23,486,900	174,806,008
1916			
State Banks	547	8,297,550	96,588,176
National Banks	338	15,321,000	215,165,000
Totals	885	23,618,550	311,753,176
1918			
State Banks	581	11,057,550	142,786,799
National Banks	346	17,657,000	266,359,000
Totals	927	28,714,550	409,145,799
1920			
State Banks	622	15,433,150	194,433,476
National Banks	356	23,680,000	338,317,000
Totals	978	39,113,150	532,750,476
1922			
State Banks	464	9,187,150	94,946,210
National Banks	447	28,745,000	379,823,000
Totals	911	37,932,150	474,679,210

	Number	Capital	Resources
1924			
State Banks	381	7,434,650	92,454,818
National Banks	407	27,845,500	425,576,000
Totals	788	35,279,650	518,030,818
1926			
State Banks	359	7,269,150	96,413,325
National Banks	358	25,660,000	414,051,000
Totals	717	32,929,150	510,464,325
1928			
State Banks	336	6,792,150	94,231,087
National Banks	325	27,115,000	470,647,000
Totals	661	33,907,150	567,878,087

Of course, the 1920s trend toward decline in country banking was not evident in all sections of the state. In fact, in some areas country banks continued to thrive. For example, the small Polish community of Harrah, a few miles east of Oklahoma City, first secured the services of a banker in 1910 when Ben Miles transferred his bank there from Choctaw. Orville G. McClurg moved with him to take a position as cashier in the new First National Bank. By 1920 Harrah had a population of 700, with many of the people engaged in cotton production. In addition, ranchers contributed much to the local economy. Then in the early 1920s Oklahoma Gas and Electric established a plant in Harrah, a development that spurred growth and necessitated expansion of banking services. The town grew as did trade, especially after a hard-surface road replaced the dirt trail from Harrah to Oklahoma City. As the First National grew, so did McClurg's functions. He was always a jack-of-all-trades, serving as cashier, janitor, and bookkeeper. The latter task was quite tiresome, because McClurg did all posting longhand into a Boston Ledger. The only machine in the bank was a typewriter.[22]

Although Miles—with the help of McClurg—prospered, most country banks experienced difficulty. Early settlers in Oklahoma often repeated a story on their country bankers:

"John, did you hear about Bob? He made $50,000 in Chicago in one week."

"I don't believe it," said John.

First National Bank, Bartlesville, 1920s. Courtesy Oklahoma Bankers Association.

Exchange National Bank, Tulsa, 1920s. Courtesy Oklahoma Bankers Association.

"It's true, I can prove it by Smith. Smith, isn't it a fact that Bob made $50,000 in Chicago in one week?"

Smith replied: "Sure, but you are mistaken about it in four places. It wasn't Chicago; it was Toledo. It wasn't a week; it was a month. It wasn't $50,000; it was $5,000. And he didn't make it; he lost it."[23]

Unfortunately, the anecdote could be applied to many of the state's country bankers. The postwar recession, the general decline of agriculture, the ongoing rural-to-urban shift in population—these and other factors created crisis conditions for small banks, and many folded.

Other financiers, particularly those in urban centers, needed assistance if they hoped to survive the postwar recession. In 1920 many of the institutions that had financed the oil industry became desperate when the price of crude oil dropped from $3.50 to $1.00 a barrel. One bank forced to close after an audit by federal examiners on April 15 was the American National Bank of Tulsa. Panic struck a majority of the region's populace because all feared losing their savings. The officials of Tulsa's other banks also became concerned about their institutions because they feared runs. The panic, however, was short-lived. Robert McFarlin, a director of the Exchange National (now Bank of Oklahoma), watched from his office as an unhappy mob gathered in downtown Tulsa. He assembled his board; the board agreed to offer the American National a $100,000 loan, which would allow it to reopen and meet the demands of its depositors. McFarlin then raced out into the crowded street in front of his bank, vaulted to the top of a parked automobile, and shouted, "You have nothing to worry about . . . If you want your money, you'll be paid—dollar for dollar!" McFarlin's rapid action stopped the run.[24]

Like McFarlin, Frank English of the City National in Lawton stopped a run. Informed that many of his depositors were uneasy, English anticipated a panic and determined to thwart it. He moved tables to the sidewalk in front of his bank and brought all his ledgers out. People then gathered in long lines to close their accounts. As was prearranged by English, in the midst of the run a long, black limousine pulled up in front of the bank. The trunk and back seats of the limousine were piled high with money sacks showing dollar signs. In front of the crowd, bank guards unloaded the automobile and carted the money sacks inside. After seeing the limousine and its contents, many people in the crowd decided to put their money back in the bank; consequently, a new table was set up on the sidewalk—a table that would receive deposits. As people made deposits, clerks took the money into the bank where the currency and coin were placed into sacks to be taken to the withdrawal tables. Eventually the panic subsided and the people dispersed. Unknown to the crowd was the fact that the money sacks brought by the limousine were filled not with currency, but only with blank paper.[25]

Despite occasional panics and the decline in the number of banks in the state, notable financial developments took place in the 1920s, with many mergers creating stronger banks. One of the more important affected the entire state. In February, 1927, the First National of Oklahoma City, founded in 1889, merged with a sister institution, the American National, founded in 1901, to form the American-First National Bank. Two brothers, Frank Johnson, with the First National, and Hugh Johnson, with American National, had had controlling interests in their respective institutions, and in the consolidation the former became president and the latter chairman of the board of the new bank. With deposits in excess of $40 million, total resources of $50 million, and $3 million in paid-in capital, the new bank was one of the largest and most powerful in the Southwest. Less than three years later, in October, 1929, the American-First National was involved in another merger, being consolidated with the Security National Bank, which had been founded in 1906 by R. R. Raymond, William Raymond, and William Mee. The new institution—to be known as the First National Bank and Trust—had paid-in capital of $5 million and was the largest national bank in the Tenth Federal Reserve District.[26]

A key development that spurred other mergers in the 1920s was the rapid rise of the automobile. Although American entrepreneurs began the production of automobiles in the 1890s, the earliest motor carriages remained toys for the very rich. Even after Henry Ford established his Ford Motor Company in 1903, a decade passed before he introduced the moving assembly production technique that drove prices downward to a level that the masses could afford. By the early 1920s the ownership of an automobile was within the grasp of the middle class, a fact that had major ramifications for the banking community. As more and more cars found their way to consumers, the federal government, in conjunction with state governments, launched a new highway-building program that not only linked towns and cities in Oklahoma, but also the state to the rest of the nation. Bank customers, with their new mobility, took their money from the small banks because they wanted the security that larger institutions seemed to provide. This led to an increased number of mergers as many small country banks were forced to join larger banks at county seats.[27]

Along with consolidation, other memorable events occurred in the 1920s. In August, 1920, a branch of the Tenth Reserve District was opened in Oklahoma City, where bankers and businessmen had long waged a campaign for such a move. A memorandum branch, or one with limited powers, the bank could issue and redeem currency and engage in the collection, clearing, and transfer of checks. It could also accept applications for loans and rediscounts from member institutions. The volume of the bank's business expanded with every month's passing, and the original staff of 50 had to be increased to 100. In December, 1920, just four months after the bank opened, the transit department processed 1,051,033 items involving $180,743,803. That same month, the money department handled 314,000 items worth $2,029,975. Originally doing business from the second floor of the old Continental Building at Second and Broadway, the branch moved into its own building at the corner of Third and Harvey in 1923.[28]

By that time new banks had been opened and old ones revitalized as a result of the oil boom. The petroleum industry, always important in Oklahoma history, had antecedents in the territorial era when wildcatters first developed the industry. In 1904 production statewide rose to more than 1,000,000 barrels. Between that year and 1907 new fields were opened near Okmulgee. In addition, Glenn Pool and Wheeler Pool were developed in Tulsa and Carter counties, respectively. By 1907 production statewide reached 43,500,000 barrels. In the next decade new fields opened, and in every boom bankers had new opportunities for expansion, because oilmen needed financial backing. Indeed, the petroleum industry would become increasingly important as the decade progressed. For example, Charles Stuart, who was president of the American National Bank in Pawhuska, established the First National Bank of Shidler in April, 1922.

Shidler was a booming oil town in the Burbank Field, which had opened in 1920 and was also for a time the terminal of a railroad built from Foraker. Stuart believed that the area would be lucrative for an experienced financier. His faith was not misplaced. Beginning with a paid-in capital of $25,000, the bank had $50,000 in deposits after its first day in operation.[29]

In 1923 the state's Bank Guaranty Law finally was repealed. Always a controversial issue that had many critics, the guaranty fund had been virtually exhausted by 1921 because of bank failures. Then, in the three-year period from 1921 to 1923 there were seventy new failures of banks in the state system. As a result, the fund had no money to pay the claims of depositors. Consequently, in January, 1923 the legislature launched an investigation into the condition of the fund and later in the year repealed the guaranty law.[30]

That same year the legislature took other action that affected banking. The solons amended the state's bad-check law by providing stiffer penalties for offenses. Persons writing bogus checks in amounts of $20 or less were deemed guilty of a misdemeanor, punishable by a fine of $100 and not more than thirty days in jail. For bogus checks of more than $20, persons were deemed guilty of a felony, punishable by a fine of up to $500 and a prison sentence of up to seven years.[31]

Shortly after the bad-check law was passed, the Oklahoma Senate concluded an investigation of the department of banking. The solons blamed former Governor J. B. A. Robertson and Governor J. C. Walton for weakening the standards of the department and, in the process, for weakening the entire state banking system. Officials in the department of banking were apparently guilty of accepting bribes for issuing charters, for allowing "insiders" to liquidate banks, and for allowing select banks to carry substandard assets. Moreover, in some instances officials in the department pressed bankers for "insider" loans, even if these loans resulted in a loss to the institution involved. The investigation resulted in the tightening of restrictions on officials in the department.[32]

While the state banking department appeared to be mired in scandal, individual financiers and the Oklahoma Bankers Association exerted leadership in helping the state recover from the recession following World War I. In particular, the OBA encouraged the for-

Five leaders in banking, 1900–1930: left to right, Charles W. Brewer, I. C. Thurmond, John W. Teter, Tom J. Hartman, Dan W. Hogan. Courtesy Oklahoma Bankers Association.

mation of county associations wherein bankers met regularly and attacked the economic problems of their area. The movement paid dividends; by mid-1923 more than half of all the counties in the state had active associations, and by mid-1924 bankers in almost all counties had organized. The associations were effective. In Texas County there were nine national and two state banks. I. M. Lightner, of Guymon, was president of the local association, which held quarterly banquets and meetings. In that agricultural area the members of the association persuaded the county commissioners to employ a county agent, although some voters opposed the move, because tax dollars would be expected to pay his salary. The bankers knew that farmers of the region needed the services of an agent because of declining farm prices. Financial leaders tried to influence farmers to plant feed crops rather than the usual wheat, because wheat prices were so low. Like the association in Texas County, the Hughes County Bankers' Association also addressed itself to the problems of the region. Under President W. M. Taylor, of Holdenville, the association sponsored programs to instruct farmers on the advantages of diversified farming and on coping with the ravages of the boll weevil, a blight that had been particularly severe in 1923.[33]

Although the state's banking community continued to have great success and to experience growing stability, leaders still had difficulty in securing their institutions from robberies. During the Roaring Twenties from sixty to seventy-five banks were robbed annually. When losses continued to mount, the OBA renewed its campaign to encourage all bankers to install electric burglar alarms, equip vaults with time locks, bar windows, buy tear-gas guns, and hire guards. In addition, the OBA suggested that small, rural institutions establish shorter hours in order to close early and complete all posting before nightfall. Yet, the number of robberies increased, and insurance rates soared, from $2 a $1,000 to $20 a $1,000 annually.[34]

Because of the severity of the problem, the OBA took drastic action. Director Eugene P. Gum, who had a long career with the OBA between 1918 and 1952, was placed in charge of a crime-prevention team and charged with the responsibility of reducing the number of robberies. Occasionally, Gum engaged undercover agents in an attempt to decrease the number of holdups. Although his work usually accomplished some results, it fell short of his expectations. Moreover, undercover work sometimes mired Gum and the OBA in legal problems. Near the end of 1920, Gum hired Jim Sanders as an undercover agent to assist H. O. Brown, who represented the Burns International Detective Agency in Oklahoma, an agency retained by the OBA. Sanders infiltrated a gang that operated out of a roadhouse near Tulsa. In December, 1920, he told Gum of a plot to rob four banks—one each in Broken Bow and Sperry and two in Oklahoma City. Before Sanders could supply any details, the Roadhouse Gang robbed the bank in Sperry, a heist in which Sanders participated. While two bandits held bank employees at bay, Sanders looted the vault, taking only $1,500—enough evidence to convict the outlaws. But he left much more untouched.[35]

Sanders later reported to Gum, who decided to let the agent continue to monitor the activities of the gang. When the bandits moved into Oklahoma City, intending to rob two banks there, Gum had the four members of the gang arrested. Tried for the robbery in Sperry, all were convicted and sentenced to fifteen years in prison. Eddie Shoquette, youngest member of the gang, appealed his case, arguing that it had been Sanders who led the gang, acted as an agent provocateur, and influenced the other men to commit crimes. Shoquette won his case and was released. Although Gum lamented that the state had not used all the evidence it had against Shoquette, Attorney General Prince Freeling declined to pursue the case further. Disappointed, Gum nevertheless continued in his efforts.[36]

Bank robbers continued to plague the small country banks of Oklahoma. In one daring daylight robbery, two men tried to hold up the State Bank of Vera, a small institution that served a town of approximately 300 people and the farmers of the surrounding countryside. Appearing to be an easy mark for the bandits, it was administered solely by Mary Garlinghouse, the cashier. On the morning of September 16, 1924, the robbers drove up to the backdoor of the bank and gained entry into a back room by breaking the latch on a locked door screen. Then they entered the front room and surprised Garlinghouse at the counter while she talked to a customer and sorted through papers. With guns drawn, the bandits ordered the customer and the cashier to lie on the floor. The customer obeyed, but Mrs. Garlinghouse told the robbers "to cut out their foolishness."[37]

After a brief scuffle, one of the robbers hit the cashier and knocked her to her knees, while his companion sacked the money from the teller's tray. Meanwhile, unknown to the bandits, their entry into the bank had been detected by Leonard Stepp, a youngster who summoned help. Soon, Constable W. R. Mosley and Mayor R. C. Lapsley, with guns cocked, were marching toward the bank from opposite ends of town. The robber who had been fighting Mrs. Garlinghouse attempted to drag her out of the bank for use as a hostage in the getaway, but as soon as he walked out the backdoor, he was shot and wounded. Thus, it was easier for the cashier to subdue him. The other robber ran for the car, but was mortally wounded by two slugs when the mayor and constable simultaneously shot him.[38]

Despite the valiant efforts of bankers like Mrs. Garlinghouse, robberies in Oklahoma continued to increase in the 1920s. In the year 1924 alone, there were fifty-four robberies in the state in which bandits netted $269,000. Ultimately, the crisis became acute, and insurance companies raised their holdup rates by 100 percent in January 1925. In April they again increased the rate by 500 percent. Bankers who had been paying $1 for each $1,000 on deposit in December, 1924, found that they were paying $10 for each $1,000 five months later. One large insurance company threatened to cancel the policies of institutions in towns of fewer than 1,000 people unless bankers provided daytime guards and stood for one-fourth of the loss in case of a robbery.[39]

Searching for a solution to the problems that bandits caused the state's financial institutions, Gum examined how such states as Iowa and Kansas had coped with similar problems. Those two states had been plagued with robbers in the early 1920s, but bankers' associations had organized vigilante groups to furnish voluntary service in guarding banks and apprehending bandits. Gum knew that after Iowa organized its vigilantes, its robbery rate statewide dropped to three a year and that its insurance rate dropped from $4 to $1 a $1,000. The OBA secretary soon began organizing Oklahoma.[40]

The Kay County Bankers Association was the first group to organize, and 53 men volunteered for service. Afterward, the financial leaders in Nowata, Creek, Rogers, and Craig counties quickly formed committees with 50 expert riflemen in each. One-third of the counties in the state had vigilante protection by October, 1925, and a large majority had the service by the end of the year. By November Lincoln County had the largest contingent in the state, with two units and 113 men under arms. Apparently, the vigilante movement proved effective, for during the calendar year of 1925, fewer than fifteen bank robberies were reported, with negligible losses.[41]

The OBA also recommended the town-guard system to thwart potential robbers. Under the plan, three armed guards would be placed near each bank and signaled by an electric buzzer whenever a robbery was in progress. The guards could then prepare to capture or shoot the bandits as they left the bank. The program was successful. By June, 1929, only twelve banks that had adopted the town-guard system had been robbed. In ten of the cases, the bandits had failed in their attempted robbery and had been either killed or captured. In the two other episodes, the system had worked, but the guards had failed to do their duty. Altogether, by the summer of 1929 the OBA—with Eugene Gum working "in the field"—had convinced 145 bankers to adopt the system. Not only did the electronic system foil holdup attempts, but it also paid extra dividends, because insurance companies agreed to reduce rates by 10 percent for those banks that installed the system.[42]

Whenever lulls in crime sprees occurred, state and local law enforcement agents as well as bankers tended to breathe a sigh of relief and relax their guard, only to become concerned when crime rates soared again. However, Eugene Gum and other officials in the OBA remained active, lobbying with the association's members to take all precautionary measures possible. Beginning in May, 1926, Gum and other officers of the association solicited donations from the membership to establish a reward fund. Originally, members contributed $17.50 each to the fund, with all members paying an additional $5.00 to $10.00 in mid-1928 and other small levies whenever the fund neared depletion. When holdups occurred, the OBA established rewards for the capture and conviction of felons, the rewards usually being $250 each.[43]

Between May, 1926, and August, 1928, fifty-eight bank robbers were arrested, convicted, and sent to the penitentiary. By August of 1928, the OBA had paid $3,351 in rewards, with another $3,250 in rewards pending. Of course, the new program did not completely stop robberies. Between May 10 and August 10, 1928, there were five holdups: the Bank of Breckenridge on June 6 and 22, the Fay State Bank on July 13, the First State Bank of Lamont on July 24, and the Oklahoma National Bank of Hastings on July 30. However, most financial leaders believed that the rewards program at least retarded crime sprees and that the program convinced many would-be bandits to look for other occupations.[44]

While the financial leaders of Oklahoma began a virtual war on banditry, they prepared to take a step believed revolutionary by some critics: they began debating the merits of a service charge on demand deposits (checking accounts). For decades Oklahoma's bankers had tried to attract hoarded money and to mobilize it for the economy, and in trying to attract depositors, they offered such inducements as free checking privileges and minimum deposits to open new accounts. By the 1920s the free services had become expensive and burdensome. Executives of the OBA estimated that more than half of all the checking accounts in the state's banks had an average balance of less than $50.00. Such accounts represented less than 5 percent of the total deposits, but cost banks from $0.40 to $0.60 a month to carry. President L. K. Meek of the Security State Bank of Ponca City analyzed his institution's books and found that approximately 15 percent of his checking customers maintained a total of 600 accounts and wrote an average of 8,000 checks a month, but had an average balance of approximately $20.00. Because of the expenses involved in carrying such small accounts for individuals who wrote a large number of checks, Meek instituted a small service charge and advised other bankers to do likewise. Like Meek, other leaders across the state suggested a service charge of $0.50 per month to offset the drain on the resources of the banks, and several institutions experimented with the charge on a trial basis. Although depositors with small accounts usually expressed dissatisfaction, by 1927 more than 200 banks had instituted the charge.[45]

The decade of the 1920s also saw new interest in and controversy over the concept of branch banking in Oklahoma, a unit-banking state. In the McFadden Act of 1927, Congress permitted national banks to establish branches in states where branching was legal. The experience of metropolitan banks in large urban centers like New York City, Boston, and Los Angeles seemed to prove that branching was successful and was one way to mobilize great amounts of capital. Moreover, in the 1920s rural banks, for which the unit rule appeared ideal, had experienced much difficulty, and it seemed to many observers that only the large institutions could survive. A third alternative was also available. If not forbidden by state law, businessmen might engage in group banking, a practice in which a group of bankers formed a holding company that in turn bought controlling interest in two or more banks and made central management possible. However, group-banking developments were subject to all antitrust legislation. In Oklahoma in the 1920s both group and branch banking

E. D. Kilpatrick, president of the OBA, 1926–27. Courtesy Oklahoma Bankers Association.

found few adherents. Most financial leaders still favored the unit system. In August, 1929, R. W. Hutto, cashier of the Security National Bank of Norman, gave one of the best, if briefest, defenses of unit banking:

> In my judgment, the power of the Federal Reserve Board will pall into

L. K. Meek, president of the OBA, 1928–29. Courtesy Oklahoma Bankers Association.

> insignificance when our national banking laws permit openly branch ownership. Fixing money rates is an important aspect of this new situation (branching), but even more important is the fact that credit will be supplied only when and where it is desired by a large group . . .
>
> I view with alarm the possibility that branch banking will result in the withdrawal of banking resources from small cities and towns and the concentration of them in the nation's larger commercial centers.
>
> A system of branch banking will result in the withdrawal of funds from our lesser communities. Large corporations and large financial groups in . . . cities will be the beneficiaries of this movement.[46]

Hutto continued in his statement to summarize how giant monopolies might form and how they might have detrimental effects on small communities.[47]

Another predominant trend of the 1920s was the ever-growing number of women who entered the banking business. In Oklahoma, women had always engaged in the industry, but their roles grew in importance after America's entry into World War I, when women replaced men who had gone into the service. The aforementioned Mary Garlinghouse, who stopped a robbery attempt at Vera, was an excellent example of a woman who held a responsible position in the business, that of cashier at the Bank of Vera. The career of Katherine Shotwell provided yet another example. Shotwell was hired by the Security National Bank of Oklahoma City in 1917. Starting in the transit department, by 1927 she had become one of the most valued employees of the bank.[48] However, women occasionally experienced problems. Although most were hard-working and professional—many attended the Women's Conference of the American Institute of Banking every year—men sometimes felt insulted or threatened when they had to work with women. Moreover, men feared that women would be constantly powdering their noses, coming to work late, or requesting the easiest jobs. The fears of men notwithstanding, women were generally as capable as their male counterparts.[49]

The 1920s also saw a rise in installment loans. As the decade progressed and the economy boomed, there was an increasing demand for consumer goods—new electric appliances, radios, automobiles—and on many items consumers could not afford to pay a lump sum.

F. S. Sherwood, president of the OBA, 1929–30. Courtesy Oklahoma Bankers Association.

Thus they turned to financiers for installment loans. Beginning in a cautious manner, Oklahoma's bankers started making loans of this type. Some, however, made a distinction between "good" and "bad" notes. Most financiers believed that household items such as washing machines and electric appliances were safe, but some considered automobile loans folly. Saying that he never varied from his policy, L. K. Meek, president of the Security State Bank in Ponca City, refused to loan anyone money on a car. He feared that most car owners would not pay as long as they still had the car. Then Meek remembered one exception. In 1926 he did, in fact, loan money on a Model T Ford, when a young farmer aroused his sympathy. The farmer needed money to pay living expenses until the harvest. Learning that he had no collateral except the Model T, Meek said, "Brother, you can borrow money from me if you will go out and take the hind wheels of the car and bring them in here to the bank."[50] Later, as Meek helped the youngster roll the tires into the bank, customers laughed and asked Meek if he were "going into the second-hand car business." Despite the unusual way in which Meek immobilized the otherwise rolling collateral, his plan worked. The young farmer rapidly repaid the loan because he wanted the convenience his Model T afforded. Such rapid repayment helped bankers gain confidence in installment loans; many even decided that automobile paper was safe, and new car loans soon became the major consumer-loan items, a development that held significant ramifications for financial leaders.[51] Throughout the 1920s the automobile industry continued to expand as Henry Ford and others experimented with ways to cut costs. With purchases of new cars skyrocketing, bankers could not help but enter the new market by providing consumer loans. By the end of the decade, such loans provided financial institutions with another great source of revenue.[52]

As always, banks sometimes became the scene of uproarious events. Once in the 1920s, Orville McClurg, the aforementioned cashier at the First National Bank of Harrah, was confronted by a Polish farmer, a customer who had both a personal savings account and an agricultural loan with the bank. The farmer brought McClurg a rolled-up newspaper, put it on the banker's desk, and told McClurg to look inside. As requested, McClurg unrolled the paper only to find a blob of wet, freshly mixed cement. "Look it over and see if the sand

and other ingredients are right," said the farmer. "I don't know anything about cement," said the perplexed financier. On hearing McClurg's words, the farmer could only exclaim, "Well, you should. That's what you loaned me the money for."[53]

Although light jokes sometimes brought fun and relaxation to long days, financial leaders still had to face their problems, and one of the most serious was the farmer's plight. In the 1920s farm tenancy continued to grow and cause myriad problems for bankers. Profits from interest collected on crop loans were the lifeblood of financial institutions in rural areas. But tenants or sharecroppers, people who most often desperately needed loans, had little collateral or ability to pay. In flush years absentee landlords exacted high profits from tenants, but had no responsibility for the tenants' debts if crops failed. As a result, bankers had no recourse but to accept a loss if tenants could not repay their loans. According to H. C. Brunt, president of the Union National, of Chandler, the problem was particularly acute in such rural counties as Lincoln, where absentee owners controlled 50 percent of the farm land. Such owners usually failed to give tenants proper advice and ignored critical matters relating to improvements, rotation of crops, ditching, terracing, and maintaining the soil.[54]

Financial leaders reacted to the tenancy problem in various ways. As such men as Brunt advised, they began restricting crop loans, making real-estate loans, and investing more of their surplus in mercantile and commercial paper. In addition, with the growth of automobile production in the 1920s and with the increased manufacture of small appliances for consumer use, bankers turned to short-term installment loans of from one to two years. They quickly found that installment notes were more readily liquidated than one-payment notes. As bankers diversified their loans and investments and began denying loans to tenant farmers, absentee owners in many areas began to chafe. But through negotiations with bankers, most owners came to terms. They guaranteed loans given to their tenants and took a more active interest in their land.[55]

In retrospect, the era from 1917 to 1929 proved fruitful to those financial leaders who withstood the ups and downs of the economic cycle. Mergers, consolidations, and failures reduced the number of banks, but those that survived saw their resources soar. Problems

Beaver County Bank (now the City National), Guymon, 1930. Courtesy Oklahoma Bankers Association.

abounded—as was evident if bankers considered the plight of tenant farmers or the dislocations caused by bandits—but progress was also evident. As they looked forward to the 1930s, most financial leaders echoed the views of political leaders and common citizens when they talked of the dawn of a new era of prosperity for all. Few foresaw the disastrous collapse of the economy that would occur in 1929, or the tremendous problems that lay ahead.

CHAPTER 6.

Depression and Slow Recovery

In 1929 the booming national prosperity came to an end. Oklahoma bankers and their customers underwent an unsettling experience when on October 24—Black Monday—the stock market crashed. Actually, industrialists had begun to curtail production and lay off workers as early as the summer of 1929, but the crash was the harbinger of more severe and widespread economic collapse. By mid-November the *New York Times* industrial average had fallen more than 210 points, from 442.77 to 223.58. Speculative stocks suffered a rapid decline in value, but blue-chip issues declined as well. The stock of Radio Corporation of America, for example, fell from $92 3/8 to $28 3/4 while General Electric fell from $368 to $173 a share.[1]

The depression continued to worsen; from 1929 to 1932 the nation's income decreased from $87.8 billion to $42.5 billion a year, and the Federal Reserve System's index of industrial production fell from 110 to 58.[2] Although agriculture had not experienced the same degree of prosperity in the 1920s as the industrial sector of the economy, conditions for the farmers deteriorated even further after the crash. From 1929 to 1932 the price of cotton dropped from $0.16 to $0.06 a pound, while corn dipped from $0.86 to $0.33 a bushel, and wheat fell from $1.13 to $0.38 a bushel. Eventually the price of wheat dropped to $0.25 per bushel. Curiously, while wheat and other crops were not worth the cost of harvesting, in some areas of the country people starved. As Franklin D. Roosevelt later said, in the 1930s there was want in the midst of plenty. In addition, the average price of farm land, a factor most critical to mortgage-holding bankers, dropped by approximately 70 to 75 percent.[3]

Financial leaders in Oklahoma found themselves in a quandary. By 1930 they had a portfolio of old uncollectible loans; thus the making of new loans appeared unappealing at the exact time when the masses needed more credit. Likewise afraid, the Federal Reserve

Board clamped down, making the giving of credit more difficult for the state's leaders. Ultimately, the economy reached a standstill. Tragically, all segments of the economy, consumers and financial leaders included, suffered a loss of confidence. Great factories shut down while people throughout the state had no clothes, no shoes; thousands of acres of wheat rotted in the fields while people went hungry.[4]

The First National of Oklahoma City, one of the largest banks in the Midwest, had an experience perhaps typical; in January 1930, the institution had $65 million in deposits, but by 1933 had only $30 million, as consumers withdrew their life savings trying to cope with the depression. With such declining balances, the First had to limit its consumer credit at a time when people most desperately needed the loans.[5]

Oklahoma, still a rural state, had never fully shared in the economic prosperity of the 1920s. Nevertheless, Oklahomans experienced increasing hardships after the crash, and financiers were pressed to keep their institutions solvent and at the same time help their communities recover. Financial leaders reacted to the collapse in various ways. Edmund Kennedy, who began his banking career in Raulston and moved to Pawhuska in 1909 to become president of the State Bank of Commerce, showed amazing foresight.[6] The leader of a small country bank that served rural Osage County, Kennedy came home one day after work in August 1929 and asked his wife, Maybelle, "How long will it take you to get ready to go to Europe?" When told that making the necessary arrangements and packing would take three days, Kennedy reserved his tickets for the trip. Only after the cruise began did Maybelle ask, "Ed, why are we taking this trip?" Kennedy replied, "There is going to be the worst crash the United States has ever known. It is going to happen while we are gone. The banks in Pawhuska are going broke, but I am not going to go broke." As he explained, "I left word that while we are gone, my bank is not to loan anyone more than $200—not anyone."[7]

But Kennedy was not the stereotype of the hard-hearted, tight-fisted banker. Explaining why he left his bank at a critical time and why he established the limit on loans, he said, "If I were there, my sentiments would force me to loan more and more money to my friends [established customers of the bank], and they would break

First National Bank (in background), Oklahoma City, 1930s. Courtesy Oklahoma Publishing Company.

me."[8] The astute Kennedy saved his bank. When he returned in October, he found his bank in trouble, but still solvent. The immediate, severe effects of the crash already had occurred, and the bank had suffered as many farmers and ranchers went bankrupt, but Kennedy's institution was one of the two out of four in Pawhuska that survived. Implementing a program of retrenchment, he became more careful in his loan policy and usually loaned only small amounts. He did work, however, to help his community recover, and he continued to provide small "feeder" or "grubstake" loans to established customers, farmers, and ranchers who were diligent workers and to business associates whose organizations were sound.[9]

Like the Kennedys, many of the state's great banking families survived the depression and gave all possible help to their communities. Although the number of great families are too numerous to mention here, a few are representative: the Crawfords, of Frederick; the English family in Lawton; the Fergusons, of Woodward; the Berrys, of Sapulpa; the Norris family, of Ada; the Berrys, of Stillwater; the Vose family, of Oklahoma City; the Harbers, of Shawnee; the Masons, of Durant; the Love family, of Chandler—these and other notable banking families did yeoman's service for their communities during these difficult times.[10]

Despite the leadership of the many key banking families in the state, conditions continued to worsen during the first phase of the depression. People appeared to lose all confidence in the economy, and at the same time they became more and more concerned over their banks. Some earnestly believed that the country could not survive, that the government might fall, and that some sort of dictatorship might emerge. Many closed their accounts with commercial banks and opened accounts with postal savings, an institution that provided keen competition to commercial institutions during the hard years. Many did so because they believed that their savings would be protected and that only the fall of the government itself could jeopardize their accounts.[11]

Not all bankers in Oklahoma were as farsighted or as fortunate as Edmund Kennedy or the old-line banking families. By the scores banks folded or were forced to merge to remain solvent. Bankruptcies and defaults became commonplace. In December, 1928, there were 336 state and 325 national banks in Oklahoma with resources of

$567,878,087. Two years later there were only 301 state and 264 national institutions, and resources had declined to $474,506,598. As conditions continued to worsen, more banks failed. By December, 1932, only 477 banks—253 state and 224 national—remained solvent, and their combined resources had dwindled to approximately $327 million.[12] Oklahoma financiers were particularly hard hit because most loans in the state were based on livestock, land, or crops for security, and these items declined in value by more than 50 percent between 1929 and 1932. Therefore, many bankers were forced to reorganize with additional capital, or to close their institutions if such capital could not be found.[13]

Oftentimes, bankers could not be faulted even when their institutions had difficulty or closed. For example, one financial leader in Osage County realized in 1927 that something was wrong with the economy. Consequently, the unnamed banker began calling in loans and reducing his loan-deposit ratio. He then invested his money in United States bonds, investments he believed absolutely safe. However, after the depression mounted in 1930 and 1932, his depositors continued to make withdrawals. Such demands forced the banker to cash his bonds at a heavy discount, and eventually the banker was ruined.[14]

In 1932 the Oklahoma Bank Department developed the Moratorium Bank Plan to expedite the handling of insolvent banks, and in doing so anticipated certain provisions of the federal Glass-Steagall Bank Reform Act of 1933. In the Oklahoma plan the bank department was named as receiver when a state institution closed. The department then examined the books and organized a new bank to assume the deposits and liabilities of the old institution, to receive new deposits, and to perform other banking functions, with restrictions usually placed on amounts of money that could be loaned.[15]

If the banking community suffered upheaval, so did its customers. The threat of foreclosures became more commonplace. Although some financial leaders carried their customers with "feeder" loans, or with loans to repay at least the interest on their notes, other bankers could not be so accommodating. To maintain solvency, many country banks were forced to foreclose on nonpaying loan customers, a majority of whom were farmers. As a result, some farm families lost everything they had. But the rural folk did not suffer alone.

Armored car, Federal Reserve Bank, Oklahoma City, 1930s. Courtesy Oklahoma Publishing Company.

Many urbanites faced house mortgages that were easy to pay during the boom years of the 1920s, but next to impossible to meet during the depression, particularly because most mortgages were for only three to five years. Likewise, many city dwellers had difficulty meeting payments in smaller installment loans made for purchases of automobiles, electrical appliances, and other consumer items.[16]

The state and federal governments did little to alleviate the crisis in banking that accompanied the deepening depression. William H. ("Alfalfa Bill") Murray, governor of Oklahoma when the depression began, was a conservative who believed that natural laws would

Federal Reserve Bank, Oklahoma City, 1930s. Courtesy Oklahoma Publishing Company.

eventually balance the economy. At the federal level, President Herbert Hoover had been inaugurated fewer than eight months before the stock market crash. He believed that the only viable solution to the economic doldrums that the country faced was for the federal and state governments to reduce spending and balance their budgets.

The continuing crisis brought little state reform, but eventually forced federal action. The Hoover administration supported the Federal Reserve Board's attempts to expand credit by reducing the rediscount rate. Although the rate was reduced several times from 1929 to 1933, such manipulation had little effect on credit or flow of money. Sensing that more substantial action was necessary, the

Hoover administration in 1930 supported new spending projects to "prime" the sagging economy. The Keyes-Elliott Act appropriated approximately $330 million for construction of public buildings. That same year construction was begun on the Colorado River Dam. In October, 1931, Hoover created the National Credit Corporation (NCC), which made loans to needy banks and accepted their frozen assets as collateral. However, the NCC was of little assistance in Oklahoma; its credit requirements were too high. In fact, the corporation made loans of less than $150 million nationally, an amount too low to ensure rapid recovery.[17]

In January, 1932, Congress took new action, creating the Reconstruction Finance Corporation (RFC). The agency was empowered to make loans totaling $3.3 billion to banks, railroads, farmers, insurance companies, and state governments. That same year other measures supported by Hoover included new capital appropriations of $125 million to the Federal Land Banks and the establishment of an Agricultural Credit Corporation that could make short-term loans to farmers.[18]

Although Hoover thus supported many reforms, a number of which directly or indirectly affected the financial institutions of Oklahoma, the depression continued its disastrous course. New problems arose after the election of Franklin D. Roosevelt, who did not enjoy the unanimous support of the business community. As the time for Roosevelt's inauguration grew near, financially well-established segments of the population feared that runaway inflation might follow any drastic attempts to reform the economy. Increasingly, banks in Oklahoma faced runs, and many closed their doors.[19]

Roosevelt reacted to the banking panic by asking Congress to pass the Emergency Banking Act, which allowed the president to proclaim a national banking holiday from March 9 to March 15. Further, the president was empowered to keep any bank closed until federal examiners had analyzed its books and pronounced it sound. Then banks might be reopened on either a restricted or an unrestricted basis, with restricted institutions limited in the amounts of money they could loan, in the amounts of overdrafts they could honor, and in other services they could perform. In addition, the banking act also allowed the RFC to purchase authorized but unissued stocks of banks that were structurally sound but that experienced difficulty meeting their obligations. On a case-by-case basis, such purchases were attempts to give bank assets more liquidity. Ultimately, the purchases had an effect similar to the issuance of clearinghouse certificates, a practice common before the Federal Reserve System was created.[20]

By the time Roosevelt had proclaimed the national holiday, Governor Murray had already taken similar action in Oklahoma. A severe public panic precipitated runs on banks throughout the state and prompted the governor to proclaim a state holiday on March 2. The moratorium lasted until March 15, its length thus conforming to Roosevelt's schedule. The closing of the banks placed great strains on both merchants and consumers. In several cities around the state, financial leaders responded to the crisis in the same way earlier leaders had responded to the Panic of 1907—clearinghouses began issuing their own scrip. In Oklahoma City a Cash Reserve Association was formed, with Hubert Hudson as chairman and Edgar T. Bell as secretary-treasurer. The association's officers quickly had scrip printed, the notes being slightly larger than ordinary currency. A formal trust agreement was framed, and various civic leaders became trustees of the association. When Murray heard of the proposed issue of scrip, he questioned its reliability and declared it illegal. When several days passed and the situation in central Oklahoma had become more critical, the Cash Reserve Association decided to ignore the governor. Opening an office, Hudson sold scrip to reliable businessmen. After one day's sale $95,500 worth of notes were in circulation, and by the end of the moratorium, $140,000. More than 250 stores in central Oklahoma accepted the notes at full face value. When real money became more available after the banking holiday, the emergency scrip was retired, but the plan inaugurated by Oklahoma City proved to be one of the most successful in the nation.[21]

Like their counterparts in Oklahoma City, financial leaders in Okmulgee experimented during the depression until they found a system to help ease hard times and facilitate the flow of goods and services. In the Okmulgee trading area a voluntary moratorium had stopped foreclosures on mortgages and the collection of other debts. But those who had currency and coin were hoarding, circulation of money reached record lows, and business came to a virtual standstill. Yet, there was new work to do. The city had scheduled improvement projects on Okmulgee Lake, but had no appropriation for the work.

Many unemployed people who wanted to work saw the city's proposed project as their salvation. Businessmen in town likewise wanted money to flow into the laborers' hands. The merchants had products to sell, but workers had no money with which to buy.[22]

In late 1932, R. L. Baugh, secretary of the Retail Merchants Association and later vice-president of the Citizens National, urged cooperation of all elements of the local economy. Aided by his local bankers, he developed a plan that revived trade. Under his direction in early 1933, the city government went forward with its improvement program for the lake. Workmen accepted trade scrip for their labor, and local merchants accepted the scrip in lieu of money for purchases. Baugh designed the scrip to be self-liquidating. The notes were in denominations of $1.00, and in each transaction a $0.03 "tax" was charged, a levy paid to the city. After thirty-five consecutive transactions, the scrip thus yielded $1.05 in taxes and was then redeemable at face value. The extra $0.05 collected by Baugh offset the expenses of the program. When the state banking holiday began on March 2, $5,000 of Okmulgee's trade notes were already in circulation, and although banks were closed, the scrip continued to boost the local economy. All merchants cooperated with the scheme, accepting $2.00 in scrip for each $5.00 purchase. As a result, Baugh's program helped Okmulgee and its hinterland survive.[23]

Some Oklahoma banks did not close during the holiday, because their leaders knew that their institutions were strong enough to withstand the run. Ben Miles, president of the First National of Harrah, refused to close his bank. On the one hand, he knew it was financially strong enough to withstand the crisis, and on the other, he believed that closing would cause a local panic of tremendous proportions. Consequently, it was "business as usual." Several country banks in the state followed Harrah's lead and likewise refused to close.[24]

The Emergency Banking Act, passed in March, 1933, was only a temporary measure designed to halt a national panic. It was part of Roosevelt's "Hundred Days War" against the depression, a "war" that saw most of the first New Deal legislation become law. Much of the initial New Deal had a direct impact on the banking industry. One clause of the banking act had given the federal government the power to recall all gold and gold certificates then held in bank vaults.

On April 19, 1933, Roosevelt ordered all private holdings of gold surrendered to Federal Reserve banks in return for other currency or coin—the president had abandoned the gold standard. Then in the next two months, Congress passed legislation to stimulate the economy, legislation such as the Federal Emergency Relief Act, which appropriated monies for relief and set up the Federal Emergency Relief Administration to coordinate all federal and state efforts; the National Industrial Recovery Act, which established industrial codes relating to prices, wages, and maximum working hours per week; and the Farm Credit Act, which consolidated all rural credit agencies under the Farm Credit Administration.[25]

Most important to bankers, during the "Hundred Days War" Congress also passed the Glass-Steagall Banking Reform Act. Under its provisions the minimum capital requirement for national banks was raised to $50,000. The bill also divorced stock investment activities from normal commercial bank operations. It prohibited national banks from paying interest on demand deposits and created a permanent Open Market Operations Committee, with one member drawn from each reserve bank on a rotating basis. Finally came the capstone of the reform act: Congress created the Federal Deposit Insurance Corporation (FDIC). Charged with the responsibility of purchasing and liquidating the assets of national banks that had been closed by the comptroller of the currency, or by a vote of the directors of such institutions, the FDIC also insured, up to $5,000 on each account, the deposits of all banks that were examined and held to be entitled to such insurance. The United States Treasury subscribed to $150 million of the FDIC's stock. Participating banks subscribed varying amounts, with individual contributions totaling one half of 1 percent of the deposits to be insured.[26]

Like their counterparts across the country, many financial leaders in Oklahoma at first opposed the FDIC program. Many agreed with the editor of the *Journal of the American Bankers Association* (ABA) when he observed that the new program ran "counter to all past experience in states which have tried guaranty, always with disastrous results." The editor then warned that the law would "force sound banks to make good the losses and mistakes of poorly managed banks . . .. The plan is dangerous not only to banking but to the entire country." Perturbed officials of the ABA then offered a prize of fifty dollars for the best essay on "Guaranty of Deposits: How Can This Threat to Sound Banking Be Met?"[27]

Many Oklahomans objected, not just to the FDIC, but to other provisions in the Glass-Steagall Act. State Bank Commissioner W. J. Barnett minced no words in declaring that the act was "most radical and [would cause] a drastic change in the banking laws of the country. The new bill," he lamented, "has been written for the . . . depositors . . . not for . . . the bankers."[28] Yet, some leaders weighed potential alternatives and defended the reform legislation. Dan W. Hogan, president of Oklahoma City's City National Bank and Trust Company and a dean of banking who began his career in Yukon, Oklahoma, in the 1890s, supported the reform. That support was critical, because all bankers in the state knew and trusted Hogan and valued his opinion. He argued that the greatest troubles in banking had arisen in the past because of overspeculation and because there were too many institutions competing for a limited number of deposits, competing in a finite market place. Contending that regulation was necessary, he applauded the development of the FDIC as a beneficial program that would protect depositors. With such knowledgeable men as Hogan lobbying for reform, critics of the New Deal reforms began to reconsider their positions.[29]

Once Hogan had spoken, other leaders quickly embraced the FDIC. Jack Conn, longtime leader in Oklahoma banking, who began his career in Ada in the 1940s before moving to Oklahoma City, recalled that "the FDIC was the greatest reform in banking ever passed by Congress."[30] Another financial leader, Howard Bozarth, who was for years president of the City National of Oklahoma City before moving to the Fidelity Bank, echoed Conn's sentiments. "The FDIC stopped the runs," Bozarth said simply.[31] It also encouraged people to move their accounts from the postal savings back to banks. Roosevelt's plan, Bozarth declared, insured that small depositors could not lose their money.[32] Whereas in earlier days rumors had been sufficient to start major panics, after the FDIC was passed those rumors no longer had the same disastrous effects because depositors knew they were protected.[33]

Although he was originally critical of the Glass-Steagall Act, Barnett had embraced the reform by October 1933. The commissioner was apparently confused for a time; he questioned the rapidity

D. P. Richardson, president of the OBA, 1930–31. Courtesy Oklahoma Bankers Association.

of New Deal reforms, always pausing to wonder whether such reforms were well-conceived. But when the thoughtful man understood the benefits of the FDIC program, he quickly changed his opinions. Believing that a new era in banking had dawned, Barnett stated that "The conservative banker will come into his own," because "the hand of the 'wildcatter' has been called by the government. Hereafter banking is going to be a profession—not merely the vehicle of speculation."[34]

While financiers coped with the unstable natures of their institutions and cooperated with the recovery attempts initiated by the New Deal, widespread unemployment and economic desperation spawned a new problem: an upsurge in the number of bank robberies and attempted robberies, particularly in the rural areas of the state. It appeared that during the depression many people turned to a life of crime out of desperation and hopelessness. An attempt was made on the Farmers and Merchants Bank of Boley in November 1932. In a daring daylight robbery, a white man, later identified as George Birdwell, and a black, Pete Glass, entered the bank in the black community while two other bandits remained behind in a getaway car. Birdwell and Glass drew their guns on cashier W. W. Riley and president D. J. Turner. After sacking all the currency and silver found in the money till, Birdwell prepared to kill Turner because the latter had made disparaging comments about the former's ancestors while the holdup was in progress.[35] But before the bank robber could act, bookkeeper H. C. McCormick, who had disappeared into the vault when the holdup began, reappeared armed with a rifle and fired point blank at Birdwell. Before the bandit fell to the floor, he fired five slugs into Turner, who fell dead next to his severely wounded assailant. Glass and a third bandit, a man named Patterson, then took charge. The latter ran into the bank when the shooting started. Armed with a shotgun, he commandeered the services of a bystander whom he ordered to take Birdwell to the car. In the meantime, the bandits failed to notice McCormick because he had slipped back into the vault to reload. While Patterson, Glass, Riley, and the bystander were carrying Birdwell to the car, merchant William Hazel saw the commotion, grabbed his rifle, and shot Patterson, who fell upon the sidewalk and then staggered to his feet, firing a pistol at Hazel. Several other merchants came to Hazel's defense, shooting at Patterson as the bandit ran to his car. Just as the outlaw reached his vehicle, McCormick, who was also the city constable, fired his rifle and felled the bandit. Glass then surrendered.[36] Wiley Combs, the fourth bandit and the driver of the getaway car, escaped. Later, Combs related that "all hell broke loose—it sounded like a damn war . . .. There was so much shootin' going on, it was kinda hard to tell who shot who!"[37]

The upsurge of robberies led the Oklahoma Bankers Association and individual financiers to offer new rewards for the capture of bandits and to initiate supplementary actions as well. As the front-page headlines of the *Kansas City Star* proclaimed on November 20, 1932:

Oklahoma Bankers, Driven to Desperation by Bandits, Are to Try War of Extermination. Rewards of $500 Are Offered for Those Captured Alive—Governor Murray Would Try Whipping Post and the Stocks—The Merchants in Small Towns Are Being Trained to Serve as Vigilantes When Robbery Alarms Sound . . . Five Banks Were Held Up in One Week.[38]

The *Star* exaggerated, but in truth the OBA, state law officers, individual bankers, and their helpless depositors were driven to distraction by the wave of robberies. Probably the most notorious Oklahoma outlaw of the era was Charles ("Pretty Boy") Floyd, an Oklahoman from Sallisaw who became one of the most infamous bandits of the early 1930s. Accused of scores of crimes in one six-month period alone, he and his gang robbed seven banks in the state, beginning on August 4, 1931, with the Citizen's Bank of Shamrock. That effort netted only $400. On September 8 the Floyd gang took $1,743 from the Morris State Bank and on September 29 robbed the First National in Maud of $3,850. On October 14 they took $2,498 from the Bank of Earlsboro, which they had robbed earlier, on March 9, 1931, of $3,000. On November 5 the gang held up the First National of Conowa, taking $2,500. Six weeks later they again robbed the Morris State Bank, taking $1,162, and on January 14, 1931, got $2,600 from the First State in Castle.[39]

Floyd, who continued his depredations until 1934, when he was felled by FBI agents, led only one of the gangs that terrorized Oklahoma bankers. According to one unofficial OBA estimate, bank robberies or burglaries in the state occurred on the average of more than

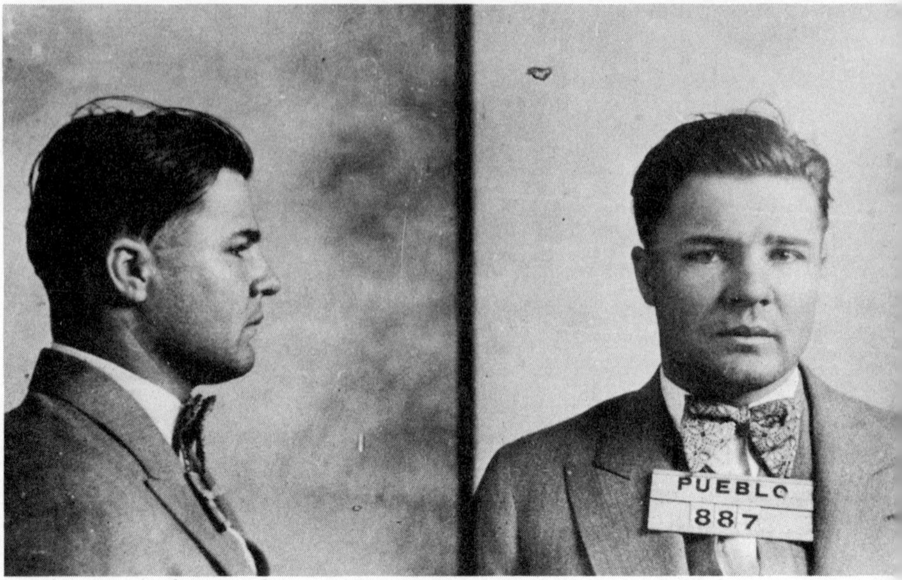

Charles Arthur ("Pretty Boy") Floyd, 1932. Courtesy Oklahoma Bankers Association.

one a week. Through the calendar year 1931 there were at least fifty-eight holdups or burglaries. Eugene B. Gum, longtime leader of the OBA, became so concerned by the outbreaks of lawlessness that he began making special studies on bank security and urged his membership to adopt up-to-date, scientific alarms and locks to ward off attackers. Yet, during the next three years, the situation worsened.[40]

On October 6, 1933, the First National Bank of Frederick was the scene of another, typical daylight holdup. Two men later identified as "Big Bob" Brady and Jim Clark, together with an unidentified driver, drove into Frederick, marched to the bank, and pulled the robbery with such military precision that the bank's patrons and officials were caught totally off guard. The bandits escaped with $3,490, but overlooked another $15,000 in drawers that they failed to search. Notified after the holdup, police chief Floyd Blair and several of his men pursued the outlaws in a high-speed chase eastward on Highway

5. After losing the outlaws, Blair later found their abandoned Ford; in it was a map that marked an escape route to the southwest, a clue that led to the bandits' undoing. Blair notified authorities in Amarillo, Texas, and Tucumcari, New Mexico. Officers in Tucumcari set up a road block, caught Brady and Clark, and recovered the bank's money. Because he had not accompanied his cohorts to New Mexico, the third unidentified bandit escaped.[41]

Despite the enforcement crackdown and an array of ingenious ploys to capture them, other bandits were successful. In November, 1934 outlaws robbed the First National Bank of Okeene. Hugh Zimmerman of Omega, one of the bank's depositors, heard of the robbery and decided to "tail" the bandits in his homemade flying machine. In previous months Zimmerman had spent his idle time tearing down an old Model T. Taking the engine, a few sideboards from an old wagon, some corrugated iron from a barn roof, and some spare parts from various farm machines, he produced a "full-fledged flying apparatus" that was held together with baling wire, but was capable of a takeoff from any yard and a perfect landing in any pasture. The mechanic boarded his Model T sky wagon and reconnoitered the Okeene countryside until he spotted the bandits' car, which he had no trouble identifying because the robbers began shooting at him.[42]

He followed the car from a safe distance until he spotted a gasoline station. He then landed his craft in an adjacent pasture, told the attendant to call the police, and took off again to resume the chase. Eventually, the robbers drove their car under a tree, but the pilot discovered their ploy and circled overhead as the police approached the scene. At the first sight of the authorities, the bandits fled. They escaped the police but could not evade Zimmerman. Each time the authorities lost the trail, the pilot spotted the outlaws. At one time there was a sizable distance between the outlaws' car and that of the pursuing policemen. Inadvertently, a third car moved between the bandits and the police. Zimmerman then flew ahead of the chase, landed and warned the innocent parties in the third car to stop.[43]

Boarding his plane again, he discovered that he had no more fuel. However, he gleefully watched as the bandits' car turned down a road that was bordered on both sides by thick woods and came to a dead end at a creek. After the pilot informed the officers of the robbers' blunder, the policemen calmly waited for the bandits. Meanwhile, the outlaws reached the creek, stopped, and doubtless lamented their poor judgment. They soon continued on their way, however, by cutting through a fence and pushing their car across the dry creek bed to another road on the other side. Although Zimmerman drew much praise for his gallant trip, the bandits escaped with the bank's deposits in tow.[44]

But Zimmerman's fast thinking had given Stanley Rogers, president of the Oklahoma Peace Officers Association, an idea that was to aid bankers in their quest for security. Rogers asked laymen and financiers to coordinate their efforts to catch bandits by finding the nearest airplane and commissioning its pilot for service should the need arise. Rogers's association then purchased an airplane and stationed it in Oklahoma City. Equipped with a two-way radio, the plane stood ready to render service to all of central Oklahoma. Rogers's idea spawned the development of a new vigilante air service that, when added to the other protective measures taken by financial leaders to increase their security, helped reduce the number of bank robberies in the state.[45]

Other factors also contributed to reducing the crime rate in Oklahoma. One point, though seldom mentioned, was the development of better roads. As bandit Whitey Combs later reflected, "The back roads were dying out—and if you can't use the back roads the way we did, you can't operate."[46] Increased activity by the Bureau of Investigation, renamed the Federal Bureau of Investigation (FBI) in 1935, also acted as a deterrent to robberies. By 1934 the agency had begun a drive to rid Oklahoma and other states of criminal elements. Bank robbers particularly feared Melvin Purvis, famed agent who reached the pinnacle of his career in the 1930s. The outlaw Combs called Purvis "a cold-blooded killer." Certainly, the competent, stern Purvis and other FBI agents worked to reduce crime.[47]

The FBI ended the careers of many bank robbers, including that of "Pretty Boy" Floyd, who had terrorized Oklahoma's bankers for years and who by 1934 was "Public Enemy Number One—the most dangerous man alive." That year, law enforcement officials began one of the most extensive manhunts in history, one designed to capture Floyd. Although Floyd evaded officers in Oklahoma, Missouri, and other states, finally in October he was tracked to a farm near East Liverpool, Ohio. Agent Purvis led a force of eight officers, four federal and four local, and laid siege to the farmhouse. When Floyd ran for a cluster of woods nearby, the agents opened fire with machine guns and pistols. The volleys stopped Floyd, who soon died from the fifteen bullet wounds he received.[48] The successful manhunt, and others like it, further reduced the crime rate in Oklahoma, and in 1935 only nine banks in the state were looted. In the period from 1936 to 1941, bandits successfully robbed only ten more, and the outlaws guilty of five of the holdups were later caught, convicted, and sent to prison, or killed.[49]

As the number of robberies declined in the state, bankers welcomed a corresponding drop in their insurance rates. In June, 1936 the National Bureau of Casualty and Surety Underwriters for Territory Four, which included Oklahoma, reduced its overall rates by 20 percent, and that reduction was followed by another of 10 percent in January, 1938. Then in August, 1938, the company trimmed 14 percent from its premium, the biggest savings going to those with small policies. In the last reduction, the bankers' rate for the first $5,000 of the coverage was cut by 25 percent, from $16 to $12.[50]

By 1938 other notable developments had taken place, developments inspired by the banking community. Throughout the 1930s financial leaders worked tirelessly on behalf of agriculture in the state, and by the latter part of the decade the work began to pay dividends. Previously, financiers and farmers had become increasingly concerned about the disastrous effects of the dust bowl, and they experimented with techniques designed to hold the topsoil. Terracing proved a partial solution, but many farmers failed to utilize that method to stop erosion. Many were uninstructed in the methods of scientific agribusiness; many were too poor to rent machinery, or to pay an expert capable of running levels. As a result, by 1930 farmers in Oklahoma had terraced fewer than 100,000 acres.[51]

The state's bankers, particularly those in northeastern and central Oklahoma, initiated a bold project in the mid-1930s to spur the farmers to action. Working with the extension agricultural engineer at Oklahoma A&M College (later Oklahoma A&M University), bankers in the northeastern part of the state scheduled a series of countywide meetings in which the engineer, W. H. McPheters, presented programs on scientific management, including discussions on terracing. A total of 103 meetings in seventeen counties was held in 1937, with 9,464 people attending. Then the bankers hired C. T. Studivant, one of McPheters' assistants, and engineer H. L. Morrisett to conduct terracing schools. By the end of the year 235,218 acres had been terraced in northeastern Oklahoma. Hundreds of thousands of acres of Oklahoma topsoil were thus preserved; financial leaders who initiated and funded the conservation drive were rewarded by increased productivity in their communities, productivity that meant new, more stable business for the banks.[52]

While developing a terracing program, the financial community in the 1930s also continued to aid farm youth by supporting the 4-H movement. From 1918 to 1938 bankers provided more than $30,000 for 185 scholarships to Oklahoma A&M College for the agribusinessmen of the future. For high school youths throughout the state, bankers also financed the purchase of pure seed and purebred livestock. In the 1930s they sponsored special classes, farm tours, and special awards at county and state fairs for outstanding contributions to agriculture. As a result, by 1938 more than 164,000 youths were enrolled in 4-H clubs, 125,000 of whom, with loans from local financial institutions, were engaged in the breeding and marketing of high grade cattle, hogs, sheep, poultry, and dairy products. The experience of the First National Bank and Trust Company of Muskogee was one example of successful banker-involvement in agriculture. The president of that institution, H. H. Ogden, had for years aided the development of farming. In 1937 he assisted seventy-three boys in securing purebred Hampshire gilts at a cost of approximately $2,000. Each participant in that year's program received expert advice in developing a herd of hogs. For monies and credit advanced, each repaid Ogden in full.[53]

In 1939 Oklahoma's bankers also organized the Wheat Improvement Association. During the presidency of R. R. Jackson, of Anadarko, the OBA—in conjunction with Oklahoma A&M and the Millers Association—financed thirty plots across the state where farmers planted many varieties of wheat and tested their new crops for quality and yield. A strong, healthy standard brand was quickly developed and recommended by the OBA.[54]

Although the 1930s brought hardship and heartbreak, many stories had happy endings, stories such as W. S. "Mike" Flanagan's experience in Collinsville. A city that boomed with more than 10,000 people and scores of thriving business establishments during the World War I era, Collinsville almost "died" in the 1920s. The local economy depended primarily upon two smelters, but at the end of the war one was moved to another location and the other closed. Most of the populace moved away, and by 1930 only 1,500 people remained. The deepening depression threatened to destroy what was left of the viability of the town. The town's three banks all failed in the late 1920s, but the American Exchange Bank, organized in 1928, survived to serve the town. By 1933 more than 400 men, almost all heads of households, held government relief jobs as conditions continued to worsen.[55]

Mike Flanagan, a native of Wagoner, joined the American Exchange in 1930 and, seven years later, bought controlling interest in the institution. Only twenty-eight years old, he decided to name a local druggist, S. C. Bryant, as president, while taking the titles of cashier and vice-president for himself. Determined to do what he could to save the community, Flanagan decided that proper use of acreage provided the solution. The land, worn out from overuse, was no longer suitable for crops, and most farms were small, with inadequate acreages for beef cattle. Flanagan decided that dairying held the keys to the future. However, there were few milk cows in the Collinsville trade territory.[56] Nonetheless, that year Flanagan began implementing a long-range plan to create a dairy industry for the Collinsville hinterland. First, he sponsored a monthly adult agriculture study session and brought in speakers from Oklahoma A&M and the University of Missouri to extoll the wisdom of dairying. Next, he underwrote the purchase of twenty-five dairy cattle; later he bought more. Then he financed individual farmers who wanted two, five, or ten of the cattle. Farmers paid on their notes twice monthly, a schedule that followed payments made by a Tulsa milk-processing plant to suppliers. Next, Flanagan began financing young members of FFA (Future Farmers of America) who were going into dairying, while the chamber of commerce sponsored an annual dairy day with speakers from Oklahoma A&M. Soon a tricounty dairy fair became an annual event, with dairymen from Tulsa, Rogers, and Washington counties participating. Eventually Flanagan's efforts helped save Collinsville; within a few years the town had grown to 3,000, with a monthly dairy income of the surrounding area exceeding $100,000.

Known as the "dairy capital of Oklahoma," Collinsville survived—with the help of the American Exchange and Mike Flanagan.[57]

While bankers continued to show interest in agricultural reforms and in agribusiness loans, they noticed a new—and to some of them an alarming—trend. Under Roosevelt's New Deal, the federal government increasingly entered areas of finance that previously had been reserved for banks and other private lending institutions. The Resettlement Administration and other New Deal agencies absorbed an ever-growing number of farm mortgages, lending more money at cheaper rates than banks could provide. Moreover, the government underwrote loans for a much longer time than private financiers. Nevertheless, the growth of installment financing—a godsend according to some bankers, a curse according to others—enabled bankers to enlarge their lending markets despite government competition and regulations.[58]

Indeed, installment financing represented salvation for many Oklahoma banks, especially the rural institutions. The First National Bank of Coalgate, under president Lillian O'Connell, discounted installment paper worth $250,000 in the mid-1930s and suffered no losses. O'Connell found that automobile paper, especially on used cars, represented the best investment, because the auto increasingly became a necessity rather than a luxury. Likewise, washing machine paper was a stable investment. Accustomed to spending all day once a week bending over a washtub, women fortunate enough to acquire a machine made certain that the family budget included their monthly payment for such a work saver. Other good installment investments were papers on refrigerators, cookstoves, and cream separators, which farmers considered a necessity in order to market butterfat products profitably. According to O'Connell, radio paper was the only risky investment. Quick changes in design, rapid depreciation, price reductions on new models, their tendency to break down—all these and other factors had a negative effect on the consumer's willingness to pay. Yet, on the whole, installment financing gave bankers a new, lucrative market while enabling them to offer broader service to their community and to build good will with customers.[59]

Comparative figures also divulge another trend in banking. Before 1930, bankers used a predominant amount of their assets to make loans and discounts and conversely committed only a small sum to investments. In 1900 the percentage of assets in loans and discounts for banks statewide stood at 49.9 percent, while the percentage of assets invested amounted to 2 percent. In 1920, 64.3 percent of assets were committed to loans and discounts, while 8 percent were committed to investments, but by 1935 a noticeable shift had occurred. In that year, only 27.1 percent of the assets were in loans and discounts while 28 percent were committed to long-term investments.[60]

As financial leaders grappled with many new trends in the 1930s, the legislature framed a new banking code. Passed on April 28, 1937, the Banking Act provided more effective control over the creation of new financial institutions. Designed to prevent bank failures and to rehabilitate banks that were having trouble, it provided an orderly liquidation of the ones that could not survive. Unlike previous banking legislation, the Code of 1937 required that the bank commissioner, who was appointed by the governor and served for four years at his pleasure, have at least five years' experience in banking. Likewise, the assistant bank commissioner, who was appointed by the commissioner, had to have three years' experience. The act of 1937 also created fourteen positions for bank examiners. In addition, the power to grant charters was lodged with the Oklahoma Banking Board, composed of the commissioner and three other members chosen by the governor.[61]

The new regulations made it more difficult to secure a charter. Under their provisions the amount of capital needed to found a bank varied, depending on the size of the community in which the bank was to do business. In smaller towns $10,000 was required; in large metropolitan centers, $25,000. However, the banking board refused to issue charters to bankers who did not furnish the deposit insurance protections offered by the FDIC, and the FDIC required a minimum capital structure of $30,000. Thus, as a practical matter, most institutions opening after 1937 needed $30,000 paid-in capital. Other sections of the code forced a public disclosure, twice each year, of each bank's assets and liabilities. Likewise, the act directed the board to examine all institutions at least two times annually and to remove any banking officer found to be incompetent, dishonest, or unwilling to comply with regulatory statutes. To prevent concentration of funds, the code provided that 15 percent of a bank's capital and sur-

Walter B. Stephens, president of the OBA, 1933–34. Courtesy Oklahoma Bankers Association.

E. C. Love, president of the OBA, 1938–39. Courtesy Oklahoma Bankers Association.

plus was the maximum amount that could be loaned to any one person or corporation.[62]

Despite the fact that financiers could not help everyone, the Oklahoma banking fraternity's contributions during the decade of the 1930s helped the state overcome the economic stagnation that characterized the era. And bankers met the next decade with hope rather than anxiety.

Chapter 7.

The 1940s

The beginnings of the war in Europe in 1939 brought boom times to the United States economy and lush times to American bankers. War orders from Europe and a preparedness campaign at home demanded increases in production. Then, in December, 1941, the pace of economic growth quickened after the Japanese attack on Pearl Harbor drew the United States into World War II. Government expenditures spiraled upward to more than $50 billion in 1942 and $80 billion in 1943. Whereas in the 1930s the government spent $6.5 billion on public works and $10.1 billion in RFC loans, from 1940 to 1946 it spent $360 billion on national defense alone. In 1945 the federal budget reached $100 billion annually. Bankers were called upon to aid the drive in increased war production by financing the development of new industries and the expansion of old ones. Moreover, the federal government asked commercial banks to finance the large deficits that the United States incurred during the war years.[1]

The bankers of Oklahoma were quick to understand the ramifications of the events that occurred between 1939 and 1942, and they rallied to support the government. A. E. Bradshaw, president of the Oklahoma Bankers Association from 1940 to 1941, summarized the viewpoint of his colleagues when he said: "In the prosecution of [our] objective [immediate aid to Great Britain and preparedness at home] there is no place for partisan politics, for private selfishness. We must all cooperate toward one common goal."[2] Bradshaw's successor, R. B. Patton, of Henryetta, established for the OBA a National Defense Loan Committee, with N. R. Graham, of Tulsa, as chairman. For the duration of the war the committee coordinated defense financing and assisted contractors and local Oklahoma industries in obtaining defense contracts.[3] To aid small companies of 500 or fewer employees, in 1943 the government established the

Smaller War Plants Corporation, which functioned through fourteen regional offices for the purpose of making full use of the nation's manpower in defense production. Oklahoma, Texas, and Louisiana comprised Region Eight, and Fred Johnson, of the Fourth National Bank of Tulsa, was appointed to the region's board of governors. The corporation was successful. From September, 1943, to January, 1944, the agency channeled contracts worth $4,670,000 and loans and leases worth $600,000 to the small industries of Oklahoma.[4]

Oklahoma's financial leaders also cooperated fully in the national effort to sell war bonds. From a 10-cent stamp to a $10,000 issue, bankers promoted the bonds as investments in American defense and as deterrents to inflation. Between 1941 and mid-1944, financiers played a leading role in marketing five bond issues. In Oklahoma the drives were tremendously successful. A total of $145,323,074 in bonds and stamps was purchased, an amount that represented 134 percent of the state goal of $108,000,000. Every county in the state consistently oversubscribed its quota. Coal County, for example, had a goal of only $156,600, but in the five drives, with county bankers chairing promotional committees, citizens purchased $381,585 in bonds, a total representing 244 percent of the $156,600 quota. Counties of greater population had larger commitments, but, like Coal County, all surpassed their quotas. Tulsa County had the largest commitment, $25,991,000, with Oklahoma County given a goal of $23,865,000. Both surpassed their quotas: citizens in the former bought $33,456,903 in bonds, and those in the latter purchased a total of $32,911,184.[5]

In addition to leading community efforts, many bankers took initiative as individuals and thereby became models for the citizenry to follow. In 1941, Otis McClintock, president of the First National Bank and Trust Company of Tulsa, began investing heavily in war bonds, using his personal funds. Encouraging his employees to do likewise, he gave each a United States defense-savings stamp album in which the first dollar's worth of stamps had already been affixed. Such promotion was designed to ensure that a large majority of McClintock's personnel would participate in the program. Moreover, the president's actions were excellent public relations and provided "good copy" for the media. Other bond drives initiated in latter 1944 and

1945 produced similar results, with the state oversubscribing its quota in each drive.[6]

Although the bond drives were of great importance during the war years, financial leaders did not ignore their traditional work, nor could they escape their traditional problems. The depression of the 1930s had created havoc within the financial institutions of Oklahoma, but the immense government spending and the general economic expansion during the war years provided a solid financial basis for those banks that had survived. Moreover, there was closer supervision by state and national authorities. In mid-1941 there were 180 state and 207 national banks in Oklahoma. All had been examined during the year, and all passed the audits of their state or national examiner.[7] The number of banks, their relative soundness, and their growth rate remained remarkably stable in the following years. By the summer of 1942 the state had chartered three new banks, including one in Tulsa and one in Oklahoma City, but the consolidation of the First State Bank of Butler and the Farmers' National Bank of Elk City left the state with a net year's increase of two banks, a total of 182 state and 207 national banks.[8]

The war affected many bankers and their institutions in a dramatic way; many younger executives were either drafted or joined the service, and some of them remained away from their jobs for four long years. Particularly hard pressed were country banks, because they had a more difficult time replacing lost personnel than did urban banks, which had a larger pool of qualified replacements. Maybelle Kennedy, of Pawhuska, whose husband Ed was president of the National Bank of Commerce, remembered that during the war all the men in the bank were either in the service or had volunteered for government jobs and were therefore absent from the bank. Mrs. Kennedy not only had the task of managing the bank, with the aid of four other women employees, but also had to manage the family ranch.[9]

Despite the loss of personnel, during the war years the Oklahoma banking community continued its work, making agriculture a priority concern. One of many programs was the national food-for-freedom project. "The Flag is on the plow as well as on the battleship and the tank" was a contemporary saying that was taken to heart by the state's financial leaders. With the Oklahoma Bankers Association coordinating efforts, state financiers advanced virtually unlimited credit to qualified producers and processors of foodstuffs. Financial leaders held food-for-freedom meetings in every county to acquaint farmers with the credit program. In addition, bankers encouraged all patrons—whether rural or urban dwellers—to plant victory gardens for their own consumption, which would help to expand total food production for the war effort.[10]

The private financial institutions also cooperated with the programs of the federal Agricultural Adjustment Administration (AAA), which was designed to conserve the soil, to improve the land, and/or to increase crop yield. In the 1940s the AAA initiated a program that encouraged farmers to apply lime to their soil and to make other improvements. Participating agribusinessmen were paid for their expenses later when their annual allotments came due. However, many farmers lacked the ready cash required to make improvements. In cooperation with the AAA, bankers in Oklahoma advanced money for improvements, using the allotments as collateral. Financiers then collected directly from the AAA.[11]

While they coordinated the federal government's attempts to help the state's farmers, Oklahoma bankers also prompted and helped finance other improvements in agribusiness, improvements that had been needed for a long time and that were absolutely necessary during the war years. Periodically during the 1930s—particularly in 1934 and 1936—farmers and financial leaders lost immense sums of money because of a shortage in feed crops. Livestock had to be sacrificed to a poor market at whatever prices farmers could get. Meeting in several conferences in the latter part of the decade, bankers developed a program to solve the dilemma. Knowing that in flush years the farmers could harvest enough feed to last for two years, enough to carry stock raisers through a dry season, bankers in 1941 began financing the development of trench silos to store excess food. Financial leaders began a statewide advertising campaign, which had immediate results: Agribusinessmen in all Oklahoma counties began building silos. The Oklahoma City Chamber of Commerce, led by manager Stanley Draper, became interested in the program and established contact with every chamber in the state. Draper asked that businessmen lend their credit to the silo program in areas where farmers lacked sufficient collateral to secure loans. As a result, by mid-1942 approximately 1,000 trench silos had been constructed, and the state was assured a surplus of feed.[12]

Bankers also became more interested in soil conservation. In the late 1930s the OBA employed an engineer from Oklahoma A&M College to begin a lecture and demonstration program to educate farmers wishing to engage in scientific soil conservation. In addition, the OBA also cooperated with state and federal agencies in promoting land-use reform. By the summer of 1942 fifty-six of the counties in the state were included in soil-conservation districts. More than 13,280 farmer-district agreements involving 2,230,000 acres had been made. Much of the state land that had been abandoned because of depleted soil was put under the plow once again. In such a conservation program, bankers proved invaluable. Not only did they finance many of the improvements, they also gave intangible assistance in counseling and educating farmers and in promoting the program.[13]

Crop-improvement projects and the problem of farm tenancy also attracted the bankers' attention. A wheat-improvement program was begun in 1937, and by 1942, after scores of experiments with hybrid strains, there had been marked improvements in the quality of wheat grown in the state. With bankers promoting and financing the innovations, the success of the wheat program encouraged experimentation with cotton, and testing resulted in the development of a seed of higher quality.

Bankers had less success when they turned to the problem of farm tenancy. During the depression more than 50 percent of the farm land in the state was worked by tenants or sharecroppers. The financing of land purchases, which was made available during the New Deal, and the work of local financial leaders had resulted in a decline in tenancy. However, by 1940 tenants still worked more than 40 percent of Oklahoma's farm lands. Financiers continued in the 1940s to pressure absentee landlords to take a more active interest in the management of their acreage. At the same time, financial leaders became more willing to lend money to tenants to get every arable acre under production to aid the war effort.[14]

During the war years bankers in the state redoubled their efforts to aid members of the 4-H clubs and the FFA. In 1941, for example, bankers loaned a total of $87,526 to 1,476 FFA members, with most of the money, $42,000, financing cattle breeding. That same year commercial bankers supplied 79 percent ($32,800) of the credit used by 4-H club members. Young people involved in agricultural programs proved to be good risks. They not only repaid their loans, but they also cooperated with bankers in supporting the war effort. By June, 1942, the youngsters in the 4-H program had purchased $99,500 in war bonds and stamps.[15]

Bankers also continued to improve their security to prevent robberies and burglaries. In the late 1930s the OBA began a publicity campaign to persuade its members to buy electric alarm systems. By the 1940s most bankers had installed such systems, which supplemented the work of guards and other security devices. Although there were nine robberies or burglaries in 1935, the statewide average declined to less than two per year from 1936 to 1941, a decline that law enforcement officers credited to the new electric alarms. The policies of insurance companies also encouraged banks to tighten security. Most companies inserted clauses in their contracts that required institutions to keep the bulk of their cash under time lock. Thus, only a limited amount of currency and coin could be left out as counter cash.[16]

The war years brought immense changes to Oklahoma's banking industry, changes that were harbingers of permanent trends. First, there was a tremendous growth in deposits and currency in circulation. Second, there was an increase in bank investments in government securities. Bankers became partially dependent on income from government issues to pay operating expenses. They developed a vested interest in the existing rate structure because securities would depreciate in a market with rising interest rates. A third new trend was an increase in tax liability. Before 1942 financial institutions paid little federal tax. Bankers could invest in tax-free federal and municipal bonds and could take capital losses on what was, in effect, amortization of bond premiums. But in March, 1941, federal securities became subject to regular taxes in addition to a surtax, and in January, 1942, the government forbade the practice of taking capital losses on bond amortization. The net result of the government's actions was to increase the tax liability of financial institutions.[17]

Another trend, a more disturbing one, that many bankers noted was the continuing tendency of the government to finance loans and thereby to engage in direct competition with commercial banks. Such governmental agencies as the Federal Intermediate Credit Banks, the Reconstruction Finance Corporation, the Producers Credit Associations, and the Farm Security Administration took away much of the commercial banker's loan market. By 1941, for example, there were select county statistics available that showed the percentage of non-real estate agricultural loans held by government agencies:[18]

	Percentage of Loans	
Selected County	*Held by Banks*	*Held by Government Agencies*
McCurtain	27.3%	72.7%
Choctaw	24.0%	76.0%
Creek	52.4%	47.6%
Rogers	52.0%	48.0%
Woodward	50.7%	49.3%

Further, an estimate revealed that, statewide, governmental agencies held from 35 to 40 percent of all agricultural loans. Many financiers lamented the trend but seemed powerless to reverse it, especially during the emergency created by war.[19]

Although the banking business became increasingly complex in the 1940s as bankers became involved in more and more projects, most financial leaders retained their humanity and their down-home ways. O. W. Brown, who was a cofounder of the Citizen's Security Bank in Bixby in 1924 and who served the bank for decades, always tried to follow the Golden Rule when he found customers in financial distress. When they needed money, he did all possible to make the loan. When they had difficulty repaying, he carried their "slow" notes until examiners forced him to become stricter. Of great value to his community in the depression years, he continued to serve in the war years. One of his legacies was the training he gave younger leaders. Once, in the mid 1940s, one of his young executives questioned Brown about a cattle loan made to D. H. ("Red") Aldridge, a local rancher. The younger man suggested that the sizable loan required frequent inspection of the collateral, the cattle herd. Brown waved him off saying that the bank also had Red's saddle horse Silver on the mortgage and that Red loved the mount too much to risk losing it. Doubtless, the youngster learned that personal knowledge of a customer was almost as important as collateral in approving a loan.[20]

Just a few years later George Brown was working for his kinsman at Citizen's Security Bank and had an experience regarding a loan that left him wishing he were dealing with Red Aldridge, or some other sober customer. Once he was awakened at two o'clock in the morning by a pounding on the door of his home. He recalled that:

> I opened the door to find one of the town drunks staring at me from behind a cloud of alcohol while his friends were in a car parked at our curb . . . the drunk explained to me that the most important business deal of his life-time had just presented itself. For only $10.00 he could buy a four legged chicken if he acted quickly. No doubt he saw four legs. There are some loans which one can not make.[21]

On certain occasions B. A. Norris and J. M. Carter, of Ada, had trouble collecting their notes. Norris once asked one of his county collectors why a certain note had not been paid. The collector thought for a moment and then replied, "Mr. Norris, this fellow drinks, gambles, and runs around with women." Continuing, the collector explained: "Now, you can drink a little and pay your note; you can gamble a little and pay your note; you can even run around with women and pay your note. But you can't pay your note if you do all three."[22]

Like Norris, Carter, for many years a vice-president for the Oklahoma State Bank of Ada, had difficulties. Once Carter made a loan to a less-than-desirable risk who had to find an endorser who could pay the note if he defaulted. As events developed, the customer indeed did not pay his loan. Carter called the endorser, who vocally chastised his friend for his failure to pay. Then, not understanding that he was to pay, the endorser demanded that his name be taken off the note, arguing that he would no longer be friends with anyone who failed to repay a loan.[23]

Other bankers like Brown, Norris, and Carter faced modern, complex problems in simple, direct ways. Ralph Chambers of the First State in Picher, for example, never liked new accounting procedures or new posting machines and preferred to continue to use a familiar "shorthand" system; one month's statement that he forwarded to the OBA contained the following balances:[24]

	.00*
*Bonds	628,365.22
@Cash	307,263.78
The Bank-roll	935,629.00
¢Loans	94,387.77
Fixtures	352.50
%Overdrafts	44.35
#	1,030,413.62*
Capital	25,000.00
Surplus	14,500.00
Und. Prof.	18,933.28
Our Part	58,433.28s
Dividends	3,810.00
Deposits	968,170.34
#	1,030,413.62*

* Mostly on FDR & Eleanor
@ Of little value
¢ Subject to deflation
% Borrowed without asking
\# Balances, doesn't it?

Although many leaders like George Brown thus could not make loans for all customers, and although Chambers did not appreciate modern accounting procedures, the end of World War II found most banks in Oklahoma in a viable, growing condition. Several metropolitan banks, in fact, had experienced such growth that they were listed among the largest 250 commercial banks in the country. The largest institution in the state was the First National Bank and Trust of Oklahoma City, a bank that ranked 106 nationwide and had deposits totaling $154,024,878 by 1945. The First National of Tulsa ranked 140, and the National Bank of Tulsa ranked 141, with respective deposits of $118,174,381 and $116,975,204. The Liberty National of Oklahoma City was ranked 250 with $63,115,567 in deposits.[25]

Oklahomans viewed the end of the war in the summer of 1945

with relief and jubilation. Yet, among the state's bankers and other business leaders, there were misgivings. Under the artificial stimulus of a world war, the American economy had boomed. Unprecedented levels of production had been reached, and jobs were available in abundance. But most bankers wondered if the country could continue to prosper in peacetime as wartime demands on industries and agriculture were cut and as ten million soldiers returned to civilian life to seek jobs. Financial leaders feared that a major crisis would develop. Such a situation did not materialize, however. Rather, the national economy remained healthy. At the war's end consumers released their pent-up demands for the goods and services that they could not afford in the dark decade of the 1930s and that they could not obtain during the wartime period of rationing. Industrial firms and agribusinessmen who had experienced fifteen years of capital starvation wanted to expand and modernize their facilities. The abundant purchasing power accumulated during the war matched the public demand for consumer goods, and a virtual flood tide of consumer spending provided producers with the incentive to reach record output. Between 1946 and 1949 production of consumer durables and housing doubled its average output for the preceding fifteen years, with housing construction alone climbing to three times what it had been. Production of business capital goods underwent similar expansion. Thus, unemployment represented no overwhelming problem in the immediate postwar years.[26]

Although the economy had continued to climb in the latter half of the 1940s as it had in the war years, the bankers found conditions changing as new trends were set in motion. Financiers in Oklahoma watched as the wartime high in demand deposits began to fall as consumers withdrew part or all of their funds to make purchases. At the same time, customers filed loan applications in record numbers with their bankers. Yet, as loan requests reached new highs, many of these carried a relatively low return. Under such conditions many of Oklahoma's financial leaders began to sell their early maturities and to increase the amount of money in their loan portfolios.[27]

As Oklahoma bankers increased their loans, they found that GI and FHA loans, supported by the government, were among the most stable. Under the GI Bill, bankers advanced money to returning veterans for the purchase of homes, farms, and businesses. Typical of the banking industry's experience with the GI Bill was that of the Security State Bank of Blackwell. The bank's president, Glenn Brumbaugh, established a postwar policy of meeting all realistic loan needs of veterans. By mid-1947 he had made approximately 300 GI loans, of which 270 were on homes and the remainder on farms and businesses. His portfolio on such loans totaled slightly more than $1,000, 000, with the average loan being $3,400. Most were margined at 10 percent. Brumbaugh made no loan having a pay-out period of more than ten years, and he carefully regulated his lending to insure that his borrowers had monthly payments that did not exceed 20 percent of their net incomes. Like other bankers, Brumbaugh also invested heavily in FHA loans.[28]

Statistics on home loans—FHA or conventional—divulged striking new trends in banking. In Oklahoma, as well as in the rest of the nation, a housing shortage led to new credit demands that necessitated heavy investments in real estate and in housing construction. By December, 1945, commercial bankers in the state had loaned a total of $25,308,000 for real-estate purchases; two years later that figure had risen to 49,196,000, an increase of 94.4 percent. During that same period, total loans on residential properties had risen from 15,843,000 to 30,430,000, an increase of 92.1 percent.[29]

Immediately after the war, many aspects of the reconversion problem (changing from a wartime to a peacetime economy) concerned financial leaders. They worried about the GI loan program, especially the loose provisions relating to credit. According to most bankers, veterans might receive guaranteed loans, but should stand the same credit and collateral checks as all other customers. Likewise, financial leaders became concerned about the status of the Small War Plants Corporation, an agency created during the war to help smaller plants convert to wartime production by making long-term, low interest loans. Congress extended the agency's life through 1946, and financiers feared that it might become permanent—and thus a competitor for bankers. Because the corporation had the power and resources of the government behind it, financial leaders argued that the corporation represented unfair government competition with private enterprise. In addition, many federal agencies still made loans to agriculture, while bankers lobbied for those agencies to minimize their activities.[30] These and other problems loomed large before the banking community, and years passed before adequate solutions were found.

In the latter 1940s yet another trend in banking made itself felt. The years saw the rise of the age of electronics. After World War II, many metropolitan institutions began to experiment with computer service, at first using what would later be called crude punch-card data processing machines. Although primitive, such innovations heralded the modern era when increasingly sophisticated computers would take over more and more banking functions.[31]

Although bankers thus made the transition to peacetime financing and used government guarantees when possible, many of them expressed concern about the competition received from the federal government in its various programs designed to aid consumers. Bankers feared that some form of state socialism would follow governmental control of credit. From the beginnings of the New Deal through World War II, some financial leaders had harbored fears that government regulation and competition would ultimately undermine the independent banking structure and the free enterprise system that had built the United States. Nowhere in Oklahoma were federal competition and regulations felt more keenly than in the smaller "country" banks. Yet, as some analysts pointed out, shortsighted policies on the part of lending agencies, which led to a collapse of farm credit, caused the growth of governmental financing. Private credit simply faltered; interest rates were too high, and the repayment period for loans was too short. One expert suggested that lenders arrange new methods of payment on farm loans that would meet the needs of the borrower better, while realizing that government financing might still be necessary to aid those people whose economic status was too risky for a private loan.[32]

Meanwhile, bankers continued to support programs that would attack the primary agricultural problem that rural Oklahoma faced: soil erosion. In the late 1940s it was estimated that three quarters of the state's arable land was suffering from the inroads of erosion. Eight and a half million acres had lost 75 percent of its top soil, and thirteen and a half million more had lost approximately 50 percent. By 1949 the bankers, in cooperation with the Soil Conservation Department of the United States Department of Agriculture, had devised a sophisticated program to encourage conservation. Soil districts had been created that included seventy-six of the state's seventy-seven counties. Trained technicians visited every farmer who cooperated with the program, diagnosed the farmer's land problems, and suggested such improvements as terracing, draining, repasturing, reforestation, contour cultivating, strip cropping, liming, and the building of ponds.[33]

While experts offered valuable advice to the farm community, financial leaders continued their public-relations campaign, preaching the doctrine of conservation. In addition, bankers willingly funded all projects that would lead to reform and higher yield in the future. As an added highlight to its program, the OBA sponsored regional banquets at which merit awards were given to cooperating farmers. From 1943 to 1950, bankers held 113 banquets and issued 2,214 awards. From Poteau to Checotah to Mangum, the meetings were held as financiers reached a combined audience of more than 50,000 people, a total that included businessmen as well as farmers.[34]

In addition to supporting soil-conservation programs, Oklahoma's financial leaders also expanded the credit agribusinessmen received. Such credit was necessary if the yeoman farmers were to reach middle-class status. Loans on farm lands, including dwellings and improvements, amounted to $6,464,000 in December 1945, but rose to $8,561,000 one year later. By January, 1948, the figure had increased to $9,383,000, a total increase of 45.1 percent.[35]

Financial leaders also renewed their interests in selected farm projects, particularly those designed to teach or to aid farm youth. In November, 1948, the OBA decided to sponsor a poultry project: the raising of broilers. With Clyde Fish, vice-president of the First National Bank and Trust of Muskogee, in charge, the OBA selected three pilot counties: Wagoner, Cherokee, and Muskogee. Fish and his committee chose 4-H and FFA boys and girls to participate in the program and found for each a sponsor who advanced $7.50 for the purchase of fifty chicks from a local hatchery. Counselors then instructed the participants on the care and feeding of the chicks. In the three county test areas thousands of broilers were raised; the OBA then supported broiler shows in May, giving prizes for the top four finishers. Such projects encouraged youngsters to go into the poultry-raising business and, generally—by example—influenced farm leaders to adopt efficient, scientific techniques in farm management.[36]

Some financial leaders in Oklahoma became so concerned with agribusiness that they opened special departments to cater to the needs of that sector of the state's economy. In April, 1948, W. H. Patten, president of the Security National in Norman, organized a Farm Service Department at his institution. With specialties in agricultural economics and education, Ishmael Smith was hired to head the department. Patten had long been interested in agriculture, being the owner of a "farmed-out farm" in Cleveland County. Smith and the new departmental staff performed various functions designed to service farm loans and to develop a balanced, scientific agricultural program for farm customers. Smith served as special farm representative, visited the rural countryside, and gave agribusinessmen personal advice. The Farm Service Department also established a credit-file system that listed pertinent information about individual farmers and their progress. In addition, the department sponsored various clubs, programs, and contests—all designed to further the goals of scientific management. In July, 1949, the bank sponsored an ensilage contest for Cleveland and McClain counties. As a result, more than 125 trench, snow-fence, or upright silos were constructed. Other programs included a junior dairy program wherein the bank made loans to young farmers for improved breeding of dairy cattle.[37]

As bankers maintained their involvement in all phases of community betterment, they also continued to show concern for projects having national significance. In 1950 the treasury began the "Independence Drive" to market Series E Bonds. State chairman for the drive was A. E. Bradshaw, president of the National Bank of Tulsa, under whose leadership volunteers began, on May 15, to sell $8 million in bonds. By July 17 they had sold $9,926,364, a figure that represented 124 percent of the state's goal.[38]

In general, in the latter 1940s financiers pursued a more liberal loan policy. Their support of the housing industry and agribusinessmen grew even larger. At the end of 1945 commercial and industrial leaders had borrowed $3,001,000 from Oklahoma bankers. One year later the amount had doubled, and by January of 1948 it had tripled, reaching $9,384,000, an increase of 212.7 percent. Tremendous business expansion occurred throughout the decade, but it was particularly intensified in the postwar years. Among business firms, the small and medium-sized firms constituted the vast majority of borrowers. In Oklahoma most loans went to customers who had less than $250,000 in assets. And the structure of Oklahoma's banking system, with its unit system and the many small banks dispersed over the countryside, made it easier for new and/or smaller firms to secure credit. Moreover, in many instances bankers had daily contact with local businessmen, were on friendly terms personally, and understood their problems. Most financial leaders, in fact, retained a personal sense of obligation to small businessmen. Most knew that the well-being and future development of Oklahoma communities depended upon the banks' fulfilling their proper function of supplying the credit to foster economic growth. Bankers also knew that healthy, growing communities stimulated larger and larger deposit accounts, which in turn stimulated new loans, which, of course, stimulated growth of banking income.[39]

During the 1940s more and more women rose to prominence in the ranks of the state's premier financial leaders. One of the most interesting careers was that of Lillian O'Connell, who was with the First National Bank of Coalgate. She joined the bank in 1927, working first as a bookkeeper. Elected assistant cashier in 1929, she joined with others in 1935 to purchase controlling interest from J. M. Browning, who was suffering ill health. After serving as vice-president for six years, she joined Earl Mitcham in 1941 to buy the interest of Fred Zweigel, the president. Thereupon, O'Connell became president while Mitcham became a vice-president. Under O'Connell's leadership, assets, deposits, and resources soared, and she was able to establish new, modern quarters for the bank in the latter part of 1941.[40]

Several mergers of significance occurred in the 1940s, many of which created stronger institutions. In 1948, Charles Vose, of the First National of Oklahoma City, bought E. A. Walker's Tradesmans Bank and effected a merger that strengthened banking in the capital city. Often such consolidations were not without humor. In the aforementioned instance, Walker, with his own particular brand of business acumen, drove Vose to distraction. After concluding his multi-million-dollar deal with Vose, Walker gave all his employees a two-

W. L. Stephenson, president of the OBA, 1947–48. Courtesy Oklahoma Bankers Association.

week bonus, for which Vose had no choice but to "pick up the tab." Later, when Vose sent staff workers to the Tradesmans to move all office machinery, they found that all adding machines had already been removed. Walker argued that the machines were his personal property and not a part of the deal. Finally, after all property settlements appeared to be completed, Walker came to Vose and "just raised hell." Angry with Vose's movers and registering disgust, Walker related that the workers had taken one of his personal electric extension cords. Later, he sent Vose a bill for $3.50 for the cord. Much to Vose's consternation, Walker "squeezed" as much as he could out of his sale, and Vose claimed that he "learned a lot from Mr. Walker about how to and how not to buy a bank."[41]

As it was true in earlier times and would be true in the future, the deans of banking in Oklahoma performed one more service during the 1940s that was sometimes overlooked: They trained a host of younger men who, when called upon later, emerged as premier leaders in their own right. For example, Dan Hogan, a dean of banking who made the run of 1889 and who later served as a president of the Oklahoma Bankers Association, developed an expertise that was difficult to match. Early the president of a bank in Yukon, he later became the head of the City National of Oklahoma City. In that position he determined to train two men. One was his son Dan, Jr., who died prematurely in the 1950s, and the other was Howard Bozarth, a young man who was graduated with a degree in business from the University of Oklahoma and who joined the City National in 1930. Bozarth remembered that the active Hogan, who was an avid sportsman, treated him as a son and taught him the banking business from the ground up, eventually making him president in 1957. Bozarth credits Hogan with being his greatest teacher, a man whose influence lingered long after his death. Like Hogan, scores of older leaders trained the men of a younger generation to take their places.[42]

If a banker's personality was reflected in the way he trained subordinates, certainly banks continued to reflect the personalities of their leaders, and in this way such dynamic individuals made a significant impact on their institutions. For example, in the 1930s and 1940s the City National and Fidelity competed closely in Oklahoma City and remained similar in size and outlook until Grady Harris, of the Liberty Bank, moved to Fidelity. Without detracting from his friendly competitors, the popular Harris brought many of his old Liberty accounts to Fidelity and attracted many new accounts as well. It was Harris, Bozarth maintained, who "really made Fidelity grow."[43]

The decade of the 1940s saw striking new trends in the banking industry, the most important of which were startling increases in bank resources and more relaxed loan policies. The stable banks in Oklahoma, approximately 420 in number, grew even more stable; they would be needed in the decades ahead.

CHAPTER 8.

Banking in the Modern Era

In the decades of the 1950s and 1960s the banking industry was influenced by a continuing, but accelerating, population shift from the rural countryside to urban areas. Country banks continued to decline in influence while urban financial institutions grew and became more wealthy, both in absolute and in relative terms. Between 1950 and 1960 the population of the state increased by only 4 percent, but urban growth far outstripped that average. Towns ranging from 7,000 to 15,000 in population increased by 31 percent while cities having more than 15,000 people increased by 35 percent. By 1960 thirty-three cities of 6,000 or more populations contained half the people in Oklahoma. Of the state's seventy-seven counties, two—Oklahoma and Tulsa—contained more than a third of the population, and two cities—Oklahoma City and Tulsa—contained more than a fourth. During the decade of the 1950s, Oklahoma City gained 74,140 inhabitants, a 30-percent increase, and Tulsa added 72,682, a 39-percent increase. Smaller cities likewise attracted many people moving from the countryside. Lawton increased its population by almost 80 percent, from 34,754 to 60,806; Altus increased by almost 125 percent, from 9,735 to 21,840. Six other towns in the state doubled their populations.[1]

The population shift continued into the 1960s and 1970s. Startling census figures in 1970 revealed that not only did a larger majority of the state's population live in urban areas, but that a majority of 52 percent lived in four of the state's Standard Metropolitan Statistical Areas (as defined by the Bureau of the Census): Tulsa, Oklahoma City, Lawton, and that portion of Oklahoma that was in the Fort Smith, Arkansas, metropolitan area.[2]

Many factors account for the accelerated movement to the cities. The excitement and diversity of urban areas historically have attracted many people. In addition, cities have always been centers for government, educational opportunities, and cultural events. But economic realities perhaps better explain the rural-to-urban shift. The agricultural decline of the 1920s and the deepening depression of the 1930s drove many farmers from the land. Mechanization allowed greater production per man-hour and contributed to the reduction in the amount of farm labor required. World War II, with its demand for manpower in industry and in the armed forces, also contributed to the loss of rural population, and the continuing industrial boom after the war ensured that the rural-urban shift would become a permanent trend.

Country bankers noted the foregoing trend and did all in their power to develop what was left of rural Oklahoma. Between 1944 and 1950 tremendous changes occurred in farm financing. Advances in technology caused an increase in the farmers' needs for short-term production and marketing loans, and commercial banks assumed much of the responsibility for this new financing. Although other lending institutions—agencies of the federal government and insurance companies, for example—extended credit to farmers, bankers continued to be the largest lenders. By the end of 1954, bankers had extended $90,011,000 in credit to farmers, a sum that included $76,983,000 in non–real estate loans for operations and production. A detailed listing on non–real estate loans in force as of January 1957 showed that commercial banks had $84,023,000 outstanding, while other institutions—the Production Credit Association and the Farmers Home Administration—had loaned only a total of $36,080,000. In real-estate mortgage credit, commercial houses had advanced more than $18,300,000 to farmers. By the end of 1960 bankers held loans for real estate and production totaling $152,056,000, still the largest amount of all lenders. In addition, as years passed and loan totals continued to grow, financial leaders also increased the amount of Commodity Credit Corporation (CCC) paper they held in cooperation with the government's farm price-support program, the total of CCC paper reaching $37,913,000 in January 1961. Clearly, in the 1950s and into the 1960s, commercial bankers continued, as they had in the past, to fully support agriculture in Oklahoma.[3]

Although financing for farmers, both on real estate and non–real estate loans, was the most important contribution of Oklahoma bankers to agribusiness, they made other contributions as well. Some financial leaders viewed with alarm the decrease in farm population and in farm acreage under production. In 1940 there had been 179,687 farms in the state, with an average per farm of 193.7 acres. By 1950 there were only 142,246 farms; although the average size had increased to 253 acres, total acreage under production decreased. By mid-1955 the number of farms and their total acreage continued to decline as it would through the 1960s. Yet, farms produced more goods than ever before. Because financiers saw this dominant trend, their goal was to encourage efficient agribusinessmen to become even more efficient.[4]

In earlier decades much emphasis had been placed on irrigation as a means of increasing production, and bankers' study groups had always stressed scientific agriculture when meeting with farmers. In the mid-1950s bankers started another educational program, one that stressed the benefits of effective brush control. Experts estimated that 10 million acres of Oklahoma land were covered with post oak, blackjack, and other kinds of brush. Further, some analysts asserted that the state's beef production alone could be increased by $100 million annually if blighted lands were converted into grasslands. Harry M. Elwell, agronomist at the Red Plains Conservation Experiment Station in Guthrie, demonstrated the tremendous effects of brush control: He cleared the woody pastures at his station and increased his hay and beef production by 800 percent. Such a lesson was not lost on Oklahoma's country bankers. Don Tyler, chairman of the board of the Union National Bank at Bartlesville, and Albert Kelly, vice-president of the American National at Bristow, used chemical sprays to clean brush on their own farms, as did Clark Chapman, president of the First State at Talihina. Homer Carlile, president of the First National in Stigler, helped Haskell County farmers who needed loans to begin a control program. After yields began increasing in areas like Haskell County, where bankers helped farmers inaugurate programs, more and more financial leaders began giving agribusinessmen money for brush control as a part of their regular operating loans.[5]

In addition to starting a new brush-control program, in the 1950s and 1960s bankers continued to support farm-related projects begun in earlier years. They continued to finance 4-H and FFA projects, programs that brought little immediate profit but promised dividends in the future. To encourage the growth of the poultry industry, financial leaders, working through their Oklahoma Bankers Association and its agricultural committee, began offering loans to 4-H and FFA members who would accept the guidance of county agents, vocational-agricultural instructors, and other experts in order to learn the proper way to raise poultry. Those who developed flocks competed for prizes at dressed-broiler shows. Because one of the largest poultry-processing plants in the Southwest was situated in Muskogee, the OBA launched the program in northeastern Oklahoma. However, the facility received 90 percent of its poultry from outside of Oklahoma, and the bankers' program, it was hoped, would spur intrastate production. The first poultry fairs were held in 1950, with several northeastern Oklahoma counties participating. The OBA then introduced areawide programs, sponsoring a total of five annually by 1953.[6]

The financial leaders also continued to support a wide variety of soil conservation programs, which had their beginning in 1942. In the first six months of 1953 the OBA held a number of awards banquets, giving 325 conservation certificates to farmers who had made the most significant improvements on their acreages. The program continued throughout the decade and into the 1960s. In February, 1961, the OBA had the distinction of sponsoring the world's largest banker-award meeting. Held in Pauls Valley and hosted by the banks of Garvin County, the banquet was attended by more than a thousand bankers, farmers, stockmen, and soil-conservation enthusiasts. Guy L. Berry, Jr., president of the American National Bank and Trust Company of Sapulpa, gave the principal address, wherein he stressed the benefits of scientific farm management.[7]

Although financial leaders in the postwar era did not forget agriculture, bankers, particularly those associated with large metropolitan banks, paid more attention to industrial loans as the state continued to urbanize. After World War II bankers asserted leadership in their communities by organizing local industrial-development foundations to secure new businesses and new jobs for their regions. The first such organization was founded in Oklahoma City in December, 1940. With many local businessmen and bankers concurring, Stanley Draper, manager of the local chamber of commerce, established the

Industries Foundation of Oklahoma City. Its immediate purpose was to acquire land for an army air corps base and supply depot. With 291 financial leaders pledging $294,500 to underwrite loans, Draper went to such men as C. A. Vose, Sr., president of the First National of Oklahoma City, for financing to purchase land adjacent to the Municipal Airport to accommodate the proposed depot.[8]

By April 1942, Draper's work and the support of the financial community had resulted in the War Department's decision to put Tinker Field in Oklahoma City. In the following decades the economic ramifications of that decision were stupendous. Thousands of jobs were created for central Oklahoma, because the federal government spent millions of dollars each year on the base. Moreover, analysts estimated that, in an indirect sense, the air base had been responsible for at least 25 percent of the economic activity in Central Oklahoma in the recent decades. This resulted from needed support services that made demands on hundreds of businesses, creating untold thousands of jobs. The Industries Foundation of Oklahoma City continued to strive for community development. With underwriting from the foundation, city leaders next engaged in negotiations that resulted in a decision by officials of the Douglas Aircraft Company to establish a plant in the city.[9] Through the 1950s and 1960s, the city fathers continued to use the foundation for economic expansion.

The bankers of Oklahoma City were not alone in promoting and underwriting their industrial foundation. After World War II, financial leaders across the state organized others. By 1958 forty-nine such foundations had been established, and each had as its purpose the securing of new industry, additional jobs, and bigger payrolls. Of course, bankers benefited from the expansion. They watched their communities grow in population and affluence; prosperity for the communities across the state meant prosperity for bankers who watched deposits increase. That development, in turn, enabled bank investments to soar and loans to reach record highs. Yet, local efforts could not accomplish miracles. In smaller urban areas foundations could underwrite one, two, or perhaps three small plants before they reached the limit of their financial ability. But industrial demands for low-cost loans—and consumer demands for the products that new industries could provide—remained high. Consequently, the OBA executive council lobbied for state aid to enable Oklahoma to offer a complete financial package to industrialists.[10]

Following the recommendations of the governor's Economic Development Commission, the legislature proposed a constitutional amendment in 1959; approved by the voters, the amendment authorized the legislature to establish the Oklahoma Industrial Finance Authority (OIFA). The broad goal of the authority, established in 1960, was to assist in developing industry and thereby to provide new jobs for the state. Governed by a seven-member board composed of bankers and other civic leaders, the OIFA acquired funds from the sale of bonds, money which became part of a revolving loan fund. Unable to make loans to private entities, the authority was empowered to make low-cost loans to development foundations, which in turn could partially support new industrial developments. Under the legislative act, developers had to provide 25 percent of a project's cost while the OIFA would provide a matching 25 percent to be secured by a second mortgage. With state aid, it thus became easier for a firm to get the remaining 50 percent of its financing from a private lending institution whose loan was secured by a first mortgage.[11]

The OIFA proved to be a tremendous success. The funding from the agency enabled businessmen to begin projects that they could not have hoped to implement without aid. Because private lending institutions did not have to bear the full brunt of such loans, the funding also allowed bankers to approve loan applications that under other circumstances might have been rejected.[12]

In 1970 the legislature, after receiving input from the OBA and its membership, created another agency that aided businessmen—and their bankers—in arranging financing. Operational by the end of 1973, the Oklahoma Business Development Corporation (OBDC) encouraged industrial growth by providing new businesses with short-term and intermediate funds for working capital and equipment purchases. Existing industries suffering from financial difficulties also received loans with the provision that such funds be used to preserve jobs that would have otherwise been lost. Under the statute creating the OBDC, operating funds were purchased from members who received shares in the corporation. Financial institutions wishing to become members pledged a percentage of their assets for funds to be made available for loans through the OBDC. Commercial banks pledged 3 percent of their capital and surplus. Of course, OBDC customers received loans from the corporation only after directors deemed it impossible for the borrower to obtain money through conventional sources. Thus, financiers viewed the creation of the OBDC as a service to them and their communities, not as a competitor in the banking field. In fact, OBDC loans were often made in conjunction with regular bank loans, with all parties involved emphasizing community betterment. Businessmen and bankers saw the benefit of the OBDC particularly in rural Oklahoma, for it was there that other sources of working capital were often severely limited.[13]

While they took advantage of new state aid for industrial financing, bankers in Oklahoma also participated in federal programs. In 1953 Congress created the Small Business Administration (SBA) as an independent agency to facilitate the growth of small business, a step that would stimulate the national economy. Under the statute, the SBA offered advice to all small businessmen who had financial needs. Those who operated successful enterprises and who demonstrated an ability to produce a profit could secure loans from the agency once private sources were exhausted. The SBA made direct loans, but, more important to bankers in Oklahoma, it also worked with qualified individuals to secure additional private funding by guaranteeing up to 90 percent of a bank loan, a practice that encouraged bankers to approve the loan. In addition to guaranteeing loans for individuals, the agency also aided local development companies, formed and owned by people in a community, by granting direct loans or by guaranteeing private loans. By the mid-1970s the program of the SBA had proven beneficial to Oklahomans. The agency had granted or guaranteed more than $6 million in direct loans to businessmen in the state and in the process had helped create 2,100 new jobs. Bankers in the state benefited directly in handling guaranteed loans and indirectly as well, sharing in the economic expansion that such loans brought.[14]

In 1965 a new federal program was created when Congress passed the Economic Development Administration (EDA). The new agency made loans that created permanent industrial facilities in "redevelopment areas," designated by the secretary of labor in regions where unemployment was chronic and annual income low. The EDA made loans of up to 65 percent of the cost of fixed assets and, in addition, guaranteed up to 90 percent of working-capital loans that were secured from private sources. Again, most bankers in the state cooperated with the program, knowing that there was low risk in guaranteed loans and knowing that they would gain as their communities benefited from industrial expansion. By the mid-1970s the EDA had made direct loans totaling $13,635,000 to businessmen in the state and had guaranteed working-capital loans of $315,000.[15]

One factor that increasingly attracted the attention of bankers, particularly metropolitan financial leaders, was the importance of securing adequate financing for the petroleum industry, one of the bulwarks of Oklahoma's economy. Before Edwin Drake brought in his well in Pennsylvania, the presence of oil was known in Oklahoma. Much earlier, Indians in the region had found petroleum in seepages from rocks and in streams and had used it for medicinal purposes. Of little utility in those early years, oil flowed from a well sunk in 1886 near Chelsea at the rate of half a barrel per day. It was sold as cattle dip, because no other market existed. In 1897 a commercial well drilled near Bartlesville produced fifty to seventy-five barrels daily, but again it was capped because of the lack of demand. After the beginning of the twentieth century, however, industrial and automotive markets for petroleum products made oil big business in Oklahoma. The state became alive with activity and new fields soon dotted the countryside as new wealth poured from the ground.[16]

By the mid-1950s the value of oil and gas produced in the state reached $570,000,000, a value greater than that of all the crops and livestock marketed that year. The effects of the industry's growth and the ramifications of that growth on the general economy of the state were widespread indeed. The industry provided jobs for more than 46,000 production workers and paid those laborers an aggregate of $220 million. Another $50 million was paid to the thousands who processed the oil in refineries. Millions of additional dollars found their way into the pockets of those indirectly serving the industry in a number of positions such as accountants, engineers, salesmen, gasoline station managers, scientific researchers, and tool and equipment manufacturers. The petroleum industry's annual purchase of supplies and equipment in Tulsa alone was more than $500 million in 1954.[17]

The support of Oklahoma's banking community proved crucial to the petroleum industry. To continue expansion, the industry needed a tremendous amount of credit, credit that only the large metropolitan financial institutions could provide. In 1954, for example, oilmen required $300 million to drill new wells, and more than 70 percent of that total came in the form of bank credit. While out-of-state institutions like the First National Bank of Kansas City helped finance oilmen, increasingly, Oklahoma's bankers assumed more of the burden.[18] When referring to the ease of securing financial backing, K. S. Adams of Phillips Petroleum exclaimed, "This [the oilmen's relationship with state bankers] is a far cry from going to London to secure financial backing as a Muskogee group had to do in 1897."[19] Indeed, some state financiers began to focus actively on the petroleum industry and devoted a large part of their staff's time to it.

Calling itself the "Oil Bank of America," the National Bank of Tulsa became the first to create and to maintain a petroleum engineering department, which offered complete engineering services to oilmen who were potential customers and to correspondent banks that were considering making loans to the petroleum industry. Such services attracted new customers, and, as a result, through the 1950s and 1960s the bank's portfolio of petroleum loans continued to increase.[20] The First National of Oklahoma City, the largest bank in the state, also increased its loans to the petroleum industry. Led by Charles Vose, Sr., and Charles Vose, Jr., chairman of the board and president, respectively, the institution by 1978 had approximately $100 million in petroleum financing, an amount that was by far the largest item in its loan portfolio.[21]

The importance of bank financing was dramatically shown when wildcat drilling began around Hobart, Oklahoma, in the Anadarko Basin. Potentially the richest reserve of natural gas in the world, the basin presented many problems to oilmen. The reserves were miles underground, and the deep wells that had to be sunk were costly. Although many banks participated in funding the drilling, again the National Bank of Tulsa asserted leadership. Board chairman A. E. Bradshaw personally promoted the development of the Anadarko Basin by conducting tours into the region. Businessmen and other bankers learned firsthand of the economic wealth found

J. L. Branen, president of the OBA, 1954–55. Courtesy Oklahoma Bankers Association.

in the area and became more willing to help finance the effort.[22]

Thus in the post–World War II era, while bankers remained active in agricultural and industrial financing, they expanded into many other areas, all of which involved, albeit some indirectly, community betterment. One development of the mid-1960s, which gave bankers outlets for surplus funds, aided needy individuals and families and promised future benefits for society. The federal government began a guaranteed student loan program and invited state banks to participate. Returns on such loans were not as lucrative as higher-risk loans to private entrepreneurs, but the government-guarantee program insured sound investments. By 1966 more than 135 banks, from Broken Bow to Ponca City and from Lawton to Stilwell, had signed agreements to participate in the program. In metropolitan Oklahoma City alone, ten banks had joined, while four in Tulsa participated.[23]

In the years following World War II, commercial bankers expanded their services and adopted innovative techniques to meet apparent ever-growing demands, demands made by industrialists, agribusinessmen, oilmen, consumers, and students. But greater innovative steps were necessary because of the challenge mounted by other financial intermediaries. In the decades of the 1950s and 1960s, intensified competition developed, with commercial banks and other institutions vying both for the savings dollar and for loan accounts. By the late 1950s commercial banks appeared to be losing the struggle, and those bankers who sounded warning cited alarming national statistics: Although the total assets of financial institutions had grown from $18 billion in 1900 to $691 billion in 1956, commercial banks suffered a relative decline; they held 56 percent of the nation's total assets in 1900 but only 31 percent by 1956. From 1946 to 1957, the commercial banks' share of savings accounts fell from 53.7 percent to 41.6 percent. In that same period their share of consumer installment loans dropped from 48.6 to 43.3 percent. Their share of residential mortgage loans also dipped, as did overall profits in commercial banking. Savings and loan associations and, to a lesser degree, mutual savings banks profited from the decline of the banks. The specialized services of the former, and their higher rates of interest on savings, helped them increase their business at the expense of the bankers.[24]

By the late 1950s commercial bankers were reacting to the intensified competition. In Oklahoma, leaders began a statewide advertising campaign, which merged with a larger national effort. Many joined the National Foundation for Commercial Banks, an agency with several broad objectives: to recapture the words "bank" and "banker" for the exclusive use of commercial institutions; to encourage members to adopt innovative programs that would deliver more services to customers; to assure "small" customers that the bankers also worked for them; to begin a public relations campaign, which would enhance the bankers' public image; and to show the public that banks promoted the prosperity of the nation.[25]

Rapidly, commercial bankers in Oklahoma started expanding their services. Many leaders began construction of new drive-in facilities to make banking more convenient for customers. Although some institutions, such as the First National of Tulsa, had added these facilities earlier, the 1950s and early 1960s saw most banks acquire some kind of drive-in service. Many bankers saw their efforts to secure drive-in services mired in difficulty, however. Tending to interpret laws against branch banking most literally, the Oklahoma Legislature in its banking code originally permitted drive-in facilities only if such facilities were physically attached to the main bank. Several financial leaders, nevertheless, tended to interpret the code liberally. Some constructed drive-in facilities hundreds of feet away from their main banking establishment and then "physically" connected the structures with television cables and telephone lines. Ultimately, in the mid-1960s, with the OBA officers leading the way, the legislature allowed financial leaders to place their drive-in a distance of up to 300 feet—later changed to 1,000 feet—away from the parent institution.

While the drive-in facility controversy was being resolved, many banks, such as the First National and the Fidelity in Oklahoma City, began utilizing computers to increase their speed in processing accounts, a development that increased the efficiency of the banks and, in addition, proved more convenient to customers. To compete with savings and loan associations, many banks also instituted new programs for savers who wished to channel monies into time deposits. Many also began to offer the now-familiar charge-card services.[26] The First National of Oklahoma City became the first institution to offer Bankamericard (Visa) service to the region's customers, and in so doing quickly amassed a Bankamericard credit portfolio of $28 million.[27]

Another leader, who was destined to become one of the great leaders of Oklahoma banking, had a key role in establishing the Bankamericard service. J. W. "Bill" McLean, a native of Okmulgee who grew up in Muskogee, was attracted to the investment field after service in World War II and was employed by Merrill Lynch. After working for a time in Tulsa, he became president of Texas National Bank in Houston, Texas. Next, he joined the Bank of America in California, where he served in international banking and later became the institution's director of marketing. Active in his national association, McLean chaired the National Credit Conference and the National Marketing Conference of the American Bankers Association. In one of his major achievements, McLean inaugurated the nationwide licensing of Bankamericard and personally enrolled the first ten major banks. Lured back to Oklahoma in 1967, he took over the Liberty National Bank of Oklahoma City, a bank that experienced rapid growth under McLean. Named as regional banker of the year by *Finance* magazine in 1972, McLean was later inducted into the Oklahoma Hall of Fame.[28]

Another leader who came to the forc in the late 1960s and whose accomplishments mirror those of his colleagues in the banking fraternity, was Eugene L. Sweringen. A Nebraskan who was educated in Oklahoma and at Harvard University, Sweringen had a distinguished academic career at Oklahoma State University and the University of Tulsa, where he served as president from 1967 to 1968. Joining the Bank of Oklahoma as president in 1968, he later became chairman of the board. Like Jack Conn, of Oklahoma City, and others, Sweringen was very active in civic affairs and in the affairs of the ABA, in addition to pushing the Bank of Oklahoma to the forefront of the state's business community.[29]

Another destined to exert leadership in the current era and one who typifies his colleagues was Jack Conn. Born in Ada, Conn was graduated from East Central College and later the University of Oklahoma's Law School. Associated with law firms in Ada and Oklahoma City, he became a member of the board of directors of the Oklahoma State Bank of Ada in 1947 and president of the institution

Jack T. Conn, president of the OBA, 1958–59. Courtesy Oklahoma Bankers Association.

in 1951. From 1958 to 1959, he served as president of the OBA and in 1966 served as president of the ABA. Moving to Oklahoma City in 1964, he became chairman of Fidelity Bank, N.A. Inducted into the Oklahoma Hall of Fame in 1969, Conn remained very active in civic affairs, particularly in the Oklahoma Heritage Association.[30]

The programs of the aggressive competitive leaders in the banking community had the desired effect. Commercial banks began in the middle and late 1960s to reclaim much business that had been lost to other institutions. One general indicator, the ratio of bank assets to the Gross National Product (GNP), revealed the resurgence of commercial banks. Their assets, having a ratio of 76.02 percent of the GNP in 1945, had declined to 50.74 percent by 1959. However, by 1970 the ratio slowly had climbed upward, to 57.05 percent of the GNP.[31]

Occasionally, bankers added new innovative programs and services to entice customers, but on one occasion in the 1960s a new financial house became overextended and found itself mired in difficulty. The New Southern Hills National Bank opened in August, 1963, with $1 million in capital and, as a lure to customers, promised free checking accounts to charter depositors. The president of the bank, Harry W. Clester, and directors James C. Leake, S. Lee Braxton, and S. Paul Hazen, hoped the free offer would attract a base of customers that might otherwise have taken years to acquire. Some leaders, such as State Banking Commissioner Carl Sebring, were critical of the Southern Hills promotion. Informed sources estimated that it cost from $10 to $15 to open new accounts. Thus Southern Hills would take an immediate loss on all accounts. And from the time the new bank was opened, business was brisk. Within two weeks the institution had 31,000 accounts, $5.5 million in deposits, and more than $1,000,000 in loans. Because of the undreamed-of success in securing new accounts, more than 100 bookkeepers were hired, that number bringing the staff up to 170 and the payroll up to $80,000 a week. The employees could not keep pace with the deluge of business, however, and ultimately had problems complying with a state requirement that gave banks only forty-eight hours to clear their checks.[32]

When James Saxon, Comptroller of the Currency, learned of the problem, he ordered the bank temporarily closed on November 8 and sent Normal Dunn, a regional examiner, to investigate. Later,

Saxon appointed William Greenfield of Dallas, Texas, as conservator. Meanwhile, as workers tried to sort through masses of backlogged paper work, critics and supporters of the efforts of Southern Hills made themselves known.[33]

Leland Gourley, president of the State Capitol Bank in Oklahoma City—a bank that had made an offer similar to that made by Southern Hills—believed the idea was sound if a bank was well-prepared to handle increased traffic. After Gourley's offer, the State Capitol Bank gained 15,000 customers and $3 million in deposits in fifteen days.[34] "The offer did nothing but help us," Gourley asserted. "It gave us a depositor base that would have taken eight or ten years to acquire otherwise."[35] But critics pointed out that a bank should not offer too many free services unless it was fully automated and thus able to handle increased paper work. The State Capitol Bank was automated; the Southern Hills was not. Its items had to be flown each night to a bank in Texas for processing.[36]

Ultimately, Saxon and Greenfield allowed Southern Hills to reopen on December 2 after it was reorganized with Lynn R. Helms as chairman of the board and with the bank's stock in the hands of new stockholders. A normal checking charge was instituted, although hundreds of people closed their accounts. Scandal touched the bank once more in January, 1964, when $330,000 was discovered missing. Management problems and mistakes in paper work were blamed for the error. Apparently, Commissioner Sebring offered good advice when he urged banks not to assume more work than they could handle.[37] Ultimately, the bank survived its crisis, later merging into the Mercantile National, an institution that has grown and gained stability, with Bill Foster in charge as it heads toward the 1980s.

In the last decade the condition of commercial banks in Oklahoma improved, relative to other financial institutions, but increasingly the state's bankers became concerned about a problem destined to overshadow all others, a problem apparently only the federal government could solve: inflation. As federal deficits soared, the national debt rose to unprecedented sums, and inflation spiraled upward. Some financiers like Jack T. Conn, chairman of the board of Fidelity National in Oklahoma City, tried to view the problem philosophically. As Conn pointed out, many financial leaders at first regarded the federal government's financial problems in a way similar to the proverbial West Texas rancher who pondered the problems of his spread and said stoically, "If it ain't the hogs it's the windmills."[38] Yet, the events of the 1960s forced financial leaders in Oklahoma to reexamine their stoicism and to speak out. Inflation, termed by some as the "cancer of the body politic," was caused, many leaders believed, by fiscal irresponsibility. Increasingly, by the late 1960s and early 1970s such leaders as Conn spoke out, warning the populace and its political leaders against rampant inflation and a debased currency. Yet, despite their arguments, bankers in Oklahoma lost in their drive to control inflation; only strong federal efforts could reverse the inflationary trends.[39]

In the 1960s most financial leaders in Oklahoma, particularly those in urban centers, became more interested in community development programs, realizing that progress that benefited society also benefited them. Many supported urban-renewal drives. Among the financial leaders who pointed the way was Jack Conn. In 1967, then president of the American Bankers Association, Conn suggested that by launching programs of their own, bankers could encourage local businessmen to contribute to the redevelopment of central business districts. Observing the decaying business districts, he realized that communities had limited funds, which at best were meagerly supplemented by state and federal aid, and he asserted that "rejuvenation . . . must depend on businessmen who see the wisdom of making an investment in the future of their local economy." Bankers, he continued, had "a responsibility to demonstrate economic leadership."[40]

While bankers became more interested in community development, they also continued to strengthen their profession with educational programs. In 1958 the OBA urged participation in several out-of-state programs, including the Southwestern Graduate School of Banking in Dallas, Texas, which was launched by Southern Methodist University. In order to complete the program, students were required to attend three summer sessions and to write a thesis. In addition to courses on banking, the school stressed the humanities, offering courses in the arts, philosophy, sociology, and history. Nine Oklahomans joined the first class. Among them were J. H. Brokaw, of Tulsa; Curtis A. Brooks, of Chickasha; and Clarence M. Clark, of Shawnee. All completed the requirements by 1960 and were graduated with distinction. By 1960 there also were two Oklahoma bank-

Art F. Barnes, president of the OBA, 1961–62. Courtesy Oklahoma Bankers Association.

ers on the school's faculty: Falkner C. Broach and Ernest L. Stucker, both with the First National Bank of Tulsa.[41]

In 1967 yet another in-state program began. The Oklahoma Intermediate School of Banking was founded by the OBA. Glenn P. Ward, a vice-president at the Fourth National Bank in Tulsa, agreed to direct the new school, and Alma Barnes, a vice-president of the Guaranty National Bank of Tulsa, later became associate director. Held at Oklahoma State University each year, the week-long institute stressed broad education, exposing students to all aspects of banking rather than training them in specific areas. The faculty for the institute included some of the best minds in the state—bankers, attorneys, businessmen, and college professors. A unique and successful program, the first of its kind in the nation, the institute was open to individuals who were employed by member institutions in the OBA. The school graduated students who had a more thorough knowledge of the problems of banking and who could return to contribute more to their home institution.[42]

Although they expanded their facilities, utilized the latest technological advances to increase efficiency, and exposed their staffs to a continuing education program, bank executives found that in the 1950s and 1960s they had to continue to cope with robberies and burglaries. Because of their isolated nature, small rural banks faced more danger than their larger, more secure urban counterparts. Perhaps typical were the robberies at Maud and Harrah in 1957. On October 16, William Paul West and George W. Jernigan, who were partners in buying and selling used cars and who were in debt $47,000, held up the First National Bank of Maud and escaped with $22,456, most of which they used to pay debts. Joined by another used-car dealer, Stephen E. Rose, the pair committed another daring daylight holdup on November 6, this time taking $10,444 from the First State Bank of Harrah. Although the bandits remained at large for several days, special agents of the Federal Bureau of Investigation arrested Rose in Norman and the other two suspects in Fort Worth, Texas. The case was broken when all three confessed, but the money could not be recovered.[43]

Occasionally, bandits were foiled by the actions of spunky bank executives. On December 31, 1956, two masked outlaws tried to rob the First National Bank of Pauls Valley. Early in the morning they broke into the bank and waited for janitor Joe Jones, who arrived punctually at 5:00 A.M. After overpowering and binding Jones, the pair waited until 8:00 A.M. when the bookkeepers arrived. Armed with a rifle and pistol, the two bandits easily corralled the staff and forced one employee to begin unlocking the vault.[44] At the same instant, bank vice-president Albert Foss entered the front door to find one of the bandits' guns leveled at him. The outlaw near the door ordered Foss to a corner of the room where the second bandit was watching the bookkeepers. Although guns were still drawn on him, Foss walked only a few paces before bolting out a back door. When the executive ran to call the police, the bandits panicked and fled, leaving the First National's money intact.[45]

Although most bandits were either foiled in their attempts to loot Oklahoma banks or caught later, attempts seemed to be never-ending; even in the modern age of the mid-twentieth century, financial leaders were forced to remain alert. Institutions in rural areas and small Oklahoma towns were in greatest jeopardy, but those in urban areas were not entirely safe. For example, in an approximate five-and-a-half-year period from June, 1963, to November, 1968, there were ten bank robberies committed in Oklahoma City, a statistic that stood in contrast to an earlier period, 1946 to 1963, when there were no bank holdups in the city. The earlier period of tranquility was broken on June 7, 1963, when two gunmen looted the First State Bank and Trust of $26,000.[46] There followed an average of two holdups a year until October 23, 1968, when a lone gunman robbed the May Avenue Bank of $12,800. After the holdup, bank president Ben T. Head muttered, "This is getting to be too much." He was referring to an earlier robbery in December, 1964, when a gunman took $27,000 from the bank. "Just like the last time," Head lamented, "I didn't know a thing about it until someone ran into my office and said that the bank had just been robbed."[47] Four of the ten robberies remained unsolved.[48]

Only occasionally were would-be robbers thwarted, and if they were, their own ineptitude usually was to blame. Five teenagers—two girls included—tried to loot the Penn Square National Bank in May 1965. One of the girls handed a teller a threatening note demanding money. "You must be kidding," the teller replied, as she handed the note back to the girl. When the bank employee made no further sound or gesture except to look at the motley crew, the youths panicked and ran.[49]

The robbery of the May Avenue Bank seemed to be a part of a wave of similar robberies that occurred in smaller Oklahoma towns. Between September 20 and December 5, six banks were attacked, beginning with the State National Bank in Depew, where a lone burglar took $19,000. Then the Bank of Red Oak was burgled on September 23; the bandits made off with $15,735. In November robbers broke into the First National of Nash, where they burned the dial off the vault door but failed to gain entry into the vault. Later in the month two institutions in small Oklahoma towns were looted within fifteen minutes of each other, and yet one more was robbed only days later.[50]

Ultimately, in 1968 the widespread rise in bank robberies forced the federal government to intervene; Congress passed the Bank Protection Act. Affecting all banks that were insured by the Federal Deposit Insurance Corporation or other federal agencies, the statute required each institution to designate a security officer to administer a protection program. The act required that all exterior doors of a bank be equipped with deadbolt locks, key-operated from both sides, and that all windows not readily observable by a regular police street patrol be secured by bars or grills. Further regulations required that an electronic surveillance system be installed in each bank, one that would include at least one camera. Installation of proper lighting systems and electronic alarms also were required along with training programs that would instruct employees in proper conduct both during and after a robbery. The penalty for noncompliance with the act's regulations was set at $100 for each day of violation.[51]

Although such statutes as the Bank Protection Act of 1968 had positive effects, in the postwar era bankers generally became dismayed over the increase of federal and state regulations. As one unidentified executive said in 1975: "I am tired of being regulated and legislated to death. It takes one of our employees full time trying to keep up with the volume of new rules and regulations passed by some state or federal agency or another." The banker continued, "Let's end some of this nonsense by leaving prudent management up to those responsible within their own banks."[52]

The unnamed executive made a point that was well-understood by many of his fellows. By the late 1960s the federal government had increased its regulations of banking by passing such acts as the Real Estate Settlement Procedures Act, the Truth-in-Lending Act, the Civil Rights Act, the Financial Institution Recordkeeping Act, and a number of other statutes. As Oklahoma State Bank Commissioner H. E. Leonard pointed out in 1976, honest, hard-working financial leaders suffered because of the actions of a few unscrupulous financiers who charged high interest and excessive closing costs on homes, or engaged in other unethical practices.[53]

Although government regulations were cumbersome, increasingly Oklahoma's financial leaders realized that to avoid total governmental control—a development that surely would come if the small group of unscrupulous financiers were allowed to operate unchecked—they had to launch a program of strict self-regulation. State Commissioner Leonard in 1976 argued for just such an approach. He contended that bankers, perhaps acting through their own association, the OBA, should establish committees to consider criteria for licensing bank officials and establish a code of ethics for the profession.[54]

The continuing debate over the concept of branch banking as opposed to that of unit banking was as important as the issue of federal and state regulation of banking. An interesting case arose in 1957, one that did not directly involve branching but involved one bank's control over another. That year the holding company for the First National in Oklahoma City, headed by Charles Vose, Sr., purchased the Idabel National. Whereas holding companies for banks had been allowed to control other business concerns, many financial leaders in the state opposed Vose's maneuver, fearing that such a multibank holding company might someday control scores of institutions, a condition that could conceivably lead to monopoly. Pressured by many state leaders, the Oklahoma Legislature in 1957 prohibited multibank holding companies; such companies were allowed, however, to control a bank and affiliated organizations.[55]

Although historically opposed by a majority of both the state's banking and political communities, branch banking did appeal to a few leaders. Some financiers with interests in large metropolitan institutions, which had resources sufficient to engulf banks with smaller assets, believed that branching belonged to the wave of the future. Those in favor of branch banking argued that the system would be more efficient than the unit system and pointed out that a majority of states in the Union already allowed branching. Yet, supporters of the unit concept resisted branching because they believed that large conglomerates would overwhelm smaller banks. Such a trend, opponents of branching pointed out, would lead to monopoly, which would be disastrous.[56] Even many of the leaders of large metropolitan institutions opposed branching. For example, Charles Vose, Sr., mentioned above, head of the largest bank in Oklahoma, was against branching "in general."[57]

Branch banking, never widely supported in Oklahoma, remained prohibited by law, but many leaders eventually began a push for the installation of a remote electronic funds-transfer system. The modern economy, advocates of such a system declared, demanded a more rapid transfer of funds and a faster posting procedure than the older system provided. In 1976 the legislature reacted to this need by passing a Consumer Banking Electronic Facility Act. Signed by Governor David Boren on March 17, the statute allowed banks to establish away from their principal place of business a "manned or unmanned" electronic facility that would provide those services legally performed at the banks' home offices. However, the term "manned" referred to retailers or other business persons in whose establishments the electronic equipment was placed. The law forbade people employed, directly or indirectly, by any bank to assist or perform any service for customers who used the facility. Hence, the state government tried to accomplish two objectives. By allowing the establishment of electronic facilities away from a bank's home office, the lawmakers sought to take advantage of modern technology to speed the transfer of funds, but in strictly regulating the operation of such facilities, the solons hoped to preserve the concept of unit banking.[58]

Executives in large banks quickly established such systems as were provided under the new law, including point-of-sale retail terminals. Then a data-processing company, Computer Congenerics Corporation, established Electronic Funds Transfer Network, Incorporated (EFT Network), to serve smaller banks. With computer centers in Oklahoma City, Tulsa, and Ardmore, the EFT Network by the end of 1976 was serving independent banks in Tulsa, Stillwater, Ponca City, and Lawton. The rise of electronic systems and computer services under the umbrella of a new equitable law provided opportunities for both large and small banks to increase their efficiency and expand their marketing regions.[59]

In the 1950s and 1960s many new banks were chartered in Oklahoma. Those destined to survive into the 1970s are enumerated below:[60]

New Banks, 1950–1969 (Still in operation in 1978)

Bank Name	Date Founded	Chief Executive Officer (as of 1978)
First Security Bank and Trust Co. (Oklahoma City)	1951	Nathaniel Ross
Peoples State Bank (Blair)	1951	Bailey Snow
Northwest Bank (Oklahoma City)	1952	Dale Cain
Union Bank and Trust Co. (Oklahoma City)	1952	John R. Browne
Community Bank and Trust Co. (Tulsa)	1952	Finis Smith
Utica National Bank and Trust Co. (Tulsa)	1953	Victor M. Thompson, Jr.
Admiral State Bank (Tulsa)	1954	J. R. Forrester
Security National Bank (Sapulpa)	1955	Dwight W. Maulding
First State Bank (Lone Wolf)	1956	Daryl Davis
North Side State Bank (Tulsa)	1958	R. J. Pleasant
Del State Bank and Trust Co. (Del City)	1959	Virgil Tague
First State Bank (Waynoka)	1959	Orville Walker
The Sheridan Bank and Trust Co. (Lawton)	1960	Frank J. Sovell
Capital Hill State Bank and Trust Co. (Oklahoma City)	1960	Wayne Lawler
Penn Square Bank, N. A. (Oklahoma City)	1960	William P. Jennings
City Bank and Trust Co. (Tulsa)	1960	John E. Deas
Community Bank (Oklahoma City)	1961	D. W. Garrett
Cyril State Bank (Cyril)	1962	Curtis A. Brooks

Bank Name	Date Founded	Chief Executive Officer (as of 1978)
Citizens State Bank (Maud)	1962	Emery J. Magruder
Grant Square Bank and Trust Co. (Oklahoma City)	1962	J. D. Bottoms
Republic Bank (Oklahoma City)	1962	N. L. McClain
The Village Bank (Oklahoma City)	1962	Thomas L. Legan
First Bank of Owasso (Owasso)	1962	Alan C. Anderson
First Bank in Atoka (Atoka)	1963	Gerald Douglas
Plaza National Bank (Bartlesville)	1963	Leon A. Orr
American National Bank of Midwest City (Midwest City)	1963	Paul Hudiburg
Security Bank and Trust Co. (Midwest City)	1963	James Evans
Exchange National Bank of Moore (Moore)	1963	Royce G. Wilmoth
Guaranty Bank and Trust Co. (Oklahoma City)	1963	George B. Payne
First National Bank (Temple)	1963	John E. Dowlen
Mercantile Bank and Trust Co. (Tulsa)	1963	G. William Foster, Jr.
First National Bank (Turkey)	1963	B. J. Smith
Lincoln Bank and Trust (Ardmore)	1964	John W. Grissom
Community Bank and Trust (Enid)	1964	Harold W. Wilson
Cache Road National Bank (Lawton)	1964	Wiley G. Sartin
Park State Bank (Nicoma Park)	1964	William J. Hogan
American Exchange Bank and Trust Co. (Norman)	1964	Jack E. Black
Norman Bank of Commerce (Norman)	1964	Robert W. Bumgarner
First State Bank (Oilton)	1964	Donald Milstead
Founders Bank and Trust Co. (Oklahoma City)	1964	Ed Miller
Friendly National Bank (Oklahoma City)	1964	James Daniel
Southwestern Bank and Trust Co. (Oklahoma City)	1964	John M. Reardon

Bank Name	Date Founded	Chief Executive Officer (as of 1978)
First National Bank (Sallisaw)	1964	James L. Monroe
University Bank (Stillwater)	1964	Richard L. Wheatley, Jr.
Guaranty National Bank (Tulsa)	1964	Larry J. Lanie
Republic Bank and Trust Co. (Tulsa)	1964	Wesley R. McKinney
First National Bank (Weatherford)	1964	Donald M. Kelley
First National Bank (Henryetta)	1965	W. R. Stubbs
Peoples State Bank and Trust Co. (Holdenville)	1965	Victor W. Pryor, Jr.
Kingfisher Bank and Trust Co. (Kingfisher)	1965	Waynard Hasenfratz
First Bank and Trust Co. (Sand Springs)	1965	Darrell Jones
First State Bank and Trust (Shawnee)	1965	Murlin Derebery
Citizens Bank and Trust Co. (Ada)	1967	Ralph F. Smith
Shepherd Mall State Bank (Oklahoma City)	1967	Harry L. Deupree, Jr.
Bank of Commerce (Chouteau)	1968	Matthew A. P. Schumacher
The Service Bank (Tonkawa)	1968	Leon Carver
Bank of Tulsa (Tulsa)	1968	Houston Adams
The First Mustang State Bank (Mustang)	1969	Gary Huckabay
The Security Bank (Warner)	1969	Jack Moore

A perusal of the foregoing list shows a striking new trend. Fifty-nine new banks were established between 1950 and 1970, with all but twelve being founded in the expansive decade of the 1960s.

Banking in modern, postwar Oklahoma saw many new trends, one of the most pronounced of which was the widespread use of elaborate computerized systems. The decade of the 1970s would see a continuation of these trends as financial leaders devised new techniques to solve the problems of the banking industry.

Citizens National Bank, Oklahoma City. Courtesy Oklahoma Publishing Company.

Interior, Citizens National Bank, Oklahoma City. Courtesy Oklahoma Publishing Company.

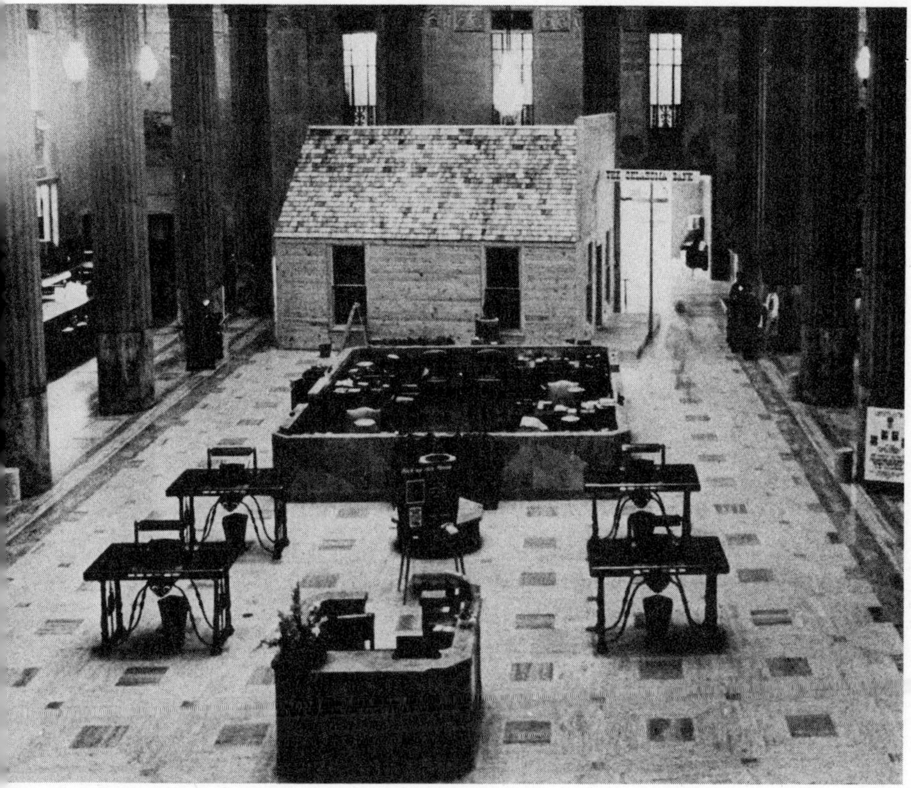

Interior, First National Bank, Oklahoma City. Courtesy Oklahoma Publishing Company.

Interior, First National Bank, Oklahoma City. Courtesy Oklahoma Publishing Company.

Fidelity National Bank, Oklahoma City. Courtesy Oklahoma Publishing Company.

CHAPTER 9.

Current Trends

In the 1970s the banking network in Oklahoma continued to expand. Consistent with the United States Comptroller's desire to ensure that all communities were well-served by financial houses, there were fifty-two institutions founded between 1970 and 1978 that were destined to survive the decade. The following table demonstrates the tremendous expansion:[1]

New Banks, 1970–1978 (Still in operation in 1978)

Bank Name	Date Founded	Chief Executive Officer (as of 1978)
First Bank of Catoosa (Catoosa)	1970	Alma Barnes
American Bank and Trust (Edmond)	1970	Robert L. Brookshire
Sequoyah State Bank of Muldrow (Muldrow)	1970	Robert Harmon
American Bank of Muskogee (Muskogee)	1970	John A. Baker
American Bank of Commerce (Oklahoma City)	1970	Ronald Peeler
Poteau State Bank (Poteau)	1970	J. Mike Snapp
American State Bank (Tulsa)	1970	Leroy Thomas, Sr.
Citizen's Bank (Velma)	1970	J. P. Reynolds
American Bank of Commerce (McAlester)	1971	E. L. Balkman, Jr.
American Bank (Tulsa)	1971	John L. O'Brien
Cashion Community Bank (Cashion)	1972	Robert L. Williams
Chickasha Bank and Trust Co. (Chickasha)	1973	Lindel Pettigrew
Exchange National Bank of Del City (Del City)	1973	J. Robert Wootten
Bank of Inola (Inola)	1973	Donald R. Garner

Bank Name	Date Founded	Chief Executive Officer (as of 1978)
First National Bank (Jenks)	1973	Robin Buerge
City Bank (Muskogee)	1973	John T. Hannah
Medical Center State Bank (Oklahoma City)	1973	Wilbert Johnson
Lakeside Bank (Salina)	1973	J. T. McFarlin
United Bank (Tulsa)	1973	William R. Nash
Wright City State Bank (Wright City)	1973	James W. Burks
Choctaw State Bank (Choctaw)	1974	Ray T. Rogers
Northwest Bank of Enid (Enid)	1974	James S. Spencer
Texoma Bank (Kingston)	1974	Darrell Stovall
Bank of Newcastle (Newcastle)	1974	W. R. Griffith
Quail Creek Bank, N.A. (Oklahoma City)	1974	Robert L. Moser
Sulphur Community Bank (Sulphur)	1974	Philip R. Key
Security Bank (Tulsa)	1974	George B. Hariger
First State Bank (Watonga)	1974	James Goodson
Grand Lake Bank (Grove)	1975	D. E. Heyburn
Citizen's National Bank (Lawton)	1975	Gilbert C. Gibson
The Crossroads State Bank (Oklahoma City)	1975	Robert R. Bryan
Nichols Hills Bank (Oklahoma City)	1975	Homer Paul
Southeast Plaza Bank (Oklahoma City)	1975	Monte M. Deere
Western Trust and Savings (Oklahoma City)	1975	Daniel W. Allred
Southwest Tulsa Bank (Tulsa)	1975	M. P. Young
Union National Bank (Tulsa)	1975	Roy G. Cartwright
Bank of the Lakes (Langley)	1976	R. R. Guest
Bank of the Panhandle (Guymon)	1976	Horace D. Eaton
Central State Bank (Edmond)	1976	Kenneth W. Frisby
Lakeside State Bank (Oologah)	1976	Paul D. Kolman
Miami National Bank (Miami)	1976	Frank H. Moores
Rolling Hills State Bank (Piedmont)	1976	Robert W. Brawley
Woodland Bank (Tulsa)	1976	Douglas L. Jackson
The Bank of Bixby (Bixby)	1977	Carroll G. Bernard
American State Bank (Broken Bow)	1977	Ronald E. Bond
Washita State Bank (Burns Flat)	1977	Rudolph Ferrari
Lakeshore Bank, N.A. (Oklahoma City)	1977	John H. Harris

Bank Name	Date Founded	Chief Executive Officer (as of 1978)
First State Bank (Tahlequah)	1977	Robert M. Johnson
Eastland Bank (Tulsa)	1977	Leland L. Konklin
Harvard Tower Bank (Tulsa)	1977	Robert L. McGoffin
Western National Bank (Tulsa)	1977	Les G. Goddard
First Community Bank (Lone Grove)	1978	Wayne Griffin

Despite the expansion of the banking network—a factor that indicated the viability of that network—the 1970s could well be called the "stormy seventies," a period fraught with problems for the national and state economies. The Gross National Product steadily declined as the balance of trade increased. The large metropolitan institutions in Oklahoma, such as the First National in Oklahoma City, and the smaller institutions, like the Harrah State, all felt the unsettling conditions of the decade. In some years erratic weather conditions hampered farm and ranch production, and in others bumper crops drove prices down. New energy problems took their toll. Increases in the price of gas, oil, and petroleum-related products were passed along to industry, whose costs lowered production and thus put laborers out of work. The consumer felt the squeeze on his pocketbook and the cost of living soared. His food, housing, utilities, clothing, car and maintenance, taxes, and credit—all cost more, and thus his standard of living declined as he was caught in the spiral of inflation.

As leaders in their respective communities, Oklahoma bankers, themselves also consumers, strove to meet these problems and others related to the banking industry: public image, educational efforts, community service, financial marketing, competition, governmental regulation, changes in currency, and the rise in robberies.

Enhancing the image of banking and imparting knowledge about what banks are and what they do for the community, as well as the individual or the business, was a partial solution for several of the aforementioned problems. In 1970 the OBA approved an extensive public relations program "designed to reduce and eliminate the widespread lack of knowledge and misunderstanding about banks and banking activities which exists among large segments of the public, legislators, press and other groups who exercise influence and [affect] the conditions under which banks must operate."[2] Developed and recommended by the OBA's Public Relations and Marketing Committee, the program sought to improve Oklahoma banking's internal image in home institutions, to stabilize the basic image of the banking industry among legislators and the press, to acquaint the public with the advantages of commercial banking services over those of competing institutions, and to call attention to banking's many contributions to the development of individual communities and the state.[3]

Of course, as individuals, bankers enhanced the industry's image by remaining ever active in community affairs. Many continued to serve on local and statewide socio-cultural committees, some of which were established by the state government and some of which originated in the private sector. For example, several bankers played key roles in establishing and/or perpetuating the Oklahoma Heritage Association, a society born of private enterprise that accepted no state funds. When Stanley Draper, longtime leader in Oklahoma City, joined the association in the late 1960s to help revitalize it, he called upon such leading bankers as Charles A. Vose, Sr. for help. Jack Conn and Howard Bozarth also gave yeomen's service to the association, Conn serving as president and Bozarth as treasurer. Such community involvement spoke well for the financial leaders of Oklahoma.[4]

The first step in the long-range public relations program, a step toward meeting the challenges of the 1970s, was education. As mentioned earlier, Oklahoma bankers encouraged continuing education, such as the intermediate and graduate schools of banking, for themselves and their employees. Between 1969 and 1975, the profession, through the OBA, held special seminars in commercial lending, installment credit, and the effect of economic development on business and agricultural finance.[5] Taking advantage of the problem-solving abilities of women bankers, the profession by 1969 boasted of more than 7,000 members in the National Association of Bank-Women. All of these women were officers of commercial banks, savings banks, and trust companies, and many were involved in educational programs. For example, the Women's Committee of the Oklahoma City Chapter of the American Institute of Banking provided job improvement programs for women and encouraged them to participate in classes sponsored by the American Institute of Banking. The com-

87 YEARS OF BANKIN

TODAY'S BANKS 1976
PREDECESSOR BANKS

- **THE FIRST NATIONAL BANK & TRUST CO.**
  OF OKLAHOMA CITY
  - SECURITY NATIONAL BANK
  - AMERICAN-FIRST NATIONAL BANK
  - AMERICAN NATIONAL BANK
  - FIRST NATIONAL BANK IN OKLAHOMA CITY
  - STATE NATIONAL BANK
  - WESTERN NATIONAL BANK
  - OKLAHOMA CITY SAVINGS BANK
  - SOUTHWEST NATIONAL BANK
  - SOUTHWEST RESERVE BANK
  - STOCKYARDS STATE BANK
  - STATE EXCHANGE BANK
  - CITY STATE BANK
  - BANK OF OKLAHOMA CITY
  - OKLAHOMA CITY NATIONAL BANK
  - CENTRAL RESERVE BANK
  - CENTRAL STATE BANK
  - COMMERCIAL NATIONAL BANK
  - OKLAHOMA BANK AND TRUST CO.
  - FIRST NATIONAL BANK OF OKLAHOMA CITY
  - THE OKLAHOMA BANK
  - TRADESMENS NATIONAL BANK
- **LIBERTY NATIONAL BANK & TRUST CO.**
  - GUARANTY STATE BANK
  - OKLAHOMA NATIONAL BANK
  - OKLAHOMA STOCKYARDS NATIONAL BANK
  - BANK OF MIDAMERICA SAVINGS AND TRUST CO.
- **CITY NATIONAL BANK & TRUST CO.**
- **FIDELITY NATIONAL BANK & TRUST CO.**
  - FIRST STATE BANK
- **OKLAHOMA NATIONAL BANK**
  - SOUTH OKLAHOMA NATIONAL BANK
- **STOCKYARDS BANK**
- **CENTRAL NATIONAL BANK**
  - THE MORRIS PLAN COMPANY
- **CITIZENS NATIONAL BANK**
- **FIRST STATE BANK & TRUST CO.**
- **NORTHWEST NATIONAL BANK**
- **MAY AVENUE BANK**
- **PENN SQUARE NATIONAL BANK**
- **CAPITOL HILL STATE BANK & TRUST CO.**
- **GRANT SQUARE BANK & TRUST CO.**
- **REPUBLIC BANK** STATE CAPITAL BANK
- **THE VILLAGE BANK**
- **GUARANTY NATIONAL BANK**
- **FOUNDERS NATIONAL BANK**
- **FRIENDLY NATIONAL BANK OF OKLAHOMA CITY**
- **SOUTHWESTERN NATIONAL BANK OF OKLA. CITY**
- **AMERICAN BANK OF COMMERCE**
- **COMMUNITY NATIONAL BANK**
- **MEDICAL CENTER STATE BANK**
- **NICHOLS HILLS BANK**
- **QUAIL CREEK BANK, N.A.**
- **SHEPHERD MALL STATE BANK**
- **SOUTHEAST PLAZA BANK**
- **WILL ROGERS BANK**
- **CROSSROADS STATE BANK**
- **LAKESHORE BANK, N.A.**

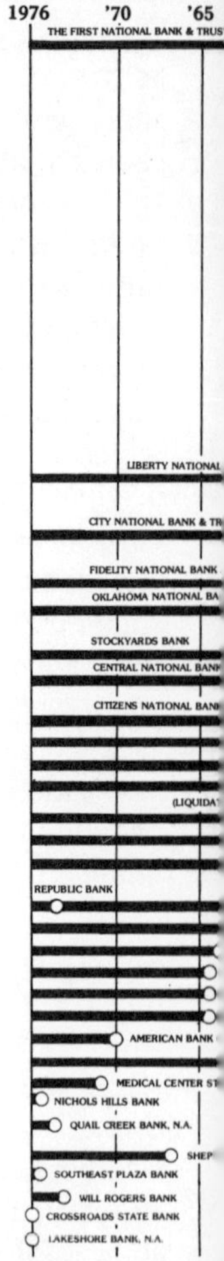

FROM 1889 TO 1976 OKLAHOMA CITY HAS HAD THEM . . . AS COMPLETELY AND AS ACCURATEI MEMORIES PERMIT . . . THERE HAVE BEEN 75 BA THEIR NAMES; SOME SOLD OUT; OTHERS LIQU FAILED . . .

Eighty-seven years of banking in Oklahoma C

OKLAHOMA CITY

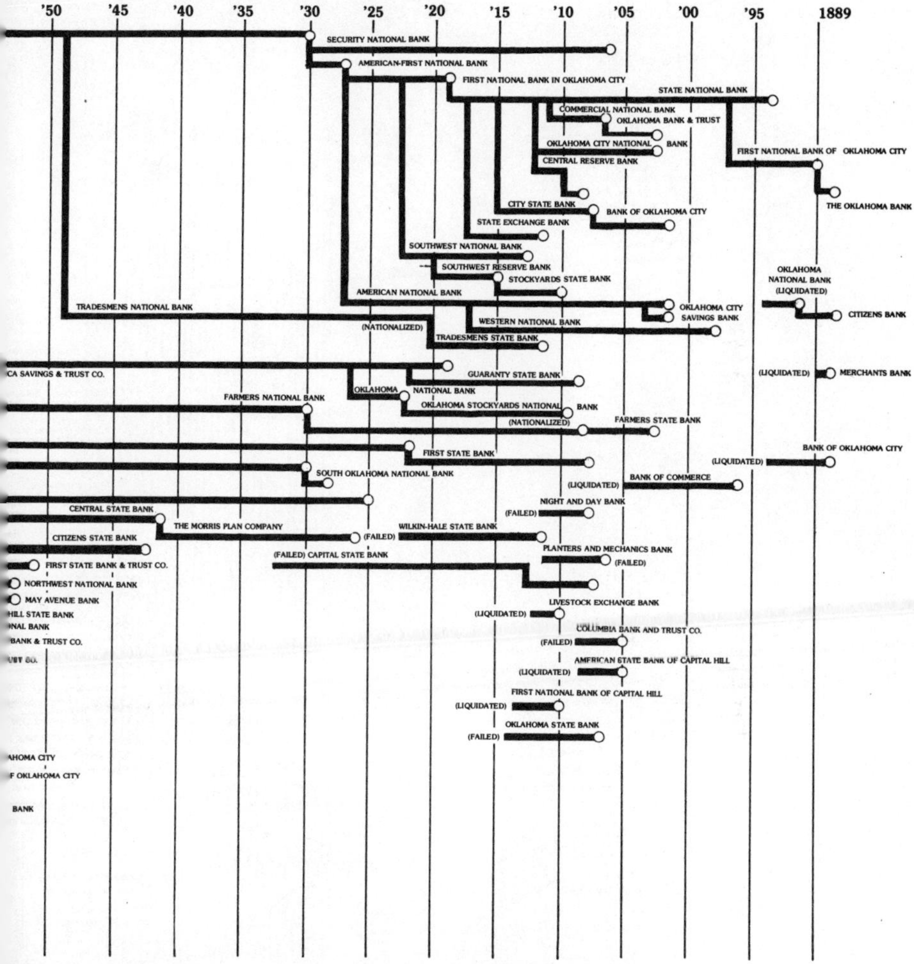

KS . . . HERE IS WHAT HAPPENED TO
STING RECORDS AND HUMAN
NAMES AT LEAST . . . SOME CHANGED
SEVERAL CONSOLIDATED; SIX

urtesy of Oklahoma Bankers Association.

The Bank of Oklahoma, Tulsa: in 1917, at left; in 1929, center; in 1975, at right. Courtesy Oklahoma Bankers Association.

mittee also helped to promote and to publicize the educational programs of the chapter.[6]

Oklahoma bankers also participated in other educational programs for young people. In 1970 the First National of Tulsa sponsored the Junior Achievement Bank. Sixteen Tulsa high school students learned about the many facets of commercial banking by establishing their own "bank." In yet another program, the First National of Tulsa and Oklahoma National Bank and Trust Companies of Chickasha cooperated with the First National Bank of Rush Springs to permit four students from the Oklahoma College of Liberal Arts of Chickasha to learn the operations and all aspects of banking by working in each department. As part of a five-week independent study program, the sponsoring institutions gave the young people a first-hand knowledge of general banking practices. Other beneficiaries of banking support were the 4-H clubs. In 1969, for instance, more than thirty-three Oklahoma financiers contributed funds to send 4-H representatives to the National 4-H Leader Forum. The state's financial leaders also sponsored many young Oklahomans in studying abroad, knowing that those leaders of tomorrow would share their knowledge with their communities.[7]

Perhaps one of the most important educational programs sponsored by the OBA was the student intern program. The idea originated from conversations between Frank G. Kliewer, Jr., an officer of Cordell National Bank, and K. C. Davis, a professor at Oklahoma State University. For several years they had discussed the problems in banking and agriculture and realized that by working together, they could overcome many future difficulties. Financiers quickly saw the benefits that the students and the cooperating banks might reap. Approximately 180 new bank officers were needed annually, and it was difficult to attract intelligent young graduates into the field, once other career goals had already been set. Moreover, out-of-state banks often raided Oklahoma colleges for the cream of the crop. This was an ideal opportunity, the bankers realized, to attract the best management talent to career opportunities in Oklahoma institutions before graduation through an exciting and challenging student-intern program.[8]

The student-intern also received excellent benefits. Paid $400 a month by the participating bank for which he worked, the student could help defray his educational expenses. Instruction was custom-designed for the student and the sponsoring bank, and the intern gained firsthand knowledge of banking by working in such areas as bookkeeping, operations, lending, investing, deposits, reserve management, safe deposit, and marketing. As part of the program, the student selected a topic of research agreeable to his professor and his bank. If the student completed his program to the satisfaction of all concerned, he was assured of a job upon graduation; if his experiences were unfavorable, the student could choose another career possibility. Consequently, all parties benefited: the sponsoring institution received an interested, qualified employee, and the student received financial aid, college credit for the course, individualized instruction, and a job.[9]

The OBA also cooperated with other organizations in their education efforts and problem solving. For example, OBA members were urged to support the work undertaken by the Small Business Administration in its management-training courses for businessmen in Oklahoma, courses designed to improve the business capability of young, newly emerging businessmen. Carl Echols, management specialist for the SBA, urged Oklahoma financiers to lend their prestige and knowledge to the courses, because "the small businessman must learn the principles of marketing, management, and advertising to be able to compete with the large discount and chain stores."[10] By lecturing and by participating in panel discussions, experienced financial leaders helped their respective banks in two ways: they strengthened their institution's image through public service, and they aided the business community by assisting small businessmen.[11]

One of the problems that the OBA hoped education would solve was that of financial marketing. The farm market was of prime importance to 410 of the 425 commercial institutions in Oklahoma that held farm credit in 1970. Thus, "the economic well-being of most of the banks in Oklahoma [was] directly related to the success and prosperity of individual farmers and agribusiness."[12] Even the largest institution in the state continued to carry a large agricultural loan portfolio. In early 1978 the First National of Oklahoma City had out in credit to the petroleum industry more than $100 million, and that sum was by far the biggest item in its portfolio. However, the institution still committed a large portion of its loans, $50 to $60 million, to agribusinessmen and stock raisers.[13] In his "President's Message" delivered to the OBA in 1970, H. E. Rainbolt warned financial leaders "to increase their ability to adequately serve their most important customer—the farmer."[14] Rainbolt pointed out that banks were losing their share of the farm-loan market to the fourteen production credit associations in the state, and to support this statement, he included the following table:[15]

Holding of Non–Real Estate Farm Loans

	Amount Held on 1-1-70	Change From 1-1-69	Change From 1-1-65
Banks	315,151,000.00	7%	54%
Production Credit Association	133,191,000.00	37%	161%
Farm Home Administration	20,830,000.00	− 1%	− 10%
Total	469,172,000.00	13%	69%

While agreeing that banks still had the majority of farm loans, Rainbolt noted the trend away from such loans and suggested that the average note of from $15,000 to $20,000 was not too large for banks to make. He insisted that commercial institutions require farmers to be competent businessmen and help them by hiring a qualified agricultural representative with well-defined functions and responsibilities.[16]

The general economic decline in the United States, along with unpredictable weather, hampered agribusiness during the 1970s and made the banking community's task more difficult. In late 1977 economic forecasters predicted that the state gradually was emerging from the worst price depression in forty years. To assess the agricultural loan situation, the State Department of Agriculture surveyed ten of the state's bankers. The findings were predictable: Oklahoma farmers and ranchers were hard hit, and many faced foreclosures within six months to a year. Those in the most difficulty were young wheat farmers who had received low prices on their crops (not enough to pay for loans on leased land and machinery) and who had little equity on which to borrow more funds to keep them going. Many ranchers were in no better condition. Because of the profit squeeze on beef from late 1973 through 1978, most ranchers had to refinance their loans and sell part of their cattle and/or equipment.

Only diversified farmers, those out of the wheat-growing area, seemed to be prospering.[17]

Jim Eatherly, president and chairman of the board of the First National Bank of Tonkawa, assessed the economic situation in his area as bad "because our farms are responsible for about 60 percent of all dollars that come into town." He added: "I think there will be a lot of farmers who'll have to refinance through the Farmers Home Administration, and I think they're doing a good job for farmers. They come in on a secondary basis when commercial banks can't handle the farmer's loans, and they handle them on a seven-year basis instead of a short-term basis."[18]

Long-term financing and refinancing meant problems for banks doing such business. Eatherly, who was also chairman of the OBA's agricultural committee, continued: "[My bank] has been as high as 83 percent on loan-to-deposit ratios, although it is now 79 percent. The ideal situation is for most banks to be around 65 percent, but most agricultural banks today are loaned up in . . . the high 70s and some even in the low 80s."[19] Consequently, those banks lost money because they could not take new customers; funds were simply not available.

In addition to the farm-loan market, there were two other potentially lucrative financial outlets for Oklahoma banking: the savings and consumer-lending markets. Data compiled by Dr. Walter Polner, of Madison, Wisconsin, suggested that these potentials were much larger than state data had shown previously. After examining ten savings institutions, Polner estimated the share of each in these markets.[20] First were insurance companies, which held $19.5 billion by the end of 1971. Although no exact data was available on the second institution, employee savings plans, and the third, pension and retirement plans, Polner believed the figures were significant. Mutual funds, a fourth outlet, received sales of more than $35.7 million in 1971, and securities during the 1970s took $50 million in savings bonds. A sixth alternative for savings, one for which there were no data, was the Farm Credit Administration agencies. The seventh outlet was thrift and loan companies. Credit unions and savings and loan associations, the eighth and ninth outlets, had the lion's share of the savings markets: $1.6 billion. From 1947 through 1962 these institutions surpassed banks, the tenth outlet, in savings.

In the 1970s banks reversed this trend to the extent that they acquired more savings than credit unions and savings and loan associations, but commercial banks still could not corner even 50 percent of the total real savings market.[21]

Polner continued his analysis by stating that the growth in savings paralleled the increase in consumer loans. Oklahomans borrowed money from eight institutions: insurance companies (loans against policies), savings and loan associations, finance companies, farm credit institutions, department and retail stores, auto dealers, credit unions, and banks. Graphically illustrating his points, he provided the following three tables:[22]

Table 1
Amount of Savings Held by Individuals in Oklahoma 1945–71
(Millions of Dollars)

Year	All Banks	Savings and Loan Associations	Credit Unions
1945	$ 101.3	$ 80.2	$ 1.8
1946	110.0	105.0	2.4
1947	116.1	124.8	3.3
1948	117.7	144.6	4.2
1949	122.9	161.9	5.4
1950	131.4	179.2	6.7
1951	171.2	202.8	8.4
1952	198.6	236.9	10.8
1953	242.1	274.7	14.1
1954	269.1	317.2	17.8
1955	282.3	358.8	22.2
1956	316.8	397.9	27.4
1957	368.5	442.1	33.3
1958	433.4	496.7	39.6
1959	469.6	577.2	45.9
1960	539.9	650.8	51.3
1961	635.3	730.8	58.1
1962	782.3	810.7	64.9
1963	937.2	897.7	73.6
1964	1086.4	981.1	85.4
1965	1265.1	1037.3	95.8
1966	1460.7	1083.1	107.6

Year	All Banks	Savings and Loan Associations	Credit Unions
1967	1762.2	1175.4	123.2
1968	2053.3	1229.0	144.0
1969	1774.6	1246.8	159.7
1970	2134.8	1341.4	187.9
1971	3102.6	1675.3	220.2

Table 2

Percentage of Individual Savings Held by Banks, Savings and Loan Associations and Credit Unions in Oklahoma

Year	All Banks	Savings and Loan Associations	Credit Unions
1950	41.40%	56.46%	2.14%
1951	44.77	53.03	2.20
1952	44.49	53.07	2.44
1953	45.60	51.74	2.66
1954	44.54	54.50	2.96
1955	42.55	54.09	3.36
1956	42.68	53.61	3.71
1957	43.67	52.39	3.94
1958	44.69	51.22	4.09
1959	42.97	52.82	4.21
1960	43.46	52.40	4.14
1961	44.63	51.28	4.09
1962	47.19	48.90	3.91
1963	49.10	47.04	3.86
1964	50.46	45.57	3.97
1965	52.75	43.25	4.00
1966	55.09	40.85	4.06
1967	57.57	38.40	4.03
1968	59.93	35.87	4.20
1969	44.78	39.19	5.03
1970	48.26	36.61	5.13
1971	62.08	33.52	4.40

Table 3
Installment Loans Outstanding in Oklahoma 1965–1971
(Millions of Dollars)

Year	All Banks	Insurance Policy	Finance Companies Personal Loans*	Credit Unions
1965	$123.5	$507	$425.4	$ 94
1966	143.4	557	441.0	106
1967	139.7	605	494.0	122
1968	139.5	656	516.6	143
1969	174.9	758	596.0	151
1970	180.3	761	656.3	164
1971	192.9	877	613.1	184

*Considered consumer loans

A fourth area Oklahoma bankers explored was the secondary-mortgage market. By utilizing the Federal National Mortgage Association, often called "Fannie Mae," and its mortgage markets, financial leaders availed themselves of an important source of revenue and captured newcomers for other financial services. For example, Fannie Mae purchased mortgages on long-term loans for homes, paying banks a servicing fee of 3/8 of 1 percent of the outstanding principal. Banks were not obligated to make loans on condominiums or subdivision projects, but Fannie Mae would purchase these mortgages and pay the servicing fee if any bank desired to enter the secondary-mortgage market.[23]

An organization of great help in making loans that banks could not otherwise accommodate was the Small Business Administration. Oftentimes, small businessmen needed five- or six-year terms to amortize their loans, but financial leaders were apprehensive about term lending in a time of uncertain interest rates. Here, the SBA helped by guaranteeing up to 40 percent of the loan. By using a fluctuating rate of interest, the bankers reviewed their loans every six months and adjusted them up or down according to the New York prime rate. Furthermore, the portion of the loan guaranteed by the SBA was not in competition with commercial banking and in fact helped Oklahoma bankers make loans and profits where otherwise none would have been possible.[24]

The SBA was not in direct competition with Oklahoma bankers, but the Credit Act of 1971, savings and loan associations, and credit unions posed real threats. Joe Gilliland, executive vice-president of the OBA, urged members to write their senators and congressmen for details on the proposed Credit Act of 1971—a bureaucratic method of solving the agricultural financing problem. Under the act, a proposed Rural Service Center (RSC) would assume virtually all the functions of commercial banks. More ominous, the regional credit bank could allow new associations, owned by the parent organization itself, the same powers as the parent. With its federal funds, favored tax shelter, and capital-drawing power, the RSC soon would have driven many Oklahoma banks out of business had it not been rejected by Congress.[25]

Oklahoma's financiers had an opportunity to contribute to the defeat of the Farm Credit Act of 1971, but there was nothing they could do to rid themselves of the increasing encroachment of savings and loan associations and credit unions into the state's $2-billion credit industry. Both institutions added banklike activities, checking accounts, service corporations, consumer loans, and trust services. But unlike banks, these businesses—credit unions in particular—were unregulated and could branch. Because such safeguards were lacking, 7,581 credit unions nationwide folded from 1956 to 1970.[26]

In August, 1976, the OBA sued the Oklahoma State Credit Union Board, Tinker Credit Union, and the Western Electric Credit Union, arguing that credit unions were "not authorized by Oklahoma banking statutes to transact nor pay interest on demand deposit accounts."[27] The OBA suit asked for an injunction to prohibit the continuation or expansion of the credit unions' share-draft program, a banking activity. The next month the American Bankers Association and Tioga State Bank, Spencer, New York, sued the National Credit Union Association (NCUA) on the same grounds. The bankers argued that state and federal statutes gave them exclusive authority to engage in banking activities, particularly checking accounts, and that the NCUA permitted credit unions to engage unlawfully in banking and to violate the Federal Credit Union Act.[28]

The president of the ABA, W. Liddon McPeters, warned that the credit unions' irresponsible expansion and unlawful banking activities were "not only unfair competition; it also jeopardizes the financial well-being of the credit union members and undermines the nation's economy."[29] The editor of *Oklahoma Banker* also noted that "between 1950 and 1971, the number of credit unions doubled to 22,812 and their total assets increased 38-fold." In conclusion he pointed out that credit unions provided "15.7 percent of total U.S. consumer installment credit."[30] The following table illustrates that amount of money invested in the leading credit unions of the Southwest:[31]

The Southwest's Largest Credit Unions
(ranked by assets as of June 30, 1976)

Credit Union	Assets
Government Employees, San Antonio (s)	$159,840,000
Tinker Air Force Base, Oklahoma City (f)	103,190,000
Dallas Teachers (s)	82,209,000
Security Service, San Antonio (f)	78,600,000
Texas Instruments, Dallas (s)	76,120,000
Government Employees, El Paso (s)	73,869,000
Randolph-Brooks, San Antonio (f)	62,035,000
Houston Area Teachers (s)	55,029,000
LTV Corporation, Dallas (f)	49,890,000
Phillips 66, Bartlesville (f)	42,782,000
Fort Worth Federal Employees (f)	39,178,000
Sheppard Federal, Wichita Falls (f)	34,304,000

(s)—State Chartered
(f)—Federally Chartered

More ominous than competition from savings and loan associations and credit unions were the continuing, ever-present threats of proliferating governmental regulation and attacks upon the Federal Reserve System. Most financial leaders agreed that the banking industry—operated for both profit and service—needed regulation to control the unscrupulous few, and most accepted that the industry needed regulation to insure uniformity of operation and of law. However, they believed that increasingly intricate and restrictive regulation hamstrung the entire industry. Moreover, many believed that these regulations were not for the good of the public, nor of banking, but were political attempts of a reactionary Congress to placate special groups and to remedy specific circumstances. All agreed that regulation had become so technical and so burdensome that bankers, however knowledgeable and conscientious, feared violation and jail.[32] A growing problem throughout the 1960s, federal regulation became almost unmanageable as the decade of the 1970s drew to a close.

Certainly, at the least, close regulation was costly and frustrating. Unlike other highly supervised industries, such as public utilities and telephone and transportation companies, banks paid the cost for their own regulation. This included annual audits by the comptroller of the currency, attorneys' fees, telephone calls from various regulating agencies, payments to third-party auditing firms, plus any costs involved in a challenge of any kind, whether or not a bank was at fault. For example, on one occasion the Securities Exchange Commission, only four weeks before its annual earnings statement came due, challenged a banker who had reported a loss despite the fact that the entire transaction had been previously reported. Bank officials dropped everything, prepared a lengthy document, and sent it to Washington, D.C., posthaste. The SEC rejected the report, whereupon bank officials, accompanied by an attorney charging $110 an hour, flew to Washington to settle the matter. After an hour's discussion, the SEC officials admitted they had misunderstood the bank's position; the bank was correct. The cost in frayed nerves was undetermined; the cost in salaries, plane fares, expenses, and legal fees was $15,000, which the banker, not the SEC, paid.[33]

Financial leaders also were frustrated when they were forced to keep a customer waiting while employees searched records for data in yet other reports. Although officials wanted to run their institutions as businesses and as a service to their communities, they found increasing amounts of time devoured in gathering data for reports, the making out and filing of reports, and keeping abreast of more reports and the dates on which they had to be filed. Oftentimes, regulatory agencies required special reports "due yesterday," forcing officials to drop all banking business in a hurried attempt to meet deadlines. One financier estimated that he filed several hundred reports annually. Because of the severe penalties for violation, government reports, not customer service, had to receive top priority, a fact that many leaders label a sad commentary on current banking practices.[34]

Also costly and frustrating was the practice of taking an employee from his post to put him at the disposal of inspectors "from a plethora of agencies, including the State Labor and Industries Department, the United States Labor Relations Board, the Treasury Department, all taxing agencies, all equal-employment-opportunity agencies, the Comptroller of the Currency, the FDIC, and the Federal Reserve."[35] Representatives of the Internal Revenue Service and other government agencies, armed with a subpoena, or writing one themselves, often asked for customer records. In most instances an employee, an accountant, or an attorney, paid by the bank, had to explain the material. And the costs and frustrations mounted.[36] In the face of continuing regulation, financial leaders anticipated supervisional problems and tried to fight passage of the most restrictive or ridiculous requirements.

More than costly or frustrating were the attacks upon the Federal Reserve System, attacks that struck at the very heart of the free-enterprise banking industry. The original design of the Federal Reserve was such that it would be forever aloof of partisan political control. Consequently, the board of governors and the presidents of the twelve reserve banks were appointed for long terms, and the system was self-financed so that it did not need congressional support for operating funds. Moreover, the system created a decentralized central bank; thus, decision-making and formulation of monetary policy were dispersed throughout the country, at once freeing the system from sectional control and making it more responsive to the needs of all areas of the country. However, a proposed Federal Reserve Reform Act threatened "to top the balance" and place the "money-creating" process in the hands of whatever political group was in power at the time. The representative, independent, and decentralized character of the Federal Reserve System would thus be destroyed. Financial leaders argued that the result would be "[to create more money] to finance politically desirable projects; then inflation takes over; followed by the printing of more money. Inevitably, rampant inflation so weakens the financial structure that the economy collapses, and very often so does the political structure as well."[37] Realizing the enormity of the situation, Oklahoma bankers opposed any tampering with the Federal Reserve System.

The government's desire to regulate the banking industry and to make the Federal Reserve System into a money-making tool for social legislation resulted from the bad economic situation during the stormy 1970s. James V. Baker, Senior Vice-President of Fidelity Bank in Oklahoma City, called the economic slump "the worst recession since the depression, [resulting in] the highest interest rates since General Lee surrendered at Appomatox."[38] The following table demonstrates that many Oklahomans could not pay their debts in the early 1970s, a fact that resulted in net loan charge-offs for bad debts:[39]

Loan Losses

1969	$ 4,114,000
1970	8,680,000
1971	8,498,000
1972	7,356,000
1973	9,712,000
1974	22,570,000

Attempting to help purchasers and themselves, Oklahoma's financial leaders supported the Consumer Credit Code and the formation of the Consumer Credit Counseling Service of Central Oklahoma. As to the former, bankers believed that the unwary or unsophisticated borrower paid too much for credit. Leaders argued that if this situation were remedied, fewer people would accumulate debts that they could not pay. The prime target of the Consumer Code was the loan shark, some of whom charged interest of 5 percent per week. Other justifications for supporting the code included outdated credit laws and confusion in those laws from state to state. In addition, Oklahoma's state code precluded its $2-billion-a-year credit industry from coming under the federal Truth-in-Lending Act of July 1, 1969.[40]

Organized by Central Oklahoma bankers, oil companies, credit unions, utilities, merchants, and finance companies, the Consumer Credit Counseling Service of Central Oklahoma proposed "to help those persons who had created unmanageable debts."[41] The service, barely self-sustaining in the late 1970s, charged debtors a three-dollar registration fee and arranged with their creditors to assume 90 percent of their debts, the other 10 percent to go to the service to cover operating expenses. The facility aided all concerned. Because the debtor could pay nothing otherwise, the creditors received most of their money, and the debtor acquired professional advice to help him pay what he owed, keeping his self-respect in the process.[42]

Examination of selected statistics demonstrated that the service was successful. From November 1967 through February 1969, for example, the service counseled more than 743 families who had bad debts totaling $1,457,739. Sixty-five percent of the clients followed professional counsel and paid all their bills. Approximately 17.5 percent were able to manage on their own after counseling, and only 17.5 percent dropped out of the program. Figures on bankruptcies filed indicated that the total dropped from 2,339 in 1967 to 1,887 in 1968, a significant decrease.[43] Praising the service, Judge William T. Billups, a federal referee in bankruptcy cases, declared that "bankruptcies have been going up all along, but now they are going down. The only thing I can attribute that to is the counseling service."[44]

In the 1970s financiers also had difficulty in forcing their customers to make adjustments to monetary changes, thus proving the old observation that people oftentimes respond quite differently to changes in currency or coins than the experts predicted they would. The public did not like the two-dollar bill of the 1970s. Put into circulation in April 1976, the new note was supposed to save the government $27 million over a five-year period because the Treasury Department would need to print fewer bills. Initially many people took the notes as collector's items, but later refused them in change. There were several reasons for this attitude. First, many people regarded the two-dollar bills as bad luck, recalling that the notes had been widely used earlier in the country's history by political bosses to buy votes and that in bygone days certain ladies of the evening charged a crisp two-dollar bill for their favors. In addition, many merchants disliked them because there was no separate space in the cash drawer for them. Moreover, one side of the bill could be mistaken for a five, the other for a twenty, resulting in costly mistakes. Nevertheless, the Treasury Department believed that the public would eventually accept the note.[45]

In a January 16 letter to the House coinage subcommittee, Undersecretary of the Treasury Betty B. Anderson proposed a new dollar coin, made basically of copper and sized between a quarter and a half dollar. Costing between two and three cents to produce, the new dollar would last approximately fifteen years in contrast to the paper dollar, which cost 1.7 cents, but wore out quickly. The new dollar would have on it the pattern of the liberty head with the liberty cap (the Phrygian cap) on a pole, a symbol of freedom since ancient times.[46]

Many vending-machine operators approved the idea, because they could sell items costing more than a dollar. However, some members of Congress feared that the operators would use the new coin as an excuse to raise prices. Nevada casino owners and managers protested the change to a coin on the grounds that gamblers love the large silver dollars. Objections aside, Terry Marksberry, special projects officer of the treasury, said that should congressional approval be forthcoming, the federal mints could produce 250 million new dollar coins for distribution in 1979.[47]

Even as Oklahoma moves toward the twenty-first century, bankers, particularly those in small towns and medium-sized cities, remained perplexed about one persistent problem, for which there appeared to be no perfect solution. Although most institutions followed sound security procedures and installed the latest technological wonders to fight crime, bandits still occasionally attacked the banks. On January 11, 1978, for example, two men entered the Peoples National Bank of Checotah at noon and walked back to the note department, where president Don Stidham was working. Before he noticed them, they donned makeshift masks and pulled revolvers. "At first everyone thought it was a joke," said Stidham, "but five seconds later when they pushed some people around and started cocking their guns, we knew the joke was over."[48] The two bandits ordered employees and customers, numbering approximately twenty-five, first into a kitchen and then into the vault, where the outlaws forced Stidham to fill pillowcases with currency. Before leaving, the two men locked their startled prisoners in the vault, where a tense atmosphere was relieved when the bank president produced a key that opened the door. Meanwhile, the robbers escaped, taking flight along a snow-blanketed country road.[49]

Although the 1970s saw a continuation of many old problems and the development of several new ones, the 400-plus state and national banks in Oklahoma emerged as sound institutions, dedicated to the welfare and progress of their communities.

Robbery of the May Avenue Bank, Oklahoma City, 1973. Courtesy Oklahoma Publishing Company.

Epilogue: Looking Ahead

Bankers in Oklahoma hesitate before making any predictions about the future, for most of them realize that it holds many uncertainties. Most leaders believe that new, open attitudes will prevail. Whereas in the "old days" many bankers appeared cold and unconcerned about consumer needs, today the majority realize that it requires a good rapport with customers to assure their business in a competitive market. Leaders also appear concerned about their profession while they identify many problem areas.

Increasingly in the modern age, banking has become more complex. In part, complexity stems from size. Whereas the small country banks at the beginning of the twentieth century had only a handful of workers, the managers of the large metropolitan institutions of today have hundreds of employees. The First National of Oklahoma City, the state's largest institution, has more than nine hundred persons on its payroll; other large banks have numbers that range from a hundred to six hundred employees. Such staffs require expanded personnel-service departments. Correspondingly, today's metropolitan institutions have many more accounts to process than they had in the old days.[1]

Many leaders predict that government regulations will become more strict, creating additional paper work for bankers. Pressure from the Equal Employment Opportunities Commission (EEOC) will continue and will increase regulations regarding conflict of interests. Furthermore, most financiers believe that there will be renewed insistence that banks meet the needs of their communities. Some insist that the recently passed Community Reinvestment Act may foreshadow credit allocation and that federal authorities may impose a national ceiling on interest rates during times of tight money.

Bankers continue to believe that federal regulations are on occasion unnecessarily overbearing and overburdensome. For example, in early 1978 the Bankamericard Division of the First National in Oklahoma City sent a customer a bill for $13.00, an appropriate amount corresponding to approximately 10 percent of the customer's bill. A federal audit disclosed that the proper amount should have been $12.98, and examiners chastised the officials for the error, one that added no interest to the account and that allowed the debtor to reduce his balance by a mere $.02. On another occasion, a man and his girlfriend applied for a Bankamericard, asking for a joint card despite the fact that they were not married. Appropriately, bank officers asked for two credit applications, one from each person, whereupon the woman charged discrimination based on sex. Federal examiners demanded complete explanations from the institution's officers and closed the case only upon being assured that all single people, men and women alike, had to file individual applications. In still another instance, the First of Oklahoma City found that by complying with a local city ordinance on door-entry safety, it violated federal safety rules. After being fined $50, the First spent considerable sums on compliance. On such occasions financial leaders wistfully longed for a common-sense approach that would replace "bureaucratic red tape."[2] In addition to the aforementioned problems, certain bankers express a fear that in the immediate future the "elevator effect" or the "up and down syndrome" will be felt as the Federal Reserve Board continues to try to control the economy by manipulating interest rates.

On the positive side, most bankers laud the great technological advances that enable institutions to become more efficient. The development of electronic systems has simplified work loads and created greater efficiency in all phases of banking. Charles Vose, Sr., of the First National Bank in Oklahoma City, points out that his organization—one of the first to adapt electronic innovations in the 1950s—ordered two additional computers in 1978 at a cost of $8 million. The two computers will reduce the work loads of key personnel by one half.[3]

Bankers will continue to feel the keen competition that comes from such other financial institutions as savings and loan associations. In the not-too-distant future bankers may be required to pay interest on demand deposits. A common practice in early, frontier

Oklahoma, interest on demand deposits was forbidden by New Deal legislation in 1933. In recent years, however, some states began paying interest to so-called NOW (negotiable orders of withdrawal) accounts. Such a practice could become mandatory for all banks before 1980, and, if put in force, could present commercial institutions with a "two-headed dragon." On the one hand, the paying of more interest could result in much higher service charges and, on the other, would deprive bankers of short-term "free" use of monies in checking accounts. As to the competition between commercial banks and savings and loan associations, a major "battle" is forecast. In 1978 several officers of savings and loan institutions stated that they might be willing to give up their interest-rate advantage over banks, but in return they wanted the right to offer checking accounts, make small consumer loans, and issue credit cards.[4]

Helping Oklahoma's banking fraternity lead the state toward the twenty-first century will be a number of leaders. Some, like Jack Conn, Bill McLean, the Voses (father and son), Eugene Swearingen, and many others have been mentioned in the preceding pages, although for every representative leader noted, scores of names have been left out for lack of space. There are, however, certain other leaders who bear mention. H. E. Rainbolt, chairman of the board of the Federal National of Shawnee, has far-flung interests in international as well as national concerns. His fellow townsman, Harber Lampl, of the American National, a civic leader with particular interests in education, will also be at the forefront of the state's banking fraternity. J. Ralph McCalmont, of the First National in Guthrie, a relative newcomer to Oklahoma banking, has already made his mark in Guthrie, where he emphasizes community growth along with historic preservation.[5]

Like Lampl, many other financial leaders come from banking families with a long tradition of service to Oklahoma. Representative of second-generation leaders are Edmund Kennedy, of Pawhuska; Charles Vose, Jr., of Oklahoma City; and Frank Kliewer, of Cordell; and representative of third-generation leaders are W. L. Stephenson, Jr., of the Central National in Enid; John E. Painter, of the Farmers State in Afton; and Guy L. Berry, Jr., of the Sapulpa American National. Likewise, the H. H. Champlin family has been associated, except for the years from 1899 to 1909, with the First National in

Enid since that institution was founded as a state bank in 1895. And there are some families in Oklahoma that have seen four generations of service. One of the most noted is the Sewell family, of Clinton. J. R. P. Sewell, father of F. A. Sewell, began organizing banks in west Texas and western Oklahoma in the 1890s, including those at Calvin, Texoma, and Goodwell. Later, F. A. Sewell built the First National at Texoma, selling the other banks in order to concentrate on one. In 1936, Sewell organized his bank at Clinton, where his son F. A. Sewell, Jr., and grandson F. A. Sewell, III, continue to serve.[6]

Many families with long traditions in banking rose from humble beginnings. W. L. Stephenson, Jr., remembered that his grandfather Arthur E. was a pioneer who intended to make the run in 1889, but became ill. Locating in Hennessey, he got a job sweeping floors in a bank and rose through the ranks to eventually take over the Central National in Enid, a post that was later taken in turn by his son and grandson. The Painter family represents another clan with roots in early Oklahoma and a long tradition of service. M. A. Painter, a rancher, came to the Twin Territories in 1895 and later helped organize what would become the Farmers State Bank in Afton. His son R. D. joined him in the bank in 1917 and later R. D.'s sons also worked in the bank.[7] Scores of other families who have been in banking for generations will continue to lead into the twenty-first century.

The OBA will also continue to be active, especially in accomplishing goals that individual bankers cannot accomplish alone. Three leaders of note have headed the OBA: Eugene Gum, from 1918 to 1952; Charles Filson, from 1952 to 1964; and Joe Gilliland, from 1964 to the present. Gilliland, a 1960 graduate of the University of Oklahoma, serves as director and executive vice-president of the association. Active within the ABA and with the Oklahoma congressional delegation in Washington, D.C., the OBA continues to work for programs and legislation advantageous to the banking fraternity. The association also cooperates with the FDIC and other regulatory agencies, trying to modify interpretations of legislation that leads to overregulation. In addition, the OBA helps members by negotiating for lower insurance rates and by maintaining a close watch over bank robberies and embezzlements and assisting law officers in bringing the culprits to justice. Finally, the OBA sponsors many educational programs each year, programs that occupy much of the staff's time.[8]

Most Oklahoma bankers, old-timers and newcomers, realize that the years ahead may be filled with problems. But various problems notwithstanding, most financial leaders are guardedly optimistic about the future. They believe that the general prosperity evidenced since World War II—allowing for temporary recessions—will continue as the banking fraternity tries to help its state and nation fulfill the promise of American life.

Appendix 1.

Past Presidents Oklahoma Bankers Association

1897	U. C. Guss	Guthrie
1897–1898	W. S. Search	Shawnee
1898–1899	J. W. McNeal	Guthrie
1899–1900	Otto A. Shuttee	El Reno
1900–1901	P. W. Smith	Newkirk
1901–1902	James H. Wheeler	Oklahoma City
1902–1903	D. W. Hogan	Oklahoma City
1903–1904	F. J. Wikoff	Stillwater
1904–1905	Frank Craig	McAlester
1905–1906	H. A. McCandless	Perry
1906–1907	N. T. Gilbert	Madill
1907–1908	E. P. Blake	Blackwell
1908–1909	A. D. Kennedy	Okmulgee
1909–1910	L. A. Wilson	El Reno
1910–1911	J. B. Ferguson	Enid
1911–1912	T. J. Hartman	Sulphur
1912–1913	Asa E. Ramsey	Muskogee
1913–1914	W. S. Guthrie	Oklahoma City
1914–1915	H. A. Spalding	North Enid
1915–1916	T. H. Dwyer	Chickasha
1916–1917	L. E. Phillips	Bartlesville
1917–1918	H. A. McCauley	Sapulpa
1918–1919	Guy C. Robertson	Lawton
1919–1920	A. L. Churchhill	Vinita
1920–1921	P. C. Dings	Ardmore
	D. N. Fink	Muskogee
1921–1922	D. S. Wolfinger	Hobart
1922–1923	G. E. Dowis	Blackwell

1923–1924	F. W. Bryant	Tulsa
1924–1925	H. N. Wilson	Bokchito
1925–1926	S. L. Morley	McAlester
1926–1927	E. D. Kilpatrick	LeFlore
1927–1928	G. S. Weitzenhoffer	Oklahoma City
1928–1929	L. K. Meek	Ponca City
1929–1930	F. S. Sherwood	Hugo
1930–1931	D. P. Richardson	Union City
1931–1932	George D. Davis	Claremore
1932–1933	H. G. Hendricks	Bristow
1932–1933	Phil C. Kidd	Norman
1933–1934	W. B. Stephens	Hobart
1934–1935	S. A. Bryant	Cushing
1935–1936	J. J. Hamre	Arnett
1936–1937	M. L. Stockton	McAlester
1937–1938	K. W. Rowe	Broken Arrow
1938–1939	E. C. Love	Chandler
1939–1940	R. R. Jackson	Anadarko
1940–1941	A. E. Bradshaw	Tulsa
1941–1942	R. B. Patton	Henryetta
1942–1943	Hugh L. Harrell	Oklahoma City
1943–1944	L. C. Wright	Blackwell
1944–1945	R. W. Hutto	Norman
1945–1946	R. W. Hutto	Norman
(Continued in office; no convention held in 1945 because of the war)		
1946–1947	T. E. Burch	Wewoka
1947–1948	W. L. Stephenson	Enid
1948–1949	J. R. Meek	Ponca City
1949–1950	George M. Reeves	Vinita
1950–1951	W. D. Finney	Fort Cobb
1951–1952	H. D. Hinson	Prague
1952–1953	L. L. Males	Cheyenne
1953–1954	R. Elmo Thompson	Tulsa
1954–1955	J. L. Branen	Marshall
1955–1956	Thos D. Tarpley	Muskogee
1956–1957	K. G. Braley	Cherokee
1957–1958	O. H. Kirk	McAlester
1958–1959	Jack T. Conn	Ada

1959–1960	Guy L. Berry, Jr.	Sapulpa
1960–1961	Joe H. Carson	Stilwell
1961–1962	Art F. Bower	Fairview
1962–1963	R. S. Carmack	Hinton
1963–1964	Harvey L. Hinkle	Oklahoma City
1964–1965	R. F. Faust	Turley
1965	John L. Burford	Miami
1965–1966	Ford Simmons	Ardmore
1966–1967	R. Y. Empie	Oklahoma City
1967–1968	Marvin Millard	Tulsa
1968–1969	Hugh Jones	Woodward
1969–1970	Philip C. Kidd, Jr.	Norman
1970–1971	H. E. Rainbolt	Shawnee
1971–1972	Frank G. Kliewer, Jr.	Cordell
1972–1973	H. E. Leonard	Elgin
1973–1974	Glenn P. Ward	Tulsa
1974–1975	Morrison G. Tucker	Oklahoma City
1975–1976	Tracy Kelly	Bristow
1976	Pat Moore	Thomas
1977–1978	Walter V. Allison	Bartlesville

Appendix 2.

Oklahoma Bankers Association Fifty Year Club, 1978*

Acott, Melvin E., First National Bank, Hominy.

Armfield, Miss Floy, Cordell National Bank, Cordell.

Armstrong, S. W., Vian State Bank, Vian.

Autrey, A. H., Federal National Bank & Trust Company, Shawnee.

Bassett, Raymond E., Sand Springs State Bank, Sand Springs.

Bastin, Louis, First National Bank & Trust Company, Ardmore.

Batis, Robert, First National Bank & Trust Company, Ardmore.

Beach, James Levi, First State Bank of Altus, Altus.

Bender, Carl H., Community National Bank of Warr Acres, Oklahoma City.

Billingsley, C. L., Security State Bank, Wewoka.

Blocker, Bryan W., First National Bank, Broken Arrow.

Boggs, Willard, Liberty National Bank & Trust Company, Oklahoma City.

Briggs, Mrs. Maude Butts, First National Bank, Nash.

Brown, O. W., Citizens Security Bank & Trust Company, Bixby.

Brumbaugh, G. E., Security Bank & Trust Co., Blackwell.

Bunch, Fred, State Bank of Rocky, Rocky.

Burnett, Lester J., Homes State Bank, Hobart.

*If retired, present hometown listed.

Buttram, O. R., Tulsa Clearing House Association, Tulsa.

Camp, John N., Waukomis State Bank, Waukomis.

Chambers, Mrs. Lina B., First State Bank, Picher.

Charles, J. L., First National Bank, Lindsay.

Cole, Mrs. Theresa B., First State Bank, Cache.

Collins, Albert E., Oklahoma National Bank & Trust Company, Chickasha.

Cowherd, R. L., Bank of Commerce, Jenks.

Crawford, Charley M., First National Bank in Frederick, Frederick.

Dennis, Lester, Security State Bank, Comanche.

Dikeman, N. J., First State Bank, Anadarko.

Doughty, Horace, First State Bank of Altus, Altus.

Downing, W. E., Fourth National Bank of Tulsa, Tulsa.

Duncan, Louis W., Commercial Bank & Trust Co., Muskogee.

English, Exall, Security Bank & Trust Co., Lawton.

Ferguson, A. C., First National Bank, Hobart.

Ford, O. H., First State Bank, Grandfield, Green Valley, Arizona.

French, J. A., First National Bank of Sayre, Sayre.

Fruin, Carlotta M., First National Bank of Coyle, Coyle.

Fugate, J. H., Binger Community Bank, Binger.

Gear, G. R., City National Bank & Trust Co., Guymon.

Gearheard, R. W., First National Bank in Tonkawa, Tonkawa.

Gibbs, Raymond O., First National Bank, Rush Springs.

Glass, Roy G., Liberty National Bank & Trust Co., Oklahoma City.

Glidewell, Web, Helena National Bank, Helena.

Graalman, O. G., State Guaranty Bank, Okeene.

Green, Ira, State National Bank, Marlow.

Guiou, R. J., State National Bank, Eufaula.

Hagle, Gilbert H., City National Bank & Trust Co., Lawton.

Hampton, M. W., American National Bank & Trust Company, Shawnee.

Herrlan, C. F., First National Bank & Trust Co., Enid.

Hollis, L. V., First National Bank & Trust Co., Okmulgee.

Huckabay, T. C., Bank of the Wichitas, Snyder.

Hughes, Edward R., Stock Exchange Bank, Woodward.

Huls, Phil, Farmers & Merchants Bank, Eufaula.

Hutts, Mrs. Katherine Price, First National Bank & Trust Co., Vinita.

King, L. W., Bank of Oklahoma, Tulsa.

Kliewer, Mrs. Fay E., Cordell National Bank, Cordell.

Klima, Miles, Fourth National Bank of Tulsa, Tulsa.

Lee, George W., First National Bank, Nowata.

McClurg, O. G., First State Bank, Harrah.

McCoy, R. B., City National Bank, Lawton.

McLaury, Ray T., Farmers National Bank, Cushing.

Males, L. L., Security State Bank, Cheyenne.

Mason, Albert W., First National Bank, Durant.

Meibuhr, Arthur C., Security Bank & Trust Co., Ponca City.

Miller, Spence A., City National Bank & Trust Co., Oklahoma City.

Mitchell, C. Denton, First National Bank, Pryor.

Morris, M. Stone, First National Bank, El Reno.

Mueller, L. C., Cleveland National Bank, Cleveland.

Mullen, J. W., First National Bank, Dewey.

Owens, H. W., National Bank of McAlester, McAlester.

Painter, R. D., Farmers State Bank, Afton.

Pate, J. R., City National Bank & Trust Co., Guymon.

Patzkowsky, Ruben, Farmers & Merchants National Bank, Fairview.

Pearson, Mrs. Cornelia D., American National Bank, Lawton.

Pittman, W. H., First National Bank, Seiling.

Pralle, Walter E., Bank of Garber, Garber.

Priddy, C. L., National Bank of McAlester, McAlester.

Ross, Jess, Citizens National Bank of Muskogee, Muskogee.

Rupp, Mac W., Bank of Commerce, Tulsa.

Seals, Denver F., Security Bank & Trust Co., Miami.

Shafer, Charles E., First National Bank, Nowata.

Sherman, E. L., McClain County National Bank, Purcell.

Snodgrass, J. H., First National Bank & Trust Company, Ardmore.

Stidham, G. W., Peoples National Bank, Checotah.

Stottisberry, Homer, Central National Bank, Poteau.

Symcox, J. Raymond, City National Bank & Trust Co., Norman.

Tabor, E. E., First National Bank, Carter.

Thompson, D. R., First State Bank, Jones.

Thompson, V. M., First National Bank of Weatherford, Weatherford.

Toews, Henry G., Security National Bank of Enid, Enid.

Turner, Clyde B., Oklahoma National Bank & Trust Co., Chickasha.

Upton, H. B., First National Bank, Tahlequah.

Van Noy, W. W., First Wagoner Bank & Trust Co., Wagoner.

Vaughn, William H., Utica National Bank & Trust Co., Tulsa.

Wells, Darvin Earl, Bank of Hunter, Hunter.

Whitten, George C., City National Bank & Trust Co., Lawton.

Wilbanks, P. R., Security National Bank, Coweta.

Winder, James H., Oklahoma National Bank & Trust Co., Chickasha, Westminster, California.

Wright, James Ralph, First National Bank & Trust Co., Muskogee.

Wynn, Ivy M., Fourth National Bank of Tulsa, Tulsa.

Notes

PREFACE

1. Interview, Tom J. Hartman, May 13, 1937, in Grant Foreman, comp., "Pioneer and Indian History," 112 vols., Indian Archives, Oklahoma Historical Society, Oklahoma City, 18: 386 (hereafter cited as "Pioneer-Indian History").

CHAPTER 1

1. *Daily Oklahoman,* April 23, 1939. For more detail on Bernard de la Harpe see Ralph A. Smith, ed. and trans., "Account of the Journey of Bernard de la Harpe," *Southwestern Historical Quarterly,* 62 (1962): 75–86, 246–59, 371–85, 525–41.
2. *Daily Oklahoman,* April 23, 1939; Edwin C. McReynolds, *Oklahoma: A History of the Sooner State,* pp. 20, 26–27.
3. E. H. Kelley, Notes, 1955, Kelley Collection, Archives (hereafter cited as KCA), Oklahoma Historical Society, Oklahoma City (hereafter cited as OHS).
4. McReynolds, *Oklahoma,* pp. 62–65.
5. Harry R. Stevens, "Hugh Glenn," in LeRoy R. Hafen, ed., *The Mountain Men and the Fur Trade of the Far West,* 2: 165–69. Also see Phillip D. Thomas, "Thomas James, Hugh Glenn, and Jacob Fowler, 1821–1823," in Joseph A. Stout, Jr., ed., *Frontier Adventures,* pp. 61–79.
6. James Neal, Notes, 1942, Archives, Oklahoma Bankers Association, Oklahoma City (hereafter cited as OBA).
7. Ibid.
8. Glenn Shirley, *Henry Starr: Last of the Real Badmen.*
9. James Neal, Scrapbook, 1942, Archives, OBA.
10. *Sunday Oklahoman* (Oklahoma City), February 24, 1963.
11. *Daily Oklahoman,* April 23, 1939; McReynolds, *Oklahoma,* p. 170.
12. *Daily Oklahoman,* April 23, 1939.
13. Kelley, Scrapbook, 1955, KCA, OHS; *Daily Oklahoman,* April 23, 1939.
14. *Daily Oklahoman,* April 23, 1939.
15. E. H. Kelley, "Notes on Early Banking in Oklahoma," *Oklahoma Banker,* April, 1955, p. 19.
16. McReynolds, *Oklahoma,* pp. 270–75; Roy Gittinger, *The Formation of the State of Oklahoma, 1803–1906,* p. 186.
17. Kelley, Scrapbook, 1955, KCA, OHS.

18. B. L. Phipps, "Banking in Indian Territory During the 1880s," *Chronicles of Oklahoma,* 7 (June, 1929): 186–87.

19. Interview, Hartman, May 13, 1937.

20. Bert Willis, "Memories," pp. 25–26, typescript copy, Archives, OBA.

21. Interview, Henry Vogel, February 19, 1937, "Pioneer-Indian History," 2: 89–96.

22. Kelley, "Notes on Early Banking in Oklahoma," *Oklahoma Banker,* October, 1954, p. 8.

23. Interview, Jake Simmons, February 24, 1937, "Pioneer-Indian History," 9: 345–409.

24. Interview, W. Jack Conn, March 12, 1977, Oklahoma Banking Collection (hereafter cited as OBC), Oklahoma Heritage Association, Oklahoma City.

25. Ibid.

26. *Daily Oklahoman,* April 23, 1939.

27. Interview, Sam Erwin, June 15, 1937, "Pioneer-Indian History," 24: 96.

28. Phipps, "Banking in Indian Territory During the 1880s," pp. 186–87.

29. Interview, Hartman, May 13, 1937.

30. *South McAlester* (Okla.) *Capitol,* January 6, 1898; James D. Morrison, "Problems in the Industrial Progress and Development of the Choctaw Nation, 1865–1907," *Chronicles of Oklahoma,* 32 (Spring, 1954): 91.

31. Kelley, "Notes on the Early History of Banking in Oklahoma," *Oklahoma Banker,* August, 1954, p. 14.

32. Ibid.

33. Ibid., July, 1954, p. 7.

34. Ibid., October, 1956, p. 29.

CHAPTER 2

1. Kelley, Scrapbook, 1948, KCA, OHS.

2. Ibid.

3. Ibid.

4. *Lexington* (Okla.) *Leader,* June 11, 1891; *Oklahoma Daily Journal* (Oklahoma City), June 4, 1891.

5. Kelley, Scrapbook, 1948, KCA, OHS.

6. Ibid.; *Oklahoma Daily Journal,* November 21, 1890.

7. *Oklahoma Daily Journal,* November 22–23, 1890; Kelley, Scrapbook, 1948, KCA, OHS.

8. *Oklahoma Daily Capitol* (Guthrie), July 20, 1891.

9. Kelley, Scrapbook, 1948, KCA, OHS.

10. Ibid.

11. Interview, Hartman, May 13, 1937.

12. *Daily Oklahoman,* April 23, 1939.

13. *Oklahoma Daily Capitol,* September 18, 1889.

14. Charles J. Kappler, ed., *Indian Affairs: Laws and Treaties,* 4 vols. (Washington, D.C.: Government Printing Office, 1904), 3: 48–54.

15. Ibid.

16. Oklahoma Bankers' Association, *Proceedings: Sixth Annual Convention, 1902* (Guthrie: State Capital Printing Company, 1902), pp. 34–37.

17. State of Kansas, Corporation Book No. 35, 1889–1891, Archives, Kansas Historical Society, Topeka; Kelley, "Notes on Early Banking in Oklahoma," *Oklahoma Banker,* March, 1954, p. 97.

18. William B. Moore, "John Henry Dill, 1868–1942," *Chronicles of Oklahoma,* 20 (September, 1942): 289–91.

19. Wyatt W. Belcher, "Political Leadership of Robert L. Owen," *Chronicles of Oklahoma,* 31 (Winter, 1953–1954): 361–71.

20. *Oklahoma Banker,* June, 1950, pp. 9–10.

21. Interview, Daniel Lanning, undated, "Pioneer-Indian History," 104: 487.

22. Interview, H. R. Warren, March 31, 1937, ibid., 2: 396.

23. Interview, Thomas Howell, August 30, 1937, ibid., 30: 244; Interview, W. C. Morris, September 30, 1937, ibid., 30: 144.

24. Kelley, "Notes on Early Banking in Oklahoma," *Oklahoma Banker,* July, 1954, p. 7.

25. *Oklahoma Banker,* April, 1948, pp. 44–45.

26. Ibid., p. 45.

27. Ibid.

28. *Daily Oklahoman,* April 23, 1939.

29. Kelley, Notes, 1948, KCA, OHS.

30. Ibid.

31. *Daily Oklahoman,* April 23, 1939.

32. Ibid.

33. *Guthrie* (Okla.) *Daily Leader,* July 21, 1893; *Guthrie* (Okla.) *Daily News,* July 21, 1893.

34. Kelley, "Notes on Early Banking in Oklahoma," *Oklahoma Banker,* July, 1954, p. 7.

35. *South McAlester Capitol,* September 13, 1894, May 28, October 8, November 19, 1896, March 11, 1897.

36. *Tulsa Daily World,* July 29, 1950.

37. Kelley, "Notes on Early Banking in Oklahoma," *Oklahoma Banker,* April, 1955, p. 19.

38. Abraham J. Seay, Report of the Governor of Oklahoma to the Secretary of the Interior, October 1, 1892 (Washington, D.C.: Government Printing Office, 1893), pp. 455–65; McReynolds, *Oklahoma,* pp. 298–99.

39. Interview, H. H. Champlin, April 17, 1937, "Pioneer-Indian History," 19: 196.

40. Joseph B. Thoburn, "John J. Gerloch," *Chronicles of Oklahoma,* 10 (March, 1932): 34–43.

41. Interview, Frank Nickerson, October 20, 1937, "Pioneer-Indian History," 102: 127.

42. Interview, Robert B. Stafford, March 9, 1937, ibid., 10: 418.

43. Ibid.

44. *Oklahoma Banker,* June, 1912, pp. 311–17.

45. Kelley, Notes, 1955, KCA, OHS; *Alva* (Okla.) *Pioneer,* November 10, 17, December 1, 1893, November 23, 1894; *Alva* (Okla.) *Republican,* February 28, 1896; Banking Files, Secretary of Oklahoma Territory, June 14, 1894, Archives, OHS.

46. Exchange Bank (Perry, Oklahoma), Memo book, Ledger book, February 20, 1896, Archives, OHS; E. W. Jones, *Early Days of Perry, Oklahoma* (Perry, Oklahoma: n. p. 1931), p. 13.

47. Jones, *Early Days of Perry, Oklahoma,* p. 13.

48. John P. Hill to James Smallwood, April 23, 1978, Archives, OBA.

CHAPTER 3

1. *Oklahoma Banker,* February, 1910, pp. 250–51.

2. Interview, Robert B. Stafford, March 9, 1937, "Pioneer Indian History," 10: 000.

3. Cassius M. Barnes, *Report of the Governor of Oklahoma,* 1897 (Washington, D.C.: Government Printing Office, 1897), pp. 22–23.

4. *Daily Oklahoman,* April 24, 1897.

5. *Oklahoma Banker,* June, 1912, p. 314.

6. *Fifty Years Forward* (Oklahoma City: First National Bank, 1939), p. 5.

7. *Banking and Corporation Laws of Oklahoma, 1893–1901* (Guthrie: State Capital Printing Company, 1901), pp. 53–74; *Proceedings of the Oklahoma Bankers Association, 1902* (Guthrie: State Capital Printing Company, 1902), pp. 34–37.

8. *Banking and Corporation Laws of Oklahoma, 1893–1901,* pp. 79–100.

9. *Proceedings of the Oklahoma Bankers Association, 1902,* pp. 34–37.

10. Kelley, Notes, 1948, KCA, OHS.

11. J. A. Henry to William Jenkins, March 3, 1900, Archives, OHS.

12. H. Clay Willis to William Grimes, October 5, 1903, Archives, OHS. Grimes to Willis, October 15, 1903, ibid.

13. W. Jenkins to Donald James, March 20, 1902, ibid.; "Day of the Run," *Mid-Central Banker,* April, 1955, p. 89.

14. *Oklahoma Banker,* April, 1948, p. 44.

15. Ibid.

16. "Day of the Run," *Mid-Central Banker,* April, 1955, p. 89.

17. *Daily Oklahoman,* April 23, 1939.

18. Ibid.

19. Interview, Tom J. Hartman, May 13, 1937, "Pioneer Indian History," 18: 000; *Proceedings of the Oklahoma Bankers Association 1903* (Guthrie: Capital Printing Company, 1903), pp. 29–30.

20. See, for example, *Proceedings of the Oklahoma Bankers Association, 1903.*

21. *Proceedings of the Oklahoma Bankers Association, 1901* (Guthrie: Capital Printing Company, 1901), pp. 81–91.

22. *Proceedings of the Oklahoma Bankers Association, 1903,* p. 186.

23. *Tulsa Daily World,* July 29, 1950.

24. Ibid.
25. Ibid.
26. Ibid.
27. *Oklahoma Banker,* April, 1948, p. 44.
28. *Daily Oklahoman,* April 23, 1939.
29. *Anadarko* (Okla.) *Daily News,* June 3, 1951; Interview, Leon Fielder, January 12, 1938, "Pioneer-Indian History," 105: 331.
30. *Proceedings of the Indian Territory Bankers Association 1901, 1902* (Kansas City, Missouri: Hudson-Kimberly Publishing Company, 1902).
31. *Proceedings of the Oklahoma Bankers Association, 1903,* pp. 146–200.
32. *Proceedings of the Oklahoma Bankers Association, 1906* (Guthrie: Capital Printing Company, 1906), pp. 21–22.
33. *The Indian Citizen* (Atoka), May 3, 1906.
34. *Oklahoma Banker,* October, 1955, p. 20.
35. Ibid.
36. Ibid.
37. *Sunday Oklahoman,* April 23, 1939.

CHAPTER 4

1. *Proceedings of the Oklahoma Bankers Association, 1908* (Oklahoma City: Western Bank Supply Company, 1908).
2. See the *Constitution of the State of Oklahoma, 1907,* Article 14.
3. *Daily Oklahoman,* April 23, 1939.
4. Ibid.; Edwin C. McReynolds, *Oklahoma,* p. 319.
5. *Daily Oklahoman,* April 23, 1939.
6. *Oklahoma Banker,* November, 1942, pp. 22–24.
7. Ibid.
8. Ibid., January, 1910, p. 201.
9. *Daily Oklahoman,* April 23, 1939.
10. *Oklahoma Banker,* October, 1913, p. 109.
11. Ibid., September, 1916, pp. 80–81.
12. Kelley, Notes, 1948, KCA, OHS.
13. *Oklahoma Banker,* June, 1910, p. 376; Ibid., February, 1910, pp. 250–51.
14. Kelley, Notes, 1948, KCA, OHS.
15. Ibid.
16. Ibid.
17. *Oklahoma Banker,* May, 1913, pp. 325, 346.
18. Ibid., May, 1913, pp. 325–26; Ibid., February, 1914, p. 241.
19. Ibid., November, 1913, pp. 133–35; Ibid., December, 1913, pp. 188–90.
20. Kelley, Notes, 1948, KCA, OHS.
21. *Oklahoma Banker,* January, 1915, pp. 216–17.
22. Kelley, Notes, 1955, KCA, OHS.
23. Ibid.
24. *Oklahoma Banker,* December, 1912, p. 170.
25. *Oklahoma Farmer-Stockman* (Oklahoma City), October 25, 1915.

26. *Oklahoma Banker,* February, 1915, p. 261; Ibid., March, 1916, pp. 270–74.

27. Ibid., February, 1916, pp. 238–41; Ibid., March, 1916, pp. 270–74.

28. Garin Burbank, *When Farmers Voted Red,* p. 101; *Oklahoma Banker,* November, 1913, pp. 138–39.

29. Robert L. Williams to E. F. Rines, January 5, February 16, 1916, R. L. Williams Papers, Archives, OHS; Burbank, *When Farmers Voted Red,* pp. 91, 101.

30. *Oklahoma Banker,* May, 1910, p. 11.

31. *Johnston County Capital—Democrat* (Tishomingo, Okla.), May 19, 1977.

32. Kelley, Notes, 1948, KCA, OHS.

33. Ibid.

34. *Oklahoma Banker,* October, 1912, p. 101.

35. Ibid., pp. 101–102.

36. Ibid., January, 1913, p. 204.

37. Ibid.; *Eufaula* (Okla.) *Indian Journal,* March 15, 1915.

38. Glenn Shirley, *Henry Starr: Last of the Real Badmen,* pp. 162–81.

39. *Daily Oklahoman,* March 2, 1915.

40. See Shirley, *Henry Starr.*

41. *Chandler* (Okla.) *News-Publicist,* April 15, July 23, August 6 and 13, 1915.

42. Ibid.; Shirley, *Henry Starr,* pp. 167–81.

43. *Oklahoma Banker,* October, 1912, p. 112.

44. Ibid., March, 1920, p. 17.

CHAPTER 5

1. Kelley, Notes, 1948, KCA, OHS.

2. *Oklahoma Banker,* October, 1915, p. 111.

3. Ibid., December, 1915, pp. 166–67; Ibid., February, 1917, pp. 233–34.

4. Ibid., December, 1916, p. 171.

5. Ibid.

6. Paul Studenski and Herman F. Krooss, *Financial History of the United States,* p. 289.

7. Ibid.

8. *Oklahoma Banker,* June, 1917, p. 335; Ibid., October, 1917, p. 509.

9. Ibid., November, 1917, pp. 542–49.

10. The table is taken from Ibid., May, 1919, pp. 30, 35.

11. Kelley, Notes, 1955, KCA, OHS.

12. *Oklahoma Banker,* March, 1918, p. 686.

13. Ibid.; Kelley, Notes, 1955, KCA, OHS.

14. Ibid.

15. Timothy W. Hubbard and Lewis E. Davids, *Banking in Mid-America: A History of Missouri's Banks,* pp. 153–54.

16. Ibid., p. 154.

17. Kelley, Notes, 1955, KCA, OHS.

18. Press releases and notes, 1919, Liberty National Bank, Collection, Oklahoma City.

19. Interview, Jack Conn, May 24, 1978, OBC.

20. Ibid.; *Oklahoma Banker,* April, 1922, p. 16.

21. Oklahoma Banking Commission, Consolidated Reports, 1908–1928, Archives, OBC.

22. Interview, Frankie McClurg, June 17, 1977, OBC.

23. E. D. Kilpatrick, Notes, 1927, Archives, OBA.

24. Eugene Swearingen, Notes, n. d., Archives, OBA.

25. Interview, Conn, May 24, 1978, OBC.

26. *Oklahoma Banker,* February, 1927, pp. 15–16; Ibid., October, 1929, pp. 25–26.

27. Interview, Conn, May 24, 1978, OBC.

28. Oklahoma City, Federal Reserve Bank, Scrapbook, Archives, OBA.

29. *Oklahoma Banker,* May, 1922, p. 29.

30. Kelley, Notes, 1955, KCA, OHS.

31. *Oklahoma Banker,* April, 1923, p. 23.

32. Kelley, Notes, 1955, KCA, OHS.

33. *Oklahoma Banker,* July, 1923, pp. 9–12; Ibid., July, 1924, p. 12.

34. Eugene P. Gum, memoranda, 1924–1930, "Report on Bank Robberies and Burglaries in Oklahoma, 1920–1930," Archives, OBA.

35. Gum, "The Facts in the Case of Eddie Shoquette," 1921, MS, Archives, OBA.

36. Ibid.

37. *Oklahoma Banker,* November, 1924, pp. 13–15.

38. Ibid.

39. Gum, memoranda, 1924–1925, "Report on Bank Robberies and Burglaries, 1924–1925," Archives, OBA.

40. *Oklahoma Banker,* April, 1925, pp. 9–11; Ibid., November, 1925, pp. 19–20.

41. Gum, Notes, 1925, Archives, OBA.

42. *Oklahoma Banker,* June, 1929, pp. 16–18.

43. Gum, memoranda, 1926–1928, Archives, OBA.

44. Gum to OBA members, August 10, 1928, Archives, OBA.

45. *Oklahoma Banker,* April, 1927, pp. 12–13; Ibid., May, 1927, pp. 20–21; Ibid., August, 1927, p. 10; Ibid., September, 1927, pp. 28–30.

46. Ibid., August, 1929, p. 12.

47. Ibid., pp. 12–16.

48. Ibid., September, 1927, pp. 38–39.

49. Ibid.

50. Ibid., p. 32.

51. Ibid.

52. Interview, Conn, May 24, 1978, OBC.

53. Interview, McClurg, June 17, 1977, OBC.

54. H. L. Brunt to Gum, July 21, 1928, Archives, OBA.

55. Ibid.; *Oklahoma Banker,* September, 1927, pp. 23–24.

CHAPTER 6

1. *New York Times,* October 14, 1929.
2. Studenski and Krooss, *Financial History,* p. 353.
3. E. H. Kelley, Notes, 1955, KCA, OHS.
4. Interview, Conn, May 24, 1978, OBC.
5. Interview, Charles Vose, Sr., May 30, 1978, ibid.
6. Interview, Maybelle Kennedy, May 26, 1977, ibid.
7. Ibid.
8. Ibid.
9. Ibid.
10. Interview, Conn, May 24, 1978, ibid.
11. Ibid.
12. Oklahoma State Banking Commission, Consolidated Reports of the Commissioner, 1928, 1930, 1932, MSS, Archives, OBC; United States Comptroller of the Currency, *Annual Report, 1928* (Washington, D.C.: Government Printing Office, 1929), pp. 30, 32.
13. Kelley, Notes, 1955, KCA, OHS.
14. Interview, Conn, May 24, 1978, OBC.
15. *Oklahoma Banker,* June, 1933, p. 22.
16. Kelley, Notes, 1955, KCA, OHS.
17. United States Federal Reserve Board, *Monetary Statistics, 1943* (Washington, D.C.: Government Printing Office, 1944); Studenski and Krooss, *Financial History,* pp. 373–79.
18. William E. Leuchtenburg, *Franklin D. Roosevelt and the New Deal, 1932–1940,* pp. 71–72; Kelley, Notes, 1955, KCA, OHS.
19. Leuchtenburg, *Franklin D. Roosevelt and the New Deal,* pp. 18–40.
20. Ibid., pp. 41–45.
21. *Daily Oklahoman,* April 23, 1939.
22. Kelley, Notes, 1955, KCA, OHS.
23. Ibid.; *Oklahoma Banker,* March, 1955, p. 22.
24. Interview, McClurg, June 17, 1977, OBC.
25. Studenski and Krooss, *Financial History,* p. 383.
26. United States Federal Reserve Board, *Annual Report, 1933* (Washington, D.C.: Government Printing Office, 1934), pp. 275–95; United States, Public Law No. 66 (HR5661), 73d Congress.
27. *Journal of the American Bankers Association,* September, 1933, p. 96.
28. *Oklahoma Banker,* June, 1933, p. 21.
29. Ibid., August, 1933, pp. 5–6.
30. Interview, Conn, May 24, 1978, OBC.
31. Interview, Howard Bozarth, May 30, 1978, OBC.
32. Ibid.
33. Interview, Conn, May 24, 1978, OBC.
34. *Oklahoma Banker,* October, 1933, p. 12.
35. Ibid., December, 1932, p. 19.
36. Ibid.

37. *Daily Oklahoman,* January 2, 1978.
38. *Kansas City Star,* November 20, 1932.
39. Gum, Notes on Charles Floyd, 1933, Archives, OBA.
40. Ibid.; Gum to OBA, February 15, 1932.
41. *Frederick* (Okla.) *Press,* October 13, 1933; C. M. Crawford, Notes, 1977, Archives, OBA.
42. Kelley, Notes, 1955, KCA, OHS.
43. Ibid.
44. Ibid.; *Oklahoma Banker,* November, 1934, p. 12.
45. Kelley, Notes, 1955, KCA, OHS.
46. *Daily Oklahoman,* January 2, 1978.
47. Ibid.
48. *New York Times,* October 23, 1934.
49. Gum, "Report on Robberies and Attempted Robberies, 1932–1941," MS, Archives, OBA.
50. Kelley, Notes, 1955, KCA, OHS.
51. *Oklahoma Banker,* April, 1930, p. 36.
52. Ibid.
53. Ibid., p. 37.
54. R. R. Jackson to Tom Hartman, n. d., 1945, Archives, OBA.
55. Lloyd C. Riggs, "Mike Flanagan: Banker and Community Rebuilder," *Bank News,* April 15, 1954, pp. 26–28.
56. Ibid.
57. Ibid.
58. *Oklahoma Banker,* December, 1938, p. 4.
59. Ibid., pp. 4–6.
60. Memos, December, 1942, Archives, OBA.
61. Kelley, Notes, 1955, KCA, OHS.
62. Ibid.; *Oklahoma Banker,* December, 1942, pp. 20–23; Also see memos, 1933, Archives, OBA.
63. *Daily Phoenix* (Muskogee, Okla.), June 23, 1959; *Oklahoma City Times,* August 29, 1961; *Daily Oklahoman,* August 30, 1961; Gum to A. B. Rivers, July 12, 1943, file on J. C. Fast, Jr., Archives, OBA.

CHAPTER 7

1. Paul B. Trescott, *Financing American Enterprise,* p. 213.
2. *Oklahoma Banker,* May, 1941, p. 25.
3. Kelley, Notes, 1955, KCA, OHS.
4. *Oklahoma Banker,* January, 1944, p. 6.
5. Ibid., June, 1941, pp. 22–23; Ibid., October, 1943, p. 21; Ibid., August, 1944, pp. 40–41; Kelley, Notes, 1955.
6. *Oklahoma Banker,* June, 1941, p. 23; Kelley, Notes, 1948.
7. Consolidated Reports, 1941, Oklahoma Banking Commissioner, Archives, Oklahoma Banking Department; Comptroller of the Currency, *Annual Reports, 1941,* (Washington, D.C.: Government Printing Office, 1941), pp. 84–87.

8. Consolidated Reports, 1942, Oklahoma Banking Commissioner, Archives, Oklahoma Banking Department; *Oklahoma Banker,* July, 1942, pp. 16–17.
9. Interview, Maybelle Kennedy, May 26, 1977, OBC.
10. *Oklahoma Banker,* July, 1942, p. 22.
11. Kelley, Notes, 1948, KCA, OHS.
12. *Oklahoma Banker,* July, 1942, p. 20.
13. Kelley, Notes, 1955, KCA, OHS.
14. *Oklahoma Banker,* July, 1942, pp. 21–22.
15. Kelley, Notes, 1948, KCA, OHS.
16. *Oklahoma Banker,* July, 1941, p. 9; Ibid., December, 1941, p. 14.
17. Kelley, Notes, 1948, KCA, OHS.
18. The table in the text was taken from the *Oklahoma Banker,* May, 1942, p. 21.
19. Ibid.
20. George L. Brown, "History of the Citizens Security Bank," MS, Archives, OBA.
21. Ibid.
22. Interview, Conn, May 24, 1978, OBC.
23. Ibid.
24. The ledger sheet in the text is taken from Ralph Chambers to OBA, June 9, 1944, Archives, OBA.
25. *Oklahoma Banker,* March, 1945, p. 24.
26. Kelley, Notes, 1955, KCA, OHS.
27. *Oklahoma Banker,* July, 1947, pp. 7–10.
28. Ibid.
29. Kelley, Notes, 1948, KCA, OHS.
30. *Oklahoma Banker,* May, 1945, pp. 28–38.
31. Interview, Bozarth, May 30, 1978, OBC.
32. *Oklahoma Banker,* May, 1946, pp. 13–14.
33. Kelley, Notes, 1955, KCA, OHS.
34. Ibid.
35. *Oklahoma Banker,* July, 1948, p. 30.
36. Ibid., July, 1949, pp. 37–39.
37. Ibid., July, 1950, pp. 12–16.
38. Kelley, Notes, 1955, KCA, OHS.
39. Ibid.
40. *Oklahoma Banker,* August, 1941, pp. 13–16.
41. Interview, Vose, May 30, 1978, OBC.
42. Interview, Bozarth, May 30, 1978, OBC.
43. Ibid.

CHAPTER 8

1. United States Bureau of the Census, *U.S. Census of Population: 1960.* Volume I, *Characteristics of the Population.* Part 38, *Oklahoma* (Washington, D.C.: U.S. Government Printing Office, 1963), pp. 10–18.

2. United States Bureau of the Census, *U.S. Census of Population: 1970.* Volume I, *Characteristics of the Population.* Part 38, *Oklahoma* (Washington, D.C.: Government Printing Office, 1973), pp. 8–25.

3. *Oklahoma Banker,* October, 1955, p. 28; Ibid., September, 1957, p. 30; Ibid., July, 1958, p. 30; Ibid., September, 1961, p. 13.

4. Ibid., November, 1955, pp. 7–10.

5. Ibid.

6. Memos, 1951–1961, Archives, OBA.

7. *Oklahoma Banker,* June, 1953, p. 4; Ibid., May, 1961, p. 16.

8. Robert A. Hefner to H. A. Montgomery, January 20, 1942, Stanley Draper Collection, Archives, OHA; Jack Hull, "Tinker Air Force Base," MS Draper Collection; James Smallwood, *Urban Builder: The Life and Times of Stanley Draper,* pp. 102–107.

9. Hefner to Montgomery, January 20, 1942, Draper Collection; Smallwood, *Urban Builder,* pp. 102–105.

10. Memos, 1945–1958, Archives, OBA.

11. *Oklahoma Banker,* March, 1973, pp. 19–26.

12. Ibid.

13. Memos, 1970–1974, Archives, OBA.

14. *Oklahoma Banker,* March, 1973, pp. 19–20, 25.

15. Memos, 1973–1974, Archives, OBA.

16. Carl Coke Rister, *Oil: Titan of the Southwest.*

17. Memos, 1953–1954, Archives, OBA.

18. Ibid.

19. *Oklahoma Banker,* September, 1955, p. 7.

20. Ibid., July, 1961, p. 16.

21. Interview, Vose, May 30, 1978, OBC.

22. Ibid.

23. Memos, 1963–1967, Archives, OBA.

24. *Oklahoma Banker,* June, 1960, pp. 28–30, 50.

25. Memos, 1955–1960, Archives, OBA.

26. *Oklahoma Banker,* July, 1973, pp. 7, 9–11, 26.

27. Interview, Vose, May 30, 1978, OBC.

28. Unidentified newspaper clippings, November, 1976, Archives, OHA.

29. "Eugene L. Swearingen," Archives, OHA.

30. Unidentified newspaper clipping, March 18, 1977, Archives, OHA.

31. *Oklahoma Banker,* July, 1973, p. 9.

32. *Tulsa Tribune,* November 9, 11, 1963; *New York Times,* January 25, 1964.

33. *Tulsa Tribune,* November 9, 11, 1963.

34. Ibid.

35. Ibid., November 9, 1963.

36. Ibid., November 11, 1963.

37. Ibid., November 9, 11, 1963, January 24, 1964.

38. Ibid., April, 1968, p. 44.

39. Memos, 1967–1970, Archives, OBA.

40. *Oklahoma Banker,* June, 1967, p. 40.

41. *Oklahoma Banker,* October, 1960, p. 31.

42. Ibid., February, 1972, pp. 4–5.

43. Ibid.; *Oklahoma County Herald* (Harrah, Okla.), November 7, 1957; *Oklahoma County News* (Jones City, Okla.), November 7, 1957; *Oklahoma City Times,* November 5, 1957; Mrs. Frankie Jo McClurg, Scrapbook, Archives, OBA.

44. *Oklahoma City Times,* December 31, 1956.

45. Ibid.

46. *McAlester* (Okla.) *News-Capital,* December 13, 1968.

47. *Oklahoma City Times,* October 23, 1968.

48. Bank Robbery file and memos, 1950–1970, Archives, OBA.

49. *Daily Oklahoman,* October 24, 1968.

50. *Sapulpa* (Okla.) *Daily Herald,* September 20, 1968; *Daily Oklahoman,* September 24, 1968; *Latimer County News* (Wilburton, Okla.), September 26, 1968; *County Journal* (Medford, Okla.), November 11, 1968.

51. *Oklahoma Banker,* January, 1969, pp. 36–37; Ibid., February, 1969, pp. 7–9.

52. Ibid., January, 1976, p. 5.

53. Ibid.

54. *Oklahoma Banker,* January, 1976, pp. 5–6.

55. Interview, Vose, May 30, 1978, OBC.

56. Interview, Maybelle Kennedy, May 26, 1977, OBC.

57. Interview, Vose, May 30, 1978, OBC.

58. Memos, 1976, Archives, OBA; *Oklahoma Banker,* April, 1976, p. 20.

59. *Oklahoma Banker,* July, 1976, pp. 13, 16, 22.

60. Ibid.; Memos, 1978, Archives, OBA.

CHAPTER 9

1. Oklahoma Bankers Association, *The Official Directory of Oklahoma Bankers,* 1978.

2. *Oklahoma Banker,* March, 1970, p. 6.

3. Ibid., pp. 6–8.

4. Interview, Paul Lambert, May 30, 1978, OBC; Smallwood, *Urban Builder,* pp. 239–45.

5. Memos, 1969–1975, Archives, OBA.

6. *Oklahoma City Times,* November 10, 1971; *Oklahoma Banker,* November, 1969, p. 57.

7. Memos, 1969–1970, Archives, OBA.

8. *Oklahoma Banker,* October, 1971, pp. 6–7.

9. Ibid., March, 1971, p. 11; Ibid., October, 1971, p. 7.

10. Ibid., January, 1969, p. 30.

11. Memos, 1969–1970, Archives, OBA.

12. *Oklahoma Banker,* November, 1970, p. 7.

13. Interview, Vose, May 30, 1978, OBC.
14. *Oklahoma Banker,* November, 1970, p. 7.
15. Ibid.
16. Ibid.
17. *Stillwater News-Press,* February 12, 1978.
18. Ibid.
19. Ibid.
20. Memos, 1973, Archives, OBA.
21. Ibid.
22. The tables in the text were taken from the *Oklahoma Banker,* August, 1973, p. 9.
23. Memos, 1973, Archives, OBA.
24. *Oklahoma Banker,* March, 1972, p. 9.
25. Memos, 1970–1973, Archives, OBA.
26. Ibid.
27. *Oklahoma Banker,* October, 1976, p. 5.
28. Ibid., pp. 5–7.
29. Ibid., p. 7.
30. Ibid.
31. The table was taken from ibid., p. 22.
32. Memos, 1976–1977, Archives, OBA.
33. *Oklahoma Banker,* November, 1976, p. 22.
34. Ibid.
35. Ibid., p. 26.
36. Ibid.
37. Ibid., July, 1976, p. 22.
38. Ibid., October, 1976, p. 8.
39. Ibid.
40. Memos, 1969–1976, Archives, OBA.
41. *Oklahoma Banker,* March, 1969, p. 26.
42. Memos, 1968–1976, Archives, OBA.
43. Ibid., 1967–1969.
44. *Oklahoma Banker,* March, 1969, p. 16.
45. *Oklahoma City Times,* January 26, 1977; *Stillwater News-Press,* February 23, 1978.
46. *Stillwater News-Press,* February 23, 1978.
47. Ibid.
48. *Daily Oklahoman,* January 12, 1978.
49. Ibid.

EPILOGUE

1. Interview, Vose, May 30, 1978, OBC; Interview, Conn, May 24, 1978, OBC.
2. Interview, Vose, May 30, 1978. OBC.

3. Ibid.

4. Interview, Bozarth, May 30, 1978, OBC; *Oklahoma City Times,* June 1, 1978.

5. Interview, Gilliland, July 7, 1978, OBC.

6. Interview, F. A. Sewell, III, July 13, 1978; Interview, R. D. Painter, July 13, 1978; Interview, W. L. Stephenson, Jr., July 13, 1978; Interview, Roretta Werner, July 13, 1978; Interview, Bob Powers, July 13, 1978. OBC.

7. Interview, Stephenson, July 13, 1978; Interview, Painter, July 13, 1978. OBC.

8. Interview, Gilliland, July 7, 1978. OBC.

Bibliography

PRIMARY SOURCES

Manuscripts, Manuscript Collections, and Government Documents

Atoka State Bank of Atoka, Oklahoma. Collection. Atoka, Oklahoma.

Bank of Oklahoma. Collection. Tulsa, Oklahoma.

Bank of Commerce of Guthrie, Oklahoma. Collection. Oklahoma Historical Society, Oklahoma City, Oklahoma.

Barnes, Cassius M. *Report of the Governor of Oklahoma, 1897.* Washington, D.C.: Government Printing Office, 1898.

City National Bank and Trust of Oklahoma City. Collection. Oklahoma City, Oklahoma.

Citizens Bank of Wakita, Oklahoma. Collection. Wakita, Oklahoma.

Citizens Security Bank of Bixby, Oklahoma. Collection. Bixby, Oklahoma.

Delaware County Bank. Collection. Jay, Oklahoma.

Draper, Stanley C. Collection. Archives, Oklahoma Heritage Association, Oklahoma City, Oklahoma.

Exchange Bank and Trust Company at Perry, Oklahoma. Collection. Perry, Oklahoma.

Fidelity Bank of Oklahoma City. Collection. Oklahoma City, Oklahoma.

Financial Systems, Oklahoma District. Collection. Oklahoma City, Oklahoma.

First Bank of Haskell, Oklahoma. Collection. Haskell, Oklahoma.

First National Bank of Altus, Oklahoma. Collection. Altus, Oklahoma.

First National Bank of Frederick, Oklahoma. Collection. Frederick, Oklahoma.

First National Bank of Mountain View, Oklahoma. Collection. Mountain View, Oklahoma.

First National Bank of Rush Springs, Oklahoma. Collection. Rush Springs, Oklahoma.

First National Bank of Seminole, Oklahoma. Collection. Seminole, Oklahoma.

First National Bank of Stillwater, Oklahoma. Collection. Stillwater, Oklahoma.

First National Bank and Trust Company of Muskogee, Oklahoma. Collection. Muskogee, Oklahoma.

First National Bank and Trust Company of Oklahoma City. Collection. Oklahoma City, Oklahoma.

First National Bank and Trust Company of Tulsa, Oklahoma. Collection. Tulsa, Oklahoma.

First National Bank and Trust Company of Vinita, Oklahoma. Collection. Vinita, Oklahoma.

First State Bank of Canute, Oklahoma. Collection. Canute, Oklahoma.

First State Bank of Olney, Oklahoma. Collection. Olney, Oklahoma.

First State Bank of Picher, Oklahoma. Collection. Picher, Oklahoma.

Foreman, Grant, comp. "Pioneer and Indian History." 113 vols. Manuscript collection. Indian Archives. Oklahoma Historical Society.

Gum, Eugene P. Collection. Archives, Oklahoma Bankers Association, Oklahoma City, Oklahoma.

Indian Territory Bankers Association. *Proceedings, First Annual Convention, 1901.* Kansas City, Missouri: Hudson-Kimberly Publishing Co., 1902.

———. *Proceedings, Second Annual Convention, 1902.* Kansas City, Missouri: Hudson-Kimberly Publishing Co., 1902.

———. *Proceedings, Third Annual Convention, 1903.* Kansas City, Missouri: Hudson-Kimberly Publishing Co., 1904.

———. *Proceedings, Fourth Annual Convention, 1904.* Kansas City, Missouri: Hudson-Kimberly Publishing Co., 1904.

Kansas. Corporation Book No. 35, 1889–1891. Archives, Kansas Historical Society, Topeka, Kansas.

Kappler, Charles J., ed. *Indian Affairs: Laws and Treaties.* 4 vols. Washington, D.C.: Government Printing Office, 1903, vol. 3.

Kelley, E. H. Collection. Archives, Oklahoma Historical Society.

Neal, James. Collection. Archives, Oklahoma Bankers Association.

Oklahoma. *Constitution of the State of Oklahoma,* 1907.

Oklahoma. Legislature. *Banking and Corporation Laws, 1893–1901.* Guthrie: State Capital Printing Co., 1901.

———. *The Statutes of Oklahoma, 1890.* Guthrie: State Capital Printing Co., 1891.

———. *The Statutes of Oklahoma, 1893.* Guthrie: State Capital Printing Co., 1893.

———. *The Statutes of Oklahoma, 1897.* Guthrie: State Capital Printing Co., 1898.

Oklahoma. Sixth Legislature. *Acts of the Sixth Legislature.* Oklahoma City: Harlow Publishing Co., 1917.

Oklahoma Bankers Association. Collections and Records, 1900–1978. Archives, Oklahoma Bankers Association. This collection was by far the most important used in this study. The executive director and the staff of the OBA have, through the years, maintained copious records that include personal correspondence (received and sent), interoffice memos, public news releases, newspaper clippings, and individual files on banks and bankers. Listed immediately below and in other portions of this bibliography are only a selected few of the OBA's extensive holdings. Other materials from the collection are not mentioned below but are referred to in the notes.

———. *Proceedings, Fifth Annual Convention, 1901.* Guthrie: State Capital Printing Co., 1901.

———. *Proceedings, Sixth Annual Convention, 1902.* Guthrie: State Capital Printing Co., 1902.

———. *Proceedings, Seventh Annual Convention, 1903.* Guthrie: State Capital Printing Co., 1903.

———. *Proceedings, Tenth Annual Convention, 1906.* Guthrie State Capital Printing Co., 1906.

———. *Proceedings, Twelfth Annual Convention, 1908.* Oklahoma City: Western Bank Supply Co., 1908.

———. *Proceedings, Eighteenth Annual Convention, 1914.* Oklahoma City: Western Bank Supply Co., 1914.

———. *Proceedings, Nineteenth Annual Convention, 1915.* Oklahoma City: Western Bank Supply Co., 1915.

Oklahoma Banking Commission. Collection. Archives, Oklahoma Banking Commission, Oklahoma City, Oklahoma.

———. Consolidated Reports, 1908–1976. Archives, Oklahoma Banking Commission.

———. Miscellaneous Records, 1908–1977. Archives, Oklahoma Banking Commission.

Oklahoma-Indian Territory Bankers Association. *Proceedings, 10th Annual Convention, 1906.* Guthrie: State Capital Printing Co., 1906.

Renfrow, William. *Report of the Governor of Oklahoma to the Secretary of the Interior, November 3, 1893.* Washington, D.C.: Government Printing Office, 1893.

Seay, Abraham J. *Report of the Governor of Oklahoma to the Secretary of the Interior, October 1, 1892.* Washington, D.C.: Government Printing Office, 1893.

State Guaranty Bank of Okeene, Oklahoma. Collection. Okeene, Oklahoma.

Secretary of Oklahoma Territory. Banking Collection. Archives, Oklahoma Historical Society.

State National Bank of Eufaula, Oklahoma. Collection. Eufaula, Oklahoma.

United States. Bureau of the Census. *U.S. Census of Population: 1960.* vol. 1, *Characteristics of the Population.* Part 38, *Oklahoma.* Washington, D.C.: Government Printing Office, 1963.

———. *U.S. Census of Population: 1970.* vol. 1, *Characteristics of the Population.* Part 38, *Oklahoma.* Washington, D.C.: Government Printing Office, 1973.

———. Congress. Public Law no. 66 (HR5661). 73d Congress.

———. Department of the Treasury. "Reports of Conditions of National Banks, 1905–1910." Washington, D.C.: Government Printing Office, 1910.

———. Federal Reserve Board. *Annual Report, 1933.* Washington, D.C.: Government Printing Office, 1934.

———. Federal Reserve Board. *Monetary Statistics, 1943.* Washington, D.C.: Government Printing Office, 1944.

———. Federal Reserve Board. *Monetary Statistics, 1965.* Washington, D.C.: Government Printing Office, 1966.

———. Comptroller of the Currency. *Annual Report, December 1, 1890.* 2 vols. Washington, D.C.: Government Printing Office, 1890.

———. *Annual Report, December 7, 1896.* 2 vols. Washington, D.C.: Government Printing Office, 1896.

———. *Annual Report, 1928.* Washington, D.C.: Government Printing Office, 1929.

———. *Annual Report, 1971.* Washington, D.C.: Government Printing Office, 1972.

———. *Annual Report, 1975.* Washington, D.C.: Government Printing Office, 1976.

———. *Eighty-eighth Annual Report.* Washington, D.C.: Government Printing Office, 1951.

———. *Fifty-eighth Annual Report.* Washington, D.C.: Government Printing Office, 1921.

———. *Forty-eighth Annual Report.* Washington, D.C.: Government Printing Office, 1911.

———. *Ninety-eighth Annual Report.* Washington, D.C.: Government Printing Office, 1961.

———. *Sixty-eighth Annual Report.* Washington, D.C.: Government Printing Office, 1931.

———. *Seventy-eighth Annual Report.* Washington, D.C.: Government Printing Office, 1941.

———. *Thirty-eighth Annual Report.* Washington, D.C.: Government Printing Office, 1901.

———. *Twenty-eighth Annual Report.* Washington, D.C.: Government Printing Office, 1891.

Williams, Robert L. Collection. Archives, Oklahoma Historical Society.

Willis, Bert. "Memoirs." Typescript copy. Archives. Oklahoma Bankers Association.

Newspapers

Alva (Okla.) *Pioneer,* 1893–94.
Alva (Okla.) *Republican,* 1895–96.
Anadarko (Okla.) *Daily News,* 1951.
Bartlesville (Okla.) *Record,* 1949–55.
Caddo (Okla.) *Herald,* 1923, 1929.
Chandler (Okla.) *News-Publicist,* 1914–21.
County Journal (Medford, Okla.), 1968.
Daily Oklahoman (Oklahoma City), 1900–78.
Enid (Okla.) *News,* 1950–55.
Eufaula (Okla.) *Indian Journal,* 1914–17.
Frederick (Okla.) *Press,* 1933–37.
Guthrie (Okla.) *Daily Leader,* 1890–95.
Guthrie (Okla.) *Daily News,* 1890–95.
Indian Citizen (Atoka, Okla.), 1897–1908.
Johnston County Capital-Democrat (Tishomingo, Okla.), 1977.
Kansas City Star, 1932–35.
Latimer County News (Wilburton, Okla.), 1968–70.
Lexington (Okla.) *Leader,* 1891–95.
McAlester (Okla.) *News-Capital,* 1967–69.
Moore (Okla.) *Monitor,* 1955–60.
New York Times, 1929–74.
Oklahoma City Times, 1920–78.
Oklahoma County Herald (Harrah, Okla.), 1957–58.
Oklahoma County News (Jones City, Okla.), 1957–58.
Oklahoma Daily Capitol (Guthrie, Okla.), 1889–99.
Oklahoma Daily Journal (Oklahoma City), 1891–98.
Purcell (Okla.) *Register,* 1960–65.
Sapulpa (Okla.) *Daily Herald,* 1967–68.
Seminole (Okla.) *Producer,* 1970–78.
South McAlester (Okla.) *Capitol,* 1894–1900.
Stillwater (Okla.) *News-Press,* 1976–78.
Tulsa Daily World, 1945–78.
Tulsa Tribune, 1960–68.

Interviews

Bozarth, Howard, May 30, 1978, Oklahoma Banking Collection, Oklahoma Heritage Association, Oklahoma City.

Champlin, H. H., April 17, 1937, "Pioneer and Indian History of Oklahoma," vol. 19, comp. by Grant Foreman, Manuscript Collection, Indian Archives, Oklahoma Historical Society.

Conn, W. Jack, March 12, 1977, and May 24, 1978, Oklahoma Banking Collection.

Erwin, Sam, June 15, 1937, in "Pioneer and Indian History of Oklahoma," vol. 105, comp. by Grant Foreman, Manuscript Collection, Indian Archives, Oklahoma Historical Society.

Fielder, Leon, January 12, 1938, in "Pioneer and Indian History of Oklahoma," vol. 18, comp. by Grant Foreman, Manuscript Collection, Indian Archives, Oklahoma Historical Society.

Gilliland, Joe, May 6, June 30, and July 7, 1978, Oklahoma Banking Collection.

Hartman, Tom J., May 13, 1937, in "Pioneer and Indian History of Oklahoma," vol. 18, comp. by Grant Foreman, Manuscript Collection, Indian Archives, Oklahoma Historical Society.

Howell, Thomas, August 30, 1937, in "Pioneer and Indian History of Oklahoma," vol. 30, comp. by Grant Foreman, Manuscript Collection, Indian Archives, Oklahoma Historical Society.

Kennedy, Maybelle, by author, May 26, 1977, Oklahoma Banking Collection.

Lambert, Paul, by author, May 30, 1978, Oklahoma Banking Collection.

Lanning, Daniel, undated, in "Pioneer and Indian History of Oklahoma," vol. 104, comp. by Grant Foreman, Manuscript Collection, Indian Archives, Oklahoma Historical Society.

McCalmont, Ralph, by author, March 19, 1977, Oklahoma Banking Collection.

McClurg, Frankie, by author, June 17, 1977, Oklahoma Banking Collection.

Morris, W. C., September 30, 1937, in "Pioneer and Indian History of Oklahoma," vol. 30, comp. by Grant Foreman, Manuscript Collection, Indian Archives, Oklahoma Historical Society.

Nickerson, Frank, October 20, 1937, in "Pioneer and Indian History of Oklahoma," vol. 102, comp. by Grant Foreman, Manuscript Collection, Indian Archives, Oklahoma Historical Society.

Painter, R. D., July 13, 1978, Oklahoma Banking Collection.

Powers, Bob, July 13, 1978, Oklahoma Banking Collection.

Simmons, Jake, February 27, 1937, in "Pioneer and Indian History of Oklahoma," vol. 9, comp. by Grant Foreman, Manuscript Collection, Indian Archives, Oklahoma Historical Society.

Stafford, Robert B., March 9, 1937, in "Pioneer and Indian History of Oklahoma," vol. 10, comp. by Grant Foreman, Manuscript Collection, Indian Archives, Oklahoma Historical Society.

Stephenson, W. L., Jr., July 13, 1978, Oklahoma Banking Collection.

Swell, Frank A., III, July 13, 1978, Oklahoma Banking Collection.

Vogel, Henry, February 19, 1937, in "Pioneer and Indian History of Oklahoma," vol. 22, comp. by Grant Foreman, Manuscript Collection, Indian Archives, Oklahoma Historical Society.

Vose, Charles A., Sr., by author, May 30, 1978, Oklahoma Banking Collection.

Warren, H. R., March 31, 1937, in "Pioneer and Indian History of Oklahoma," vol. 2, comp. by Grant Foreman, Manuscript Collection, Indian Archives, Oklahoma Historical Society.

Werner, Roretta, July 13, 1978, Oklahoma Banking Collection.

SECONDARY SOURCES

Unpublished

Bowers, Cheryl D. "Seventy-Five Years of Progress." MS, 1971. Exchange Bank and Trust. Collection. Perry, Oklahoma.

Brown, George L. "History of the Citizens Security Bank." MS. Archives, Oklahoma Bankers Association.

Gates, Fred H. "The National Banks of Oklahoma During the Chaotic Years 1928–1938." (Unpublished M.A. thesis, Oklahoma State University, 1938.)

Gum, Eugene P. "The Facts in the Case of Eddie Shoquette." MS. Archives, Oklahoma Bankers Association.

Hull, Jack. "Tinker Air Force Base." MS. Draper Collection. Oklahoma Heritage Association.

Books and Periodicals

Bank News, 1950–1960.

Belcher, Wyatt W. "Political Leadership of Robert L. Owen." *Chronicles of Oklahoma,* 31 (Winter, 1953–1954): 361–71.

Binning, Arthur C. and Thomas C. Cochran. *The Rise of American Economic Life.* 4th ed. New York: Charles Scribner's Sons, 1964.

Burbank, Garin. *When Farmers Voted Red: The Gospel of Socialism in the Oklahoma Countryside, 1910–1924.* Westport, Connecticut: Greenwood Press, 1976.

Conn, Jack. "Oklahoma Banking: Past, Present and Future," *Oklahoma Banker,* June, 1967, pp. 22–24, 26, 30–31.

Geffs, Irving. *Fifty Years Forward.* Oklahoma City: First National Bank and Trust Company, 1939.

Gittinger, Roy. *The Formation of the State of Oklahoma, 1803–1906.* Norman: University of Oklahoma Press, 1939.

Hafen, LeRoy R., ed. *The Mountain Men and the Fur Trade of the Far West.* 9 vols. Glendale: Arthur H. Clark Co., 1965.

Harlow, Victor E. *Oklahoma: Its Origins and Development.* Oklahoma City: Harlow Publishing Co., 1935.

Heilbroner, Robert L. *The Economic Transformation of America.* New York: Harcourt, Brace, Jovanovich, 1977.

Hill, Luther B. *A History of the State of Oklahoma.* 2 vols. New York: The Lewis Publishing Co., 1910.

History of Mountain View, Kiowa County, Oklahoma, 1899–1970. Mountain View: *Mountain View News,* 1970.

Hubbard, Timothy W. and Lewis E. Davids. *Banking in Mid-America: A History of Missouri's Banks.* Washington, D.C.: Public Affairs Press, 1969.

Jones, E. W. *Early Days of Perry, Oklahoma.* Perry, Oklahoma: n.p., 1931.

Journal of the American Bankers Association. 1933–1965.

Leuchtenburg, William E. *Franklin D. Roosevelt and the New Deal, 1932–1940.* New York: Harper & Row, 1963.

Linzee, E. H. "Registration and Drawing for the Opening of Kiowa and Comanche Country, 1901." *Chronicles of Oklahoma,* 25 (Autumn, 1947): 289–94.

McReynolds, Edwin C. *Oklahoma: A History of the Sooner State.* Norman: University of Oklahoma Press, 1954.

McRill, Albert. *And Satan Came Also: An Inside Story of a City's Social and Political History.* Oklahoma City: Semco Color Press, 1955.

Mid-Continent Banker. 1955–1960.

Moore, William B. "John Henry Dill, 1868–1942." *Chronicles of Oklahoma,* 20 (September, 1942): 289–91.

Morrison, James D. "Problems in the Industrial Progress and Development of the Choctaw Nation, 1865–1907." *Chronicles of Oklahoma,* 22 (Spring, 1954): 70–91.

Oklahoma Bankers Association. *The Official Directory of Oklahoma Banks, 1978.* Kansas City, Missouri: Bank News, 1978.

Oklahoma Banker (Oklahoma City), 1908–1978.

Oklahoma Farmer-Stockman (Oklahoma City), 1914–1925.

One Man's Family Bank. Mountain View, Oklahoma: First National Bank of Mountain View, 1939.

Phipps, B. L. "Banking in Indian Territory During the 1880s." *Chronicles of Oklahoma,* 7 (June, 1929): 186–87.

Riggs, Lloyd C. "Mike Flanagan: Banker and Community Builder." *Bank News,* April 15, 1954, pp. 26–28.

Rister, Carl Coke. *Oil: Titan of the Southwest.* Norman: University of Oklahoma Press, 1949.

Shirley, Glenn. *Henry Starr: Last of the Real Badmen.* New York: David McKay Co., 1965.

Smallwood, James, ed. *And Gladly Teach.* Norman: University of Oklahoma Press, 1976.

Smallwood, James. *Urban Builder: The Life and Times of Stanley Draper.* Norman: University of Oklahoma Press, 1977.

Smith, Ralph A., ed. and trans. "Account of the Journey of Bernard de la Harpe." *Southwestern Historical Quarterly,* 62 (1962): 75–86, 246–59, 371–85, 525–41.

Stevens, Harry R. "Hugh Glenn." In LeRoy R. Hafen, ed., *The Mountain Men and Fur Trade of the Far West.* 9 vols. Glendale: Arthur H. Clark Co., 1965.

Stewart, Roy P. *Born Grown: An Oklahoma City History.* Oklahoma City: Fidelity Bank, 1974.

Stout, Joseph A., Jr., ed. *Frontier Adventures.* Oklahoma City: Oklahoma Historical Society, 1976.

Studenski, Paul and Krooss, Herman F. *Financial History of the United States.* New York: McGraw-Hill, 1963.

The First Seventy-five: A Story of a City and Its Bank (First National Bank and Trust, Tulsa). Tulsa: First National Bank and Trust, 1970.

Thoburn, Joseph B. "John J. Gerlock." *Chronicles of Oklahoma,* 10 (March, 1932): 34–43.

Thomas, Phillip D. "Thomas James, Hugh Glenn, and Jacob Fowler, 1821–1823." In Joseph A. Stout, Jr., ed., *Frontier Adventures.* Oklahoma City: Oklahoma Historical Society, 1976.

Trescott, Paul B. *Financing American Enterprise.* New York: Harper & Row, 1963.

Wamsley, Burkett. *Ad Libs to Bixby History,* Bixby, Oklahoma: Citizens Security Bank and Trust, 1974.

Index